1980

TONAL
HARMONY
IN CONCEPT
AND PRACTICE

TONAL
HARMONY
IN CONCEPT
AND PRACTICE

Second Edition

ALLEN FORTE

YALE UNIVERSITY

HOLT, RINEHART AND WINSTON, INC.

New York   Chicago   San Francisco   Atlanta

Dallas   Montreal   Toronto   London   Sydney

Copyright © 1962, 1974 by Holt, Rinehart and Winston, Inc.
Library of Congress Cataloging in Publication Data

Forte, Allen
Tonal Harmony in Concept and Practice, Second Edition

1. Harmony. I. Title
MT50.F713T7 1974   781.3   73-15820
ISBN: 0-03-077495-0
Printed in the United States of America
4567 038 987654321

PREFACE

The intention of this second edition is the same as that of the first: to prepare the student for advanced study of tonal music.

In carrying out the revision, the author has left the essential organization of the book intact, since it is straightforward and has proved to be sufficiently flexible to accommodate various ways of presenting the material.

Numerous small but important emendations have been made to the text. A few sections have been deleted, as have certain types of exercises that were not in accord with the spirit of the book—notably the Roman-numeral exercises, which were at odds with the figured-bass approach to voice leading and vertical structure.

To the reader who is familiar with the first edition, the most evident change in the second edition will be the addition of a new chapter (Chapter 13: Large-Scale Arpeggiations, Passing and Auxiliary Notes) and the addition of a new section, Linear Intervallic Patterns (section 220). The new chapter is intended to introduce the student to harmonic and linear events of larger dimension, while the new section deals with an important class of linear events within a harmonic context. Both additions should help prepare the reader for advanced analysis.

Finally, in addition to the Subject Index, an Index of Musical Examples has been supplied so that the student and teacher can easily refer back to illustrations of the various technical features that have been discussed.

A. F.
New Haven
December 23, 1973

CONTENTS

TONAL HARMONY IN CONCEPT AND PRACTICE

Chapter 1

STRUCTURAL CHARACTERISTICS OF THE FUNDAMENTAL MATERIALS

Composition consists in two things only. The first is the ordering and disposing of several sounds . . . in such a manner that their succession pleases the ear. This is what the Ancients called *melody.* The second is the rendering audible of two or more simultaneous sounds in such a manner that their combination is pleasant. This is what we call *harmony,* and it alone merits the name of composition.

Jean Benjamin de Laborde, 1780

By tradition, harmony study has been closely associated with the study of composition, with the study of the way in which tonal materials are organized to become music. This is not without justification, for the concepts of harmony are both basic and comprehensive. They stand at the very foundation of the art and reach forth to include its most elaborate expressions. The purpose of this book is to unfold those concepts and at the same time to present techniques that will enable the student to compose coherent and effective tonal music. To this end specific experiences are provided in the form of carefully planned exercises, exercises which contribute toward the ultimate goal: increased understanding of the art form. Without question this is the most important result of genuine technical training in music.

The primary aim of serious music study is to illuminate the subject, not to surround it with trivia and bury it beneath detail. At the same time one must realize that a technical approach to music, like a technical approach to any subject,

1

involves specific tasks that are often detailed. These include the learning of a new terminology, the memorizing of certain facts, and the intelligent working out of exercises in order to achieve basic skills. Without these one cannot hope to approach the general concepts essential to the art, nor can one attain the level of minimal ability that will enable him to enjoy the rewards of creative activity.

Let us begin by considering important characteristics of the fundamental materials.

1. Scale and Key

A scale is more than an exercise for fingers or vocal cords; it can also take the shape of a musical theme:

example 1. BEETHOVEN: *Piano Trio in B♭ major, Op. 97* ("Archduke")

Scherzo, allegro

This theme contains the seven different notes that belong to the key of B♭ major: B♭, C, D, E♭, F, G, and A. Thus it is not only an ascending scale but also a complete melodic statement of the key of B♭ major. By "key" we refer not in this instance to the key signature of two flats but to the collection of notes listed above the scale. These scale degrees, as they are called, relate to one another in certain ways that are of the utmost significance for harmony. Accordingly, we are far more interested in the relationships between the scale degrees than in their letter names.

2. Chord and Interval

If we consider the Beethoven theme in Example 1 more carefully we see that certain scale degrees are stressed, while others are passed over without emphasis. The accented notes are marked by asterisks in the next example.

example 2.

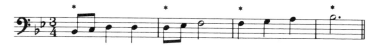

If these accented notes are extracted from the theme and arranged vertically we obtain a harmony or *chord,* a group of notes which sound simultaneously.

example 3.

The notes of the chord are separated by spaces, spaces that before were filled by the *scale degrees.* These spaces, called *intervals,* are of fundamental importance to harmony, for they are used to measure and describe chord structure and succession.

Intervals are named according to the number of scale degrees they encompass. The intervals of the chord extracted from the Beethoven theme will serve well to illustrate this:

example 4.

3rd   5th   8ve   =   chord

In Example 4 the lowest note of the chord has been paired with each of the other chord notes in succession to form intervals of three different sizes. The first of these intervals encompasses three scale degrees: Bb, C, and D. Therefore it is called a *third* (written as 3rd). The next interval, from Bb to F, encompasses five scale degrees: Bb, C, D, Eb, and F, and therefore is called a *fifth* (written as 5th). The last interval, from Bb to Bb, spans eight scale degrees: Bb, C, D, Eb, F, G, A, and Bb; accordingly it is called an *octave* (written in musical notation as 8ve).

The smallest interval in tonal music is the *second* (2nd), an interval that encompasses only two notes. This is the interval we find between one scale degree and the next—for example, from Bb to C in the Bb major scale. The 2nd has two sizes, a fact easily verified by looking at a piano keyboard. We see that within the 2nd from Bb to C lies a third key, notated either as B♮ or as Cb. Moving up to the next 2nd in the Bb scale, from C to D, we also find a third key in the middle, notated as C♯ or Db. However, the 2nd just above, from D to Eb, contains no extra key; it is smaller than the two 2nds below it. This small 2nd, the 2nd which encompasses two scale degrees with no note between (D to Eb), is called a *minor 2nd.* The large 2nd, which encompasses two scale notes with one note between (Bb to C), is called a *major 2nd.* Thus the scale consists of the fixed succession of major and minor 2nds shown in the next example.

example 5.

One can easily remember the structure of the *major scale* by noting that the minor 2nd occurs twice: between scale degrees 3 and 4 and again between scale degrees 7 and 8. All other 2nds in the scale are major.

The major scale degrees require no sharps or flats (*accidentals*) other than those in the key signature. However, if we wish to represent the notes that lie within the major 2nds we must use accidentals. Such notes which do not belong to the key are called *chromatic* notes. When all five chromatic notes are combined with the unaltered scale degrees we have a scale called the *chromatic scale*. Example 6 shows the unaltered scale, or *diatonic* scale, at (*a*). The five chromatic notes are shown at (*b*), and the combined scale or chromatic scale is shown at (*c*).

example 6.

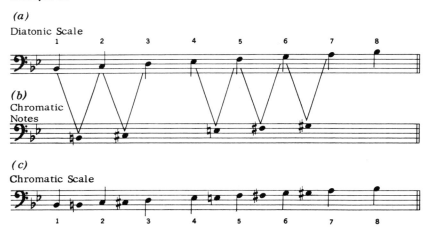

The minor 2nd is often called a half step and the major 2nd is frequently called a whole step. These terms are very convenient and we shall use them a great deal. For example, in naming intervals the diatonic scale provides the measurement of general size (2nd, 3rd, and so on) while we describe the specific size of the interval in terms of half steps. Thus we say that the minor 2nd is one half step smaller than the major 2nd, or that the major 2nd contains two half steps. The chromatic scale therefore is a series of half steps which comprises all the pitches of our equal-tempered system. From the standpoint of tonal music it is not an independent scale, but derives from the diatonic scale, as shown by Example 6.

3. Key Signatures and Diatonic Scale Structure

The sharps and flats in the various key signatures serve to fix the half steps between scale degrees 3 and 4 and 7 and 8. Thus, in the key of C no accidentals are required for the half steps. They occur naturally without accidentals.

example 7.

However, if we construct a scale upward from another note, say G, without accidentals we discover that a whole step occurs between scale degrees 7 and 8 instead of the required half step:

example 8.

This makes clear the relation between key signature and scale structure. The one sharp in the key signature of G major raises scale degree 7 to create the required half step, the leading note progression.

example 9.

If we proceed from the key of one sharp to the key of two sharps, of three sharps . . ., we discover that each added sharp applies to scale degree 7:

example 10.

Similarly, the single flat in the key of F major creates a half step between scale degrees 3 and 4.

example 11.

And each added flat applies to scale degree 4.

example 12.

4.   The Minor Scale and Chord

Like the major scale, the minor scale can also be expressed as a theme. We quote from the opening of a Bach work:

example 13.   J. S. BACH: *Concerto for Solo Harpsichord and Orchestra in D minor*

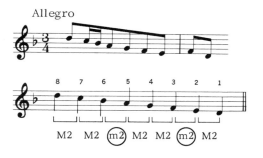

Directly below the theme is represented in equal note values the scale upon which it is based. Like the major scale this minor scale contains two minor 2nds (half steps). However, in the minor scale they occur between scale degrees 2 and 3 and scale degrees 5 and 6.

If we extract the accented notes of the Bach theme in Example 13 and arrange them in vertical order as we did those of the Beethoven theme in Example 3 the chord shown in Example 14(*a*) is obtained.

example 14.

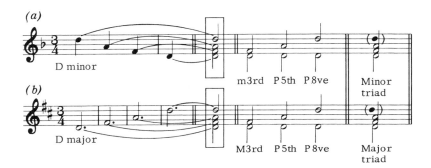

Directly below Example 14a we again present the Beethoven chord from Example 3, transposed to D major for easier comparison with the minor example. The intervals of each chord have been sorted out, as in Example 4, for identification and comparison. The lowest chordal interval in the minor key (Example 14a) is a small 3rd, encompassing three half steps. This is commonly known as a *minor 3rd* (m3rd). In contrast, the lowest chordal interval in the major key (Example 14b) is a large 3rd, or *major 3rd* (M3) encompassing four half steps.

The next chordal interval is the same in both minor and major. It encompasses seven half steps and is known as the *perfect 5th* (p5th). Lastly we find the *perfect 8ve,* which is also the same in both minor and major keys. It spans the entire array of twelve half steps and plays a special role in tonal harmony which is explained in the next section.

5. Octave Equivalence

The notes which form the 8ve always have the same letter name. One of the most fundamental axioms of tonal music is that notes which bear the same name are equivalent. We call this the axiom of *8ve equivalence.* It reads: A note which stands at the interval of an 8ve from another note and which has the same letter name is regarded as a duplication or 8ve *doubling* of that note, not as an additional and different chordal element. For this reason only three different notes are counted in the chords shown in Example 14. These three note chords are called *triads.*

6. The Triad

Defined more precisely, a triad is a three-note chord that contains the intervals of a 3rd and a 5th, measured upward from the lowest note, called the *fundamental* or *root.* The last part of the definition is of the utmost importance since in tonal music we measure chordal intervals first from the bottom up, not from the top down or from the inside out. Thus the difference between major and minor triads is a difference in the size of the first interval above the fundamental: the minor triad contains a minor 3rd, the major triad contains a major 3rd. Both triads contain perfect 5ths.

7. Arpeggiation of the Triad; Parallel Major and Minor Keys

The following examples present two themes, one based upon the major triad and one upon the minor triad.

example 15. BEETHOVEN: *Fifth Symphony*

example 16. BEETHOVEN: *Piano Concerto in C minor, Op. 37*

The theme in Example 15 opened with a horizontal statement of the major triad on C. A horizontal chord statement of this kind is also known as an *arpeggiation* of the chord. The theme shown in Example 16 opens in a strikingly similar way, but with an arpeggiation of the C minor triad.

When a major and minor scale both begin with the same note, as in the case of C major and C minor in the themes above, they are called *parallel.* Thus we say that the parallel major key of C minor is C major, the parallel minor of C major is C minor. The key which shares the same key signature but not the same first degree with another scale is called *relative.* Thus, the relative minor of C major is A minor (no sharps or flats in either key signature); the relative major of A minor is C major. The relative minor scale always begins a minor 3rd below a major scale.

We often speak of the major or minor *mode.* The term mode is held over from the pretonal period, during which it had more precise meanings. In tonal music it designates only the general character of the major scale as distinct from the minor scale, and vice versa. Thus we say "the minor mode," referring to the general characteristics of the minor scale, but "the key of C minor," meaning both the specific pitches which comprise that key as well as their relationships.

8. The Auxiliary Note and the Passing Note

The Beethoven themes above also illustrate two melodic events of fundamental significance to the study of harmony. First, in Example 15 attention is drawn to the note marked *aux.*

This abbreviation stands for *auxiliary note,* a note that stands at the interval of a 2nd above or below two occurrences of a more important harmonic note. In this instance the auxiliary note D stands between two C's, C being the more important note since it belongs to the C major triad, the *tonic* triad. The second melodic event of fundamental significance is marked *pn* in Example 16. This abbreviation stands for *passing note,* a note that passes between or connects two more important harmonic notes. Here D, the passing note, stands between E♭ and C, which belong to the C minor triad, the tonic triad in the key of C minor. The passing note differs radically from the auxiliary note. The auxiliary note departs from and returns to the same note. The passing note connects two different notes.

Auxiliary notes and passing notes are often chromatic. In such cases spelling depends upon the function of the note. For instance, in the Haydn theme below we find a chromatic passing note which connects scale degrees 1 and 2. Since the passing note ascends, it is spelled G♯, not A♭. The latter would be the correct spelling for a descending passing note.

example 17. HAYDN: *Symphony in G major, No. 94*

In the passage quoted in Example 18 the chromatic auxiliary note is spelled F♯, not G♭, since it ascends to the main note.

example 18. HAYDN: *Symphony in C minor, No. 95*

It will be observed that the auxiliary note F♯ here is not preceded by the main note, G. This is an example of one form of the *incomplete* auxiliary note. (See section 224.)

9. The Triadic Division of the Diatonic Major and Minor Scales

We have seen that both the diatonic major and the diatonic minor scales contain a triad, a triad whose fundamental note is scale degree 1. Because of its position in the scale this triad, the tonic triad, divides the scale into two parts. The largest interval of the triad, the 5th, delimits the first part of the scale, leaving the upper part of the scale within the interval of a 4th. The resultant *triadic* or *harmonic* division of the scale is illustrated in the following example.

example 19.

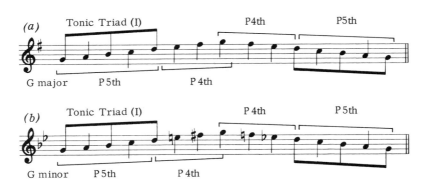

Example 19 shows the diatonic scales both in ascending and descending directions. The division of the scale into 5th and 4th is marked by brackets. The stems of the triadic notes are beamed together.

10.   The Leading Note and the Law of the Half Step

In the upper 4th of the harmonically divided scale we find two passing notes side by side: scale degrees 6 and 7. Of these two passing notes, scale degree 7 is most important since it completes the 8ve scale. It stands at the interval of a half step from the last note of the scale (the 8ve) and has a particularly strong attraction to that note. This can be verified empirically.

example 20.

If one plays or sings the incomplete scale shown in Example 20 he will remark the tendency of scale degree 7 to lead upward to the 8ve and thus to complete the scale. Because it has this strong tendency scale degree 7 is known as the *leading note.*

The leading note is only one instance of the operation of an important melodic law, the *law of the half step.* According to this law the strongest, most binding progression from one note to another is the half-step progression. If both whole-step and half-step progressions are available from a given note the half-step progression will always be preferred.

11.   Alteration of Scale Degrees 6 and 7 in Minor

The law of the half step enables us to understand a modification which is normally made in the minor scale. Whenever a melody ascends through the upper 4th, scale degree 7 is raised one half step so as to convert it into a leading note like that of the major scale. At the same time the 6th degree is also raised, for if it were not raised it would tend to descend to scale degree 5 in accord with the law of the half step rather than progress upward as an ascending passing note. Example 21 shows the descending direction of the unaltered passing notes and their ascending direction when altered.

example 21.

These alterations of scale degrees 6 and 7 are so common that we do not regard them as genuine chromatic alterations. They have been assimilated as part of the diatonic minor scale. Thus the form of the diatonic minor scale depends upon the direction of melodic progression. In both directions the lower division of the scale, the 5th, remains the same. However, with ascending motion through the upper division, the 4th, scale degrees 6 and 7 must be raised. An example follows.

example 22.   VIVALDI: *Concerto grosso in G minor, Op. 3/2*

The descending scale in the first part of the theme requires no accidentals. It is part of the *natural minor* scale. However, when the scale ascends, the 6th and 7th degrees are raised so that they may serve effectively as ascending passing notes, as explained above. In this form the upper 4th of the minor scale is identical to that of its parallel major. The total minor scale pattern in Example 22, including the descending natural pattern and the ascending altered pattern, is called the *melodic minor scale.*

When the 7th degree is raised but not the 6th, the result is a third form of the minor scale, the *harmonic minor scale.* The following theme is based upon that form.

example 23.   SCHUMANN: *First Symphony*

In accord with the law of the half step, scale degree 6 functions as upper auxiliary note to scale degree 5. Its implicit progression is shown in parentheses in Example 23.

The harmonic minor scale occurs infrequently in melodic statements such as that in Example 23. Its importance lies with harmonic progression, as we shall see in Chapter 4.

The diatonic minor scale therefore has three forms: natural, melodic, and harmonic. They are summarized in Example 24 below.

example 24.

12. The Law of the Half Step as Applied to Scale Degree 4 in Major

The tendency of certain diatonic notes to move by half step has been illustrated in the cases of the leading note and the variable 6th degree of the minor scale. Another special case is scale degree 4 in the major mode, which by virtue of its diatonic position tends to descend to scale degree 3 by half step rather than ascend to scale degree 5 by whole step. Thus, 4 often serves as an upper auxiliary note to 3, as in the next example.

example 25.   BRAHMS: *Variations on a Theme by Haydn, Op. 56*

Scale degree 4 serves as auxiliary note to scale degree 3 twice in this short melodic figure. It occurs first in a submetrical, then in a metrical value.

Because of its strong tendency to descend, scale degree 4 is a unidirectional passing note as well as an auxiliary note. Special harmonic conditions are required to make it serve as an ascending passing note.

13. The Inversion of Intervals

We have already mentioned the fact that notes which have the same letter name are regarded as equivalent. This is evident in the following theme.

example 26.   MOZART: *Symphony in D major, K.385* ("Haffner")

The half note D in the second measure is not different from the first note of the theme, but merely another occurrence of the same note in a different octave. Both notes are called D. Similarly, all the notes in the third measure are C#'s and all the notes in the final measure are A's. This reflects the operation of the principle of 8ve equivalence previously described (page 8). *Inversion,* a primary technique of chord generation, is dependent upon the principle of 8ve equivalence. We shall consider chord inversion in subsequent chapters; here discussion is limited to interval inversion. This is shown below.

Example 27.

Unison = 8ve

At (*a*) we have two voices or instruments sounding D at the same pitch level. They form the interval called the *unison.* (Actually, no "interval" is involved since the pitches are exactly the same, but the unison is commonly classed as an interval.) When one note of the unison is placed an 8ve higher, as shown at (*b*), the unison becomes an 8ve and the two intervals, unison and 8ve, are regarded as interchangeable. Thus interval inversion means the placement of the lower note an 8ve higher or the placement of the higher note an 8ve lower. Example 28 provides another illustration.

example 28.   Interval Inversion

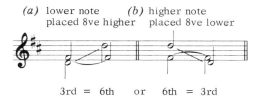

(*a*) lower note placed 8ve higher   (*b*) higher note placed 8ve lower

3rd = 6th   or   6th = 3rd

Example 28 shows that when the lower note of a 3rd is placed an 8ve higher the interval of a 6th results (*a*). Similarly, if the upper note of a 6th is placed an 8ve lower the interval of a 3rd results (*b*). We will examine inversions of other intervals after we have considered the dual classification of intervals into consonances and dissonances.

14.   Consonant and Dissonant Intervals

In music the terms consonant and dissonant have nothing whatsoever to do with the pleasant or unpleasant quality of a sound. They are technical terms applied to phenomena of motion. The adjective *consonant* is applied to stable intervals, intervals which tend to remain stationary, in contrast to more active intervals called *dissonant* intervals. The intervals that make up the tonic triad are consonant, as is the 8ve which doubles the fundamental note of the triad:

example 29.

Triad   3rd   5th   8ve   6th   4th   unison

Example 29 shows that the triadic intervals and their inversions are consonant with but one exception: the 4th. This interval, the inversion of the consonant 5th, is consonant only under special conditions. (See section 20.)

All diatonic intervals other than the triadic intervals and their inversions are dissonant intervals. There are only three types of dissonant diatonic intervals: the 2nd, the 7th, and the tritone. The first two are shown below.

example 30.

2nd   7th

Example 30 shows that the 2nd inverts to become the 7th. The 7th plays a major role in the generation of dissonant chords, as explained in Chapter 5.

Between scale degrees 6 and 7 in the harmonic minor scale there occurs a 2nd which is larger than the major 2nd by one half step. This is called the *augmented 2nd.* When inverted it becomes a small 7th called a *diminished* 7th:

example 31.

aug. 2nd   dim. 7th

The remaining dissonant diatonic interval occurs between scale degree 4 and the leading note:

example 32.

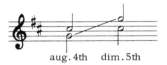

aug. 4th   dim. 5th

In comparison with other diatonic 4ths the 4th between scale degree 4 and the leading note is oversize by one half step. Whereas the others contain five half steps this one contains six. Therefore it is called an *augmented* 4th. When the augmented 4th is inverted it becomes an undersized 5th—in comparison with the other diatonic 5ths. This small 5th is called *diminished.* Both the augmented 4th and its inversion, the diminished 5th, span six half steps; therefore inversion does not affect the actual size of the augmented 4th, as it does all other intervals. In view of this fact the interval is often called a *tritone,* whether notated as an augmented 4th or as a diminished 5th. The term *tritone* refers to the fact that the interval spans three whole steps (= six half steps).

15. Perfect and Imperfect Consonances

Traditionally the consonant intervals are divided into two types: perfect and imperfect. There are four intervals of each type. Shown in Example 33 are the perfect consonances: the unison and its inversion the 8ve, the 5th and its inversion the 4th.

example 33.

unis. 8ve   5th   4th

Diatonic 3rds and 6ths are the imperfect consonances. They are shown below.

example 34.

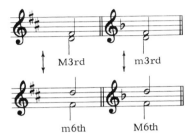

Example 34 shows that the major 3rd inverts to become the small or minor 6th, while the minor 3rd inverts to become the large or major 6th. Like the major and minor 2nds and major and minor 3rds, the two 6ths differ in size by only one half step.

16. Compound Intervals

In the theme of Mozart's "Haffner" *Symphony,* Example 26, we saw that the principle of 8ve equivalence was not affected by the number of 8ves involved. That is, D above middle C has the same harmonic meaning as D one 8ve higher, two 8ves higher, three 8ves higher, . . . From this we can derive the following rule: the addition of an 8ve to an interval does not change the function of the notes involved. A melodic example follows.

example 35.   BACH: *Fugue in B♭ minor, WTC I*

aux

Here an auxiliary note has been placed an 8ve higher so that it stands at the distance of a 9th, not a 2nd, from the main note. The addition of an 8ve does not affect the function of the note.

Example 36 shows three common compound intervals.

example 36.

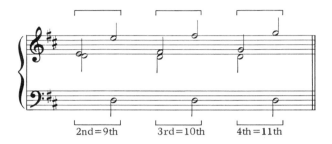

Regardless of the number of 8ves involved only one 8ve is added to the simple interval in naming the compound interval. The compound form of the 2nd therefore is the 9th, of the 3rd the 10th, of the 4th the 11th. The notes of the simple interval do not cross to form the compound interval. Therefore the process differs fundamentally from inversion.

17. Chromatic Intervals as Altered Diatonic Intervals

When one note of an interval is chromatic or when both notes are chromatic, the entire interval is called chromatic. Chromatic intervals arise by raising or lowering one or both notes of a diatonic interval, so that the interval is made larger or smaller by the interval of a half step. The rules of terminology, beginning with the smallest interval, are as follows:

> If it is made larger by one half step:
> > a minor interval is called major,
> > a major interval is called augmented,
> > a perfect interval is called augmented,
> > an augmented interval is called doubly augmented.
> If it is made smaller by one half step:
> > a minor interval is called diminished,
> > a major interval is called minor,
> > a perfect interval is called diminished,
> > a diminished interval is called doubly diminished.

Some of these *chromatic alterations* are illustrated in Example 37.

example 37.

m2nd   M2nd   m3rd   M3rd
(diatonic) (chromatic) (diatonic) (chromatic)

M3rd   A3rd   m6th   d6th
(diatonic) (chromatic) (diatonic) (chromatic)

When naming such altered intervals one must ask two questions. First, what is the name of the interval in its unaltered form? (2nd, 3rd, . . .) Second, does the chromatic alteration make the interval larger or smaller? In connection with the first question we emphasize that chromatic alteration of a diatonic interval does not change the letter names of the notes involved but only adds an accidental to one or both notes. If a letter name is changed we do not have an altered interval, but an entirely different interval. For example, D to F$^\times$ is an augmented 3rd, but D to G, which has the same appearance on the keyboard as D to F$^\times$, is a perfect 4th. Since chromatic alterations always reflect the operation of melodic forces, it is important that they be accurately represented in notation.

18. Summary of Interval Types

Example 38 summarizes the interval types explained in preceding sections. It includes only representatives of each type, not all the available intervals. The keys of C major and C minor are used to give the intervals a diatonic context. The brackets indicate intervals related by inversion. Compound intervals are not shown separately since they are entirely dependent upon the simple intervals from which they derive.

example 38.

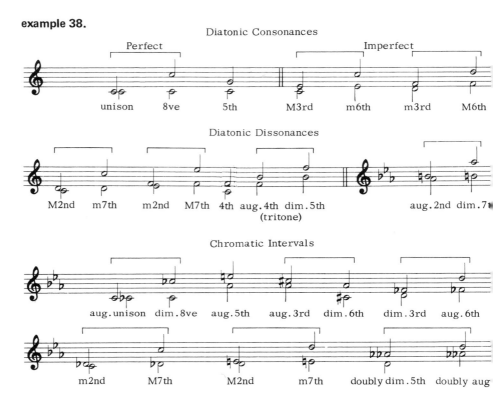

19. Summary of Inversion Nomenclature

With inversion, consonant intervals remain consonant, except for the consonant 5th which becomes a dissonant 4th. Likewise dissonances remain dissonances with inversion. The details of nomenclature are summarized below.

> When inverted,
> > perfect consonances remain perfect, but
> > imperfect consonances change as follows:
> > > major intervals become minor,
> > > minor intervals become major.
>
> When inverted,
> > minor dissonances become major,
> > major dissonances become minor;
> > augmented intervals become diminished,
> > diminished intervals become augmented.

20.   Absolute Interval Values and the Influence of Context

An interval is like a word in that it takes on specific meaning only when it occurs in context with other intervals. Thus, if we open the dictionary and look up the word "land," we find that it is defined as "the solid part of the earth's surface: distinguished from sea." However, this is only one of its meanings. In all, ten definitions are given for the nominal form of the word "land" and ten more for the verbal form. The choice of a particular meaning depends upon the context in which the word occurs. Alone it is ambiguous. Similarly, a musical interval alone is ambiguous. Its precise meaning is revealed only when it is placed in a particular musical context. For the most part, consonant intervals behave like consonances, dissonant intervals like dissonances. However, under certain conditions a consonant interval may behave like a dissonance, a dissonant interval like a consonance. Thus the qualities of consonance and dissonance are not fixed, absolute values, but are subject to the ever-present influence of other elements, other organizing forces. Two of the most important of these are meter and rhythm.

21.   Meter and Rhythm

Music is often described as the temporal art, for the dimension of time is crucial to music. In tonal music time is organized and measured out in two ways: by *meter* and by *rhythm.* Both, in turn, serve to organize and articulate melody and harmony. The functions of meter and rhythm are shown in the next example, which again uses the theme quoted at the beginning of this chapter.

example 39.

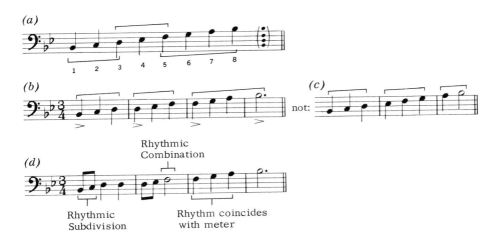

It will be recalled that the Beethoven theme in Example 1 was based upon the ascending Bb major scale. Example 39(a) now shows that scale in equal note values. In connection with Example 1 we demonstrated that the ascending scale contained the Bb tonic triad. In Example 39 the intervals of that triad are bracketed and the complete triad is represented in parentheses. However, the triad is not made evident by the succession of quarter notes shown in Example 39(c). These notes could group in several ways which would not reveal the underlying triad. But when the scale is measured out in groups of three quarter notes as at (b) the triadic intervals become distinct. This, then, is a metrical pattern. It exhibits the two fundamental characteristics of meter: (1) it is based upon a succession of notes of equal duration, and (2) the notes of equal duration are grouped in a regular and repeated pattern by accent. Both characteristics are represented in the notation. The meter signature shows the value which represents one of the equal notes, called the *metrical* unit, and also the number of those notes which form a group or measure. For example, the signature $\frac{3}{4}$ should be read as: "three quarter notes to each measure (group)." The bar line indicates the placement of metrical accent, the accent which marks off each group, or measure. This accent falls on the first note of the group. Secondary metrical accents often occur, but are standardized by tradition and not indicated in the notation.

Repetition is an important factor in the metrical organization of the Beethoven theme in Example 39. Scale degrees 3 and 5 are repeated so that the first note of each triadic interval falls on the accented first beat, or down-beat, of the measure. This repetition is essential, for if the ascending scale were to be measured out in $\frac{3}{4}$ without repetition and follow exactly the metrical succession of quarter notes the pattern shown at (c) would result. Clearly this pattern does not reveal the intervals of the tonic triad.

We have discussed the function of meter. Example 39(d) shows the function of rhythm in the articulation of the tonic triad that characterizes the Beethoven theme. In contrast to metrical pattern, which is a succession of notes of equal value grouped by regular accent, *rhythmic pattern* often consists of notes of different values, notes which are grouped in various ways, often by irregular accent. Thus, if we regard metrical pattern as the constant, underlying, repetitive pattern, rhythmic pattern is the varied and flexible pattern that is superimposed on the metrical pattern. Rhythmic pattern may act upon metrical pattern in four ways: (1) it may divide the metrical unit into notes of shorter duration; (2) it may combine metrical units into notes of longer duration; (3) it may shift or displace the metrical accent; (4) it may coincide exactly with the metrical pattern. In the Beethoven theme shown in Example 39(d) the rhythmic pattern relates to the underlying metrical pattern in three of these ways. In the first measure the rhythmic pattern subdivides the first quarter note, the metrical unit, into two shorter notes, eighth notes. In the second measure the rhythmic pattern combines two quarter notes into a longer note, the half note. In the third measure the rhythmic pattern coincides exactly with the metrical pattern. Thus each measure has a different pattern and each interval of the unfolding triad is expressed in a different way; yet the phrase as a whole is unified by the underlying metrical pattern. This careful adjustment of metrical and rhythmic pattern is not a matter of happenstance. Beethoven's sketches offer abundant evidence of the care he gave to just such details as these.

The only rhythmic operation not included in the Beethoven theme is shift or displacement. This can be seen in the following theme.

example 40.   MOZART: *Symphony in D major, K.504* ("Prague")

At (a) we see the theme as it would be without rhythmic displacement; at (b), the theme as the composer wrote it. We find a rhythmic displacement of the metrical pattern in the third and fourth measures. A displacement of this kind is often called a *syncopation.*

Of most significance to harmonic and melodic development are shift of metrical accent and division of the metrical unit. Division, in particular, is so important that when we describe the function of melodic notes we must distinguish carefully between *metrical* durations—notes that have the value of the metrical unit or larger—and *submetrical* durations—notes of lesser duration than the metrical unit. Thus in the example below we describe the melody at (a) as a metrical arpeggiation, while we describe the passing eighth notes at (b) as submetrical passing notes.

example 41.

22. Simple and Compound Meter

Before we leave the topic of meter we must review certain essential terms and classifications. Meters are simple or compound. The simple meters either have two units per measure with the primary metrical accent falling on the first ($\frac{2}{8}$, $\frac{2}{4}$, $\frac{2}{2}$ or ¢), three units per measure with the primary metrical accent falling on the first ($\frac{3}{8}$, $\frac{3}{4}$, $\frac{3}{2}$), or four units per measure with a primary accent on the first and a secondary accent on the third ($\frac{4}{8}$, $\frac{4}{4}$ or C, $\frac{4}{2}$). The two-unit meter is called *duple* meter, the three-unit meter *triple* meter, the four-unit meter *quadruple* meter.

Often the rhythmic pattern divides each metrical unit into three equal durations, as in the following excerpt.

example 42. BRAHMS: *Intermezzo in A major, Op. 76/6*

Each group of three notes is called a *triplet.* When such a triplet pattern is continued throughout a composition it becomes in effect a new metrical pattern and is usually notated as a *compound meter:* a triplet subdivision superimposed upon a simple meter. In the excerpt below, the compound meter signature $\frac{6}{8}$ represents a continuous subdivision of this kind.

example 43. BRAHMS: *Intermezzo in E♭ major, Op. 117/1*

Compound meters retain the unit and the accent pattern of the simple meter from which they derive. Thus in $\frac{6}{8}$ the unit is the dotted quarter note and the metrical pattern remains duple in essence.

Example 44 (below) shows the common metrical patterns and illustrates the three primary rhythmic operations. In each case meter and rhythm combine to form a metric-rhythmic pattern which organizes the notes of the ascending major scale.

Example 44 also makes clear the basic similarity of all the metrical patterns of a particular type. For instance, the duple meters are essentially the same whether the unit is the eighth, the quarter, or the half note.

example 44. Common Metric-Rhythmic Patterns

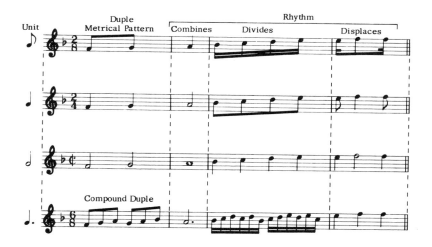

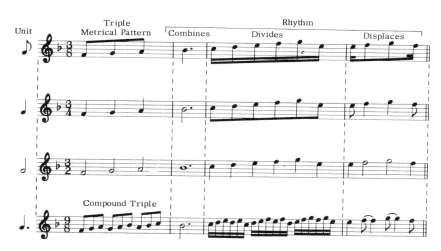

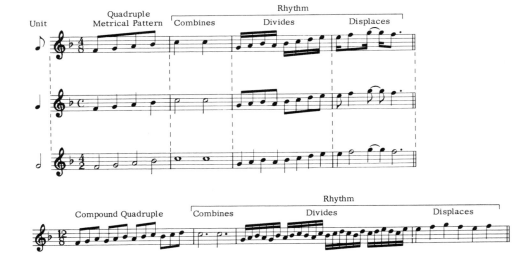

23. The Circle of 5ths

In the pages to follow we shall on many occasions refer to the entire spectrum of diatonic keys. These keys, fifteen major and fifteen minor, are customarily arranged by successive 5ths, a procedure which yields an orderly and easily memorized progression of key signatures. The arrangement is known as the *circle of 5ths* because its originator, Heinichen, represented it in the form of a circle. Here we have relinquished the circle, but retained the succession of 5ths.

example 45.

Sharp keys by ascending 5ths

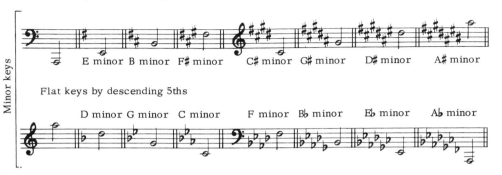

Minor keys

E minor B minor F# minor   C# minor G# minor   D# minor   A# minor

Flat keys by descending 5ths

D minor G minor C minor   F minor Bb minor   Eb minor   Ab minor

Beginning from the major tonality without key signature, C major, the keys are arranged by ascending 5ths. This produces a series of "sharp" keys in which one sharp is added to each successive key. The "flat" keys are arranged by descending 5ths beginning from C again, and there too we see a series in which one flat is added to each successive key. The minor keys begin from the minor tonality without key signature, A minor. As in the major mode, the sharp keys arrange themselves by ascending 5ths, adding one sharp with each successive key, while the flat keys arrange themselves by descending 5ths, adding one flat with each successive key.

It should be emphasized here that the circle of 5ths is a visual convenience, a mnemonic device, nothing more. It does not represent fully any important structural aspect of tonal music, as we shall see in Chapter 7 which deals with harmonic progression.

24. Harmony and the Training of the Musical Ear

The musician cannot be content simply to hear; he must know what he hears and be able to communicate that knowledge. The systematic study of harmony provides an excellent opportunity to develop those skills.

Memorization plays an important role in hearing music. We remember melodies, harmonies, and rhythms just as we remember faces. And as one's acquaintance with tonal music widens, he must also learn the names of the various events which become familiar, for in that way both the sound and its structural meaning in the musical composition are fixed in mind.

To direct and encourage the development of the musical ear specific exercises are given at the end of each chapter. These begin with basic keyboard and aural exercises in the material newly introduced. If he consistently practices these exercises the student will find that his aural capacities will develop simultaneously with other musical skills.

25. Chapter Summary

It has been seen that the diatonic scale represents a key. It also serves as a map for locating notes and chords. Thus we refer to "scale degree 3" and "tonic chord" (I).

The diatonic and chromatic scales are used to measure intervals. Intervals, in turn, are used to measure and describe chords. We classify intervals first according to the number of diatonic degrees they span ("2nds," "3rds," . . .), then according to the number of half steps they contain ("minor 2nds," "major 3rds," . . .), and finally as consonances or dissonances. The triadic intervals, 3rd, 5th, unison, and 8ve, and inversions of triadic intervals (with the frequent exception of the 4th) are the only consonant intervals. All other intervals are dissonant.

The triad divides the diatonic scale into two unequal parts. The lower division spans the 5th, the upper spans the 4th. We explained the melodic function of certain diatonic notes within these divisions as passing notes and auxiliary notes. Particular emphasis was given to the melodic function of scale degree 7 as leading note and to the variable 6th and 7th degrees of the minor scale. In all these cases we emphasized that the half step exerts the strongest melodic attraction (law of the half step).

The principle of 8ve equivalence underlies interval inversion, which is an extremely important procedure in tonal harmony since it produces chord inversion, as we shall see. Inversion is entirely different from the shift of 8ve that produces the compound interval. A simple arithmetical formula can always be used to determine whether two intervals are related on the basis of inversion: The sum of an interval and its inversion equals 9. Thus, the 3rd is the inversion of the 6th $(3 + 6 = 9)$. But, for example, the 9th is not the inversion of the 2nd $(9 + 2 = 11)$. The 9th is a compound interval, a 2nd plus an 8ve.

We have given a brief introduction to the function of meter and rhythm. Their interaction is of vital importance to harmony.

EXERCISES

A. List of Some Important Terms to Define and Memorize

Scale degree
Chord
Chromatic scale
Triad
Relative minor
Passing note
Auxiliary note
Half step
Leading note
Melodic minor scale
Inversion

Octave equivalence
Consonant interval
Dissonant interval
Tritone
Compound interval
Augmented 2nd
Diminished 5th
Compound meter
Submetrical
Rhythm

B. Sample Diatonic Intervals

INSTRUCTIONS
Each of the following melodic fragments features a particular diatonic interval. Many perhaps are already familiar. All should be memorized without delay to provide a basis for interval recognition and for the singing of melodies and harmonies required for subsequent exercises.

exercise 1.   Ascending minor 2nd. (BEETHOVEN: *Ninth Symphony*)

exercise 2.   Descending minor 2nd. (Chorale: *Ach Gott und Herr*)

exercise 3.   Ascending major 2nd. (Chorale: *Freu dich sehr, o meine Seele*)

exercise 4.   Descending major 2nd. (SCHUMANN: *Third Symphony*)

exercise 5.   Ascending minor 3rd. (BRAHMS: *Lullaby*)

exercise 6.   Descending minor 3rd. (BERLIOZ: *Harold in Italy*)

Adagio

exercise 7.   Ascending major 3rd. (Chorale: *Es ist gewisslich an der Zeit*)

exercise 8.   Descending major 3rd. (BEETHOVEN: *Piano Sonata in E major, Opus 109*)

Adagio

exercise 9.   Ascending perfect 4th. (MENDELSSOHN: *Nocturne*)

Andante

exercise 10.   Descending perfect 4th. (SCHUBERT: *Unfinished Symphony*)

Allegro

exercise 11.   Ascending perfect 5th. (BACH: *Fugue in D♯ minor, WTC I*)

exercise 12.   Descending perfect 5th. (Chorale: *Aus tiefer Not*)

exercise 13.   Ascending minor 6th. (BRAHMS: *Fourth Symphony*)

exercise 14.   Descending minor 6th. (BACH: *Italian Concerto*)

exercise 15.   Ascending major 6th. (HAYDN: *Symphony in D major, No. 99*)

exercise 16.   Descending major 6th. (WAGNER: *Die Meistersinger*)

exercise 17.   Ascending minor 7th. (BRAHMS: *Fourth Symphony*)

exercise 18.   Descending minor 7th. (BACH: *Sixth Brandenburg Concerto in B♭ major*)

exercise 19.   Ascending major 7th. (BRAHMS: *First Symphony*)

exercise 20.   Descending major 7th and diminished 7th. (BACH: *Harpsichord Concerto in D minor*)

exercise 21.   Ascending perfect 8ve. (MOZART: *Piano Concerto in D minor, K.466*)

exercise 22.   Descending perfect 8ve. (MOZART: *Symphony in G major, K.444*)

exercise 23.   Tritone. (MOZART: *Symphony in C major, K.551*)

exercise 24.   Augmented 2nd. (SCHUMANN: *First Symphony*)

exercise 25.   Diminished 7th. (BACH: *Fugue in A minor, WTC II*)

C. Structure and Notation of the Diatonic Scales

The purpose of this exercise is to make certain that the reader has a basic familiarity with the whole- and half-step patterns in the major and minor scales and that he understands notation, including key signatures.

> INSTRUCTIONS
> A single note is given. The numeral below the note indicates its position in the diatonic major or minor scale. Supply the correct key signature and write out the complete scale, marking the position of the half steps. The procedure is demonstrated below.

exercise 26. **Major scales**

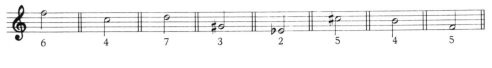

exercise 27. **Minor scales (melodic form)**

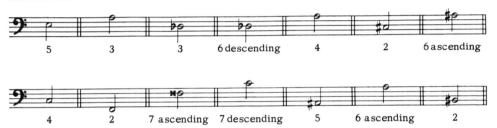

D. Intervals to Identify

INSTRUCTIONS
Each exercise contains intervals extracted from a single diatonic scale. Identify the key from the accidentals, then sing the intervals by scale degree numbers and letter names, identifying each interval by class (consonance or dissonance) and size.

exercise 28.

exercise 29.

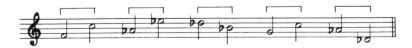

exercise 30.

exercise 31.

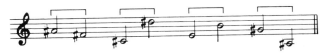

exercise 32.

exercise 33.

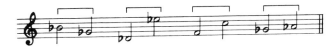

exercise 34.

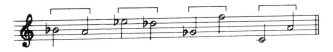

exercise 35.

E. Familiar Melodies

INSTRUCTIONS
Portions of familiar melodies are notated below without key signature and without metric-rhythmic pattern. Identify the melody and supply the missing elements. Also label all intervals between successive notes.

exercise 36.

exercise 37.

exercise 38.

exercise 39.

exercise 40.

exercise 41.

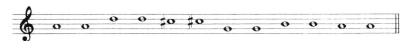

exercise 42.

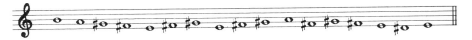

exercise 43.

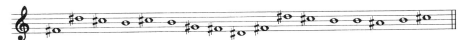

exercise 44.

exercise 45.

exercise 46.

exercise 47.

Chapter 2

THE TRIAD:
THE HARMONIC BASIS
OF TONAL MUSIC

Harmony differs from chord as whole
differs from part.

Friedrich Wilhelm Marpurg, 1755

26. How Chord Structure Is Described

The first focus in harmony study is the structure of chords. As indicated in
Chapter 1, a chord is a group of three or more different notes that sound simultaneously. A chord has at least the value of a full metrical pulse. It may even
extend over several measures, as in the following passage.

example 46. BEETHOVEN: *Piano Sonata in E♭, Op. 7*

Each measure of this excerpt contains the same chord, a chord that consists of the notes Eb, G, and Bb. A description of a chord in terms of letter names is, however, of little general significance, and therefore chord structure is described by listing the intervals which make up the chord. In this way we represent not merely the notes of the particular chord, but the general class to which it belongs. As a result, we immediately know a great deal about its probable behavior in a particular context.

The intervals which comprise a chord are always reckoned from the bass upward. Thus, in Example 46 although the distribution of the notes above the bass changes from measure to measure the *intervals* which those notes form with the bass remain the same and we say that a single chord governs the entire passage. Since the chord contains the intervals of a perfect 5th and a major 3rd above the bass it is recognized as a major triad.

27. The Triad as Basic Consonant Chord

In Chapter 1 consonant intervals were emphasized as the stable and foundational elements of tonal music. We can now extend that statement to include consonant chords. When the intervals of a chord are consonant with the bass, the entire chord is called consonant. If the chord contains an interval which is dissonant against the bass, the entire chord is called dissonant. Therefore, the triad whose fundamental note is scale degree 1 is a consonant chord since it contains the consonant intervals of a perfect 5th and a major 3rd measured upward from the lowest note, whereas the triad on scale degree 7 is dissonant because it contains the dissonant interval of a diminished 5th.

example 47.

28. The Triads in the Diatonic Major Mode

As has been indicated triads can be constructed on each note of the scale. Example 48 summarizes the seven diatonic triads in the major mode.

example 48.

Each diatonic triad is designated by a Roman numeral which shows the diatonic position of its fundamental note. In addition, each triad has a name. For the time being we will use only two of these, those that refer to the most important triads. The triad on scale degree 1 (I) is called the *tonic* triad, and the triad on scale degree 5 (V) is called the *dominant* triad.

In the major mode all triads are consonant except one, the leading note triad, VII, which is called diminished after the size of its dissonant interval. Of the six remaining triads three are major (I, IV, and V) and three are minor (II, III, and VI).

29.   The Triads in the Diatonic Minor Mode

The diatonic triads in minor are constructed both from the natural and the harmonic forms of the scale. As shown in Example 49 this means that V and VII both have two different forms, depending upon the scale from which they are drawn.

example 49.

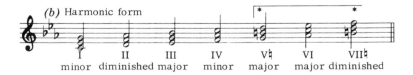

If drawn from the natural minor scale V is a minor triad, often called the *minor dominant.* If drawn from the harmonic minor scale V includes raised scale degree

7, the leading note, and therefore has the same notes as V in the parallel major mode. Similarly, if drawn from the harmonic minor scale, VII is a diminished triad, like VII in the parallel major, whereas if drawn from the natural minor scale, it is a major triad.

In connection with the harmonic minor scale as a source of diatonic chords it is important to realize that the leading note is not included as a chord note in chords whose fundamental notes lie below scale degree 5. Thus only V and VII contain the leading note. The following triad is not a functional diatonic triad:

example 50.

Occasionally one diatonic triad is drawn from the melodic minor scale: a major triad on scale degree IV. The major 3rd of this normally minor triad is raised scale degree 6 which characterizes the melodic minor scale.

example 51.

30.   Harmony in Four Voices; Doubling

Although the three-note chord, the triad, is fundamental to tonal music, compositional practice features four-note chords. One reason for this is that the lowest note or bass was initially regarded as the foundation which supported the chord, as an independent element upon which the triad was constructed. Thus we have the familiar expression "bass and chord," meaning the bass note plus the three notes of the triad. Often, however, it is more convenient to regard the bass note simply as another chord note. In that case we see that the triad becomes a four-note chord when one of its notes is duplicated, or doubled, at the interval of the unison or the 8ve. In the following distribution each chord has one note doubled, with the exception of the next to last.

example 52.   CHOPIN: *Nocturne in G minor, Op. 37/1*

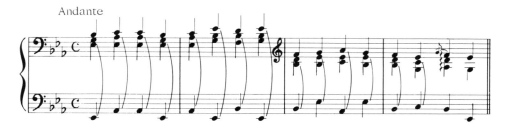

We can describe the distribution of chord notes here more accurately by saying that the bass of each chord is doubled at the 8ve.

By tradition, each note of a four-note chord is designated according to the normative arrangement of two male and two female voices in choral music, whether or not the chord is actually intended for vocal performance. Thus, the highest voice in Example 52 is called the soprano, the voice below it the alto. The voice immediately above the bass is called the tenor. A typical vocal arrangement is shown in the following composition. As is customary in the four-voice vocal composition, the stems of the notes sung by the soprano point upward, those of the alto point downward. Similarly, the tenor stems point upward, while those of the bass point downward.

example 53.   ALBRECHTSBERGER: *Miserere*

Soprano and bass are often referred to as the *outer voices,* alto and tenor as the *inner voices,* for obvious reasons. This pairing of voices is evident in the notation of many of the instrumental examples and exercises in the present volume: soprano and bass notes of the chord are each given separate stems, while the inner voices (alto and tenor) are attached to a single stem.

Voices are also called *parts*. Therefore we speak either of "four voice" or "four-part" harmony. The terms are identical in meaning. Since four-part harmony is the norm in triadic music, harmony in less than four parts may be regarded as incomplete, while harmony in more than four parts results from the doubling of more than one chord note or the tripling, quadrupling, and so on of one or more chord notes.

31. Positions of the Soprano Voice

The highest voice of the chord plays a primary role in harmonic and melodic progression. Therefore there is a special terminology to describe its position in relation to the bass of the chord. When the soprano doubles the bass we speak of the *position of the octave* (Example 54a). When the soprano carries the 3rd we have the *position of the 3rd* (Example 54b). When the 5th of the chord is in the soprano we speak of the *position of the 5th* (Example 54c).

Changes in soprano position do not affect the interval content of the chord. This is evident in the following excerpt, where only the soprano position changes in each successive statement of the chord (see Example 46).

example 54.   MOZART: *The Magic Flute (Der dreimalige Akkord)*

When the three soprano positions of the triad are considered, one of the special advantages of four-voice harmony becomes clear. With only three voices one could not obtain a complete chord in the soprano position of the 8ve. Either 3rd or 5th would have to be omitted, as shown below.

example 55.

32. Chord Spacing

When the notes of the triad lie as closely together as possible the triad is said to be in *close position.* When the notes do not lie as closely together as possible the triad is said to be in *open position.* When the triad is distributed conveniently for the keyboard so that soprano, alto, and tenor are as close as possible the chord is said to be *in close position below the soprano.* Only the bass lies apart from the other notes in this spacing, which will be used extensively in the exercises in the present volume. This spacing, which is termed four-voice keyboard spacing, is shown in the following excerpt.

example 56. BRAHMS: *Vergangen ist mir Glück und Heil, Op. 48/6*

33. Figured Bass

It has been emphasized that the bass is the foundation of harmonic structure. Its role as the bearer of harmony is evident in the system of musical notation known as *figured bass* which developed as an integral part of tonal music throughout the seventeenth and eighteenth centuries.

A figured bass consists of a series of bass notes with symbols above and below that indicate how the chords are to be completed and connected. For example, this is a fragment of an eighteenth-century bass:

example 57. MARCELLO: *Psalms*

At first this system was used only as a kind of musical shorthand which enabled composers to give minimal instructions to keyboard accompanists without the necessity of writing out all the notes. The performers, specially trained for their task, would then transform the figured bass into full-fledged accompaniments, often adding embellishments of various kinds.

Gradually the figured bass, or *thorough bass* as it was known in England, came to be used by composer-performers to notate improvisations, actually compositional sketches. From this it was only a short step to the direct use of figured bass in the teaching of composition, and thus in the eighteenth century it became one of the fundamental means by which composers learned their craft. Bach, his sons, Haydn, Mozart, Beethoven—all were introduced to music via figured bass. The following excerpt from J. S. Bach's short treatise on figured bass indicates the close connection between figured bass and composition. It also demonstrates the importance of the consonant triad in his musical thought.

> The harmonic triad belongs properly to the subject of composition, but since a figured bass is the beginning of a composition, and . . . may even be called an extemporaneous composition, made by the person who plays the figured bass, the subject of the triad may be fitly mentioned in this place.

This clearly shows Bach's regard for the figured bass, a regard shared by many. In addition to its historical validity the figured bass has to recommend it this primary educational advantage: it provides the beginner with absolutely essential experience in the construction and connection of chords. Moreover, he can obtain this experience before learning about chord relations and chord progression. These come later, after a period of systematic, guided work with the basic materials and techniques of harmony. At this elementary stage he need only follow certain simple instructions and perform certain operations. Gradually, against an accumulated background of experience with the basic materials, concepts of tonal organization will be introduced which afford a deeper understanding of triadic music. In this way conceptual knowledge increases simultaneously with skill in performing the basic operations required by the art. We now present the first of these operations, the reading of figured bass.

The figures tell the musician which intervals make up the chord above the bass: Thus, if the chord is a diatonic triad the figures would be $\frac{5}{3}$, indicating that a 5th and a 3rd above the bass combine to form that particular chord. In actual practice, since the triad is the fundamental harmony in tonal music it usually is not figured at all. Therefore any bass note without an accompanying figure means that a diatonic triad ($\frac{5}{3}$) is to be constructed above that note.

example 58.

$(\frac{5}{3})$

Thus for the accompaniment of the familiar French folk song, *Au clair de la lune,* one need only notate the bass and upper voice as shown in the next example. The melody is notated separately on the top staff.

example 59.   *Au clair de la lune*

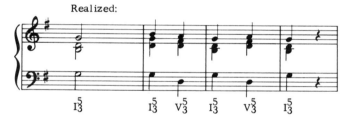

If each chord is played in close position below the soprano, that is, in four-voice keyboard spacing, an adequate accompaniment is obtained. The second part of Example 59 shows the accompaniment as it should be played, or to use the traditional term, "realized."

The figures do not indicate the soprano position or spacing of the chord. For the time being, the reader will not be concerned with these problems since the soprano will be given in all figured bass exercises and, unless otherwise stated, he will use the four-voice keyboard spacing as illustrated in Example 56 above.

Whenever a diatonic note is raised or lowered the alteration is indicated by the signs ♯, ♭, or ♮, as in regular notation. For example, in the accompaniment for the following song the bass note D is supplied with a ♯. This sign transforms the minor dominant triad into the dominant triad with the leading note. As a bass figure an accidental alone always refers to the 3rd above the bass and only to the 3rd. The numeral 3 is not required. In all other cases the accidental precedes the figure for the interval, for example ♭5.

example 60. *English Folk Song*

Realized:

Here, as in Example 59, the first task of the performer is to read the figured bass correctly and supply the indicated chord notes in close position below the soprano. He must then connect the chords in a coherent and effective way. The description of this procedure follows.

34. Chord Connection (Voice Leading)

The figured bass system provides an excellent means for learning to construct chords. It also provides an excellent means for learning to connect them. These two operations, chord construction and chord connection, are fundamental to harmony study. They must be learned before more demanding tasks are undertaken.

Influenced by the two-dimensional notation of music, we often speak of chord construction as occurring in the *vertical* dimension, whereas chord connection occurs in the *horizontal* dimension. This distinction pervades musical terminology. Thus, the techniques of chord connection are commonly called *voice leading* techniques, referring to the progression of the individual chord notes which form "voices" in the horizontal dimension.

The two basic techniques for connecting consonant chords are illustrated by the opening of a familiar song:

example 61. *America*

Here we see that when connecting one chord with another, notes common to both chords are kept in the same voice, while notes that have no counterpart in the subsequent chord move to the nearest note in that chord, preferably by stepwise motion. Sometimes there will be more than one possible stepwise progression, in which case the best choice is determined by rhythm, meter, distribution, register, and other factors which will be explained and illustrated as we proceed.

Voice leading is often described in terms of pairs of voices, for example, soprano and bass, or alto and tenor. When the voices move in the same direction and maintain the same interval we say that they are in *parallel motion.* When they move in the same direction but do not maintain the same interval they are in *similar motion.* When they move in opposite directions they are in *contrary motion.* And when one voice moves while the other remains stationary they are in *oblique motion.* These patterns are illustrated below.

example 62.

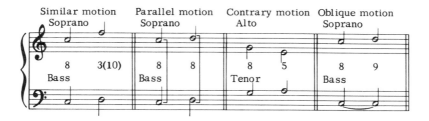

Example 62 shows soprano and bass moving in similar and parallel motion, alto and tenor in contrary motion, and soprano and bass in oblique motion. Also important are the intervals which the voices form. These are figured in Example 62.

Whenever two voices are in parallel motion particular attention must be paid to the intervals they form, lest they violate one of the most important principles of voice leading, a principle that exerts a large measure of control over melodic progression, the prohibition of parallel 5ths and parallel 8ves. By this is meant that two voices are not permitted to move from one chord to another in such a way that they form a succession of two perfect 5ths or two perfect 8ves in parallel motion. Therefore the following succession is incorrect:

example 63.

Parallel 8ves, as shown here, reduce the number of voices to three since the voice that doubles at the 8ve is not an independent voice but merely a duplication. Parallel 8ves may also confuse the functions of the voices, as here. If the upper voice succession G A is merely a duplication of the bass, then the actual soprano must be D E, the alto voice. This interpretation of course makes no sense, for it turns the texture inside out.

　　Such duplication of voice leading is not, however, the only function of 8ve doubling. In many compositions we find that voices are doubled at the 8ve for reinforcement. For example, the bass of the classical period symphonic movement is ordinarily played by cellos and contrabasses, instruments which sound an 8ve apart. This kind of doubling for reinforcement is not at all the same as the doubling of an essential voice in the register of another voice, as in Example 63.

　　Parallel 5ths are avoided because the 5th, formed by scale degrees 1 and 5, is the primary harmonic interval, the interval that divides the scale and thus defines the key. The direct succession of two 5ths raises doubt concerning the key. Example 64 illustrates.

example 64.

The prohibition of parallel 5ths is more than a pedantic dictum. It is an important negative principle that is responsible for many harmonic and melodic features of tonal music—for example, the use of inverted consonances explained in the next chapter. Without the limitation placed upon parallel 5ths and 8ves the art of tonal music would not have developed the elaborate and intricate forms which have given it such a unique position.

The problem of parallel 5ths and 8ves usually involves only two chords in succession, chords that are apt to be closely associated as a pair. Chords are often grouped in this way and we may regard the chord pair as the smallest unit of harmonic motion, the smallest harmonic context. Pairs of consonant chords are connected by stepwise voice leading as a general rule. However, nonstepwise motions ("skips") may be required in order to avoid parallel 5ths, or they may be desired in order to gain or maintain a particular register. In such cases skips are made freely and the rule of stepwise voice leading is disregarded. Different conditions obtain when dissonant chords are involved. There certain stepwise voice leadings are obligatory.

In subsequent sections closer attention will be given to the intervallic patterns formed by moving voices—in particular, to the patterns formed by the outer voices—since such patterns have very significant implications not only for the detail of tonal compositions but also for structures of longer span. (See, for instance, section 220.)

35. The Basic Cadence

Perhaps the most important chord pair in tonal music is the closing succession V I (dominant-tonic). When it occurs at the end of a composition or at the end of a longer harmonic unit this kind of succession is called a *cadence.*

example 65.

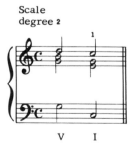

Example 65 shows the basic cadence, sometimes called "authentic." The soprano progression from scale degree 2 to scale degree 1 is supported by the cadential harmonies V I. When the soprano comes to rest on scale degree 1, as in Example

65, the effect of completion or closure is stronger than when the soprano ends on scale degree 3, as below.

example 66.

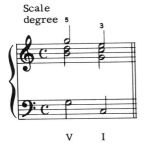

V   I

This succession closes harmonically but not melodically. (See section 137.)

36. Temporary Shift to Five Voices

In certain situations one can add a fifth to the normative four-voice texture in order to obtain both stepwise leading and complete chords. Example 67 illustrates this, using the cadential succession V I.

example 67.

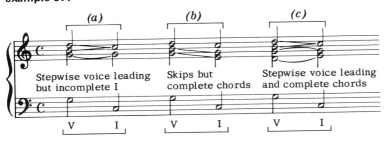

At (a) the voice leading is stepwise but the final chord lacks a 3rd. At (b) the inner voices must skip in order to achieve a complete statement of the final chord. This is the normal procedure in four voices. At (c) a fifth voice, D, is added to the V. This provides both stepwise voice leading and a complete final chord.

The temporary shift to five voices is a valuable technique that solves many voice-leading problems. However, it should be used sparingly since one must also learn to manipulate four voices in situations where a fifth voice would not be available, for example, in writing for a quartet of brass instruments.

EXERCISES

A. List of Some Important Terms to Define and Memorize

Dissonant chord

Doubling

Outer voices

Position of the 8ve

Position of the 5th

Four-voice keyboard spacing

Alto voice

Figured bass

Voice leading

Similar motion

Cadence

Skip

B. Basic Keyboard and Aural Exercises

INSTRUCTIONS

Play each exercise at the keyboard. Then before going on to the next sing the exercise in the following ways, using the keyboard to check for accuracy not to accompany the voice.

1 Sing the entire bass.
2 Sing the entire soprano.
3 Beginning from the soprano note, sing all the notes of each chord in descending order, close position. Use the neutral syllable "la."
4 Beginning from the bass note, sing all the notes of each chord in ascending order, close position.

These four steps are illustrated below.

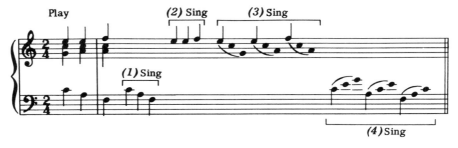

The exercises should be repeated until a certain degree of fluency is attained. With each repetition transpose the patterns to a different key and provide a different metric-rhythmic pattern. For singing, letter names should replace the neutral syllable, "la," when the exercises are repeated.

exercise 48. **Triads in all three soprano positions. Continue until all keys have been included.**

The following two exercises will be used again in subsequent chapters. For convenience, they are identified as Basic Chord Patterns 1 and 2. Both contain only diatonic triads.

exercise 49.   **Basic Chord Pattern 1**

exercise 50.   **Basic Chord Pattern 2**

C. Figured Bass Exercises

INSTRUCTIONS

The exercises are to be worked out at the keyboard first, then notated in full according to the rules given below. Each exercise should then be sung, following the instructions given above for the basic keyboard and aural exercises.

1 Each chord must be complete. No chord note may be omitted.

2 Four-voice harmony is to be maintained. This means that one note of each triad must be doubled. Select the doubling that will permit retention of common notes or stepwise connection with preceding and following chords and that will at the same time avoid impending parallel 5ths or 8ves, if any.

3 Stepwise voice leading is especially important when the half step is involved. For example, diatonic scale degrees 4 and 7 in major and all chromatic notes demand stepwise progression, whenever possible, in accord with the law of the half step.

4 Use only the diatonic notes of the key unless an accidental appears as a bass figure.

5 Use four-voice keyboard spacing. Occasionally this must be abandoned when doubling is changed to avoid parallel 5ths or 8ves.

6 To develop facility in locating the chord follow this procedure at the beginning:

   (a) Think of the triad in close position directly above the bass in the left hand (without doubling).

   (b) The notes which are required to make the triad complete in four parts should then be placed in close position below the given soprano:

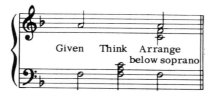

Given   Think   Arrange
                  below soprano

exercise 51. C. P. E. BACH

exercise 52. C. P. E. BACH

exercise 53. **C. P. E. BACH**

exercise 54. **Chorale:** *Wenn wir in höchsten Nöten sein*

exercise 55. **Folk song:** *Flow Gently, Sweet Afton*

exercise 56.   Chorale: *Wir Christenleut' hab'n jetzo Freud*

exercise 57.   *The Apprentice's Farewell* (German folk song)

exercise 58.   Chorale: *Was Gott tut, das ist wohlgetan*

exercise 59. *Dame d'esprit* (La Folie d'Espagne)

Moderato
Voice

exercise 60. **Chorale:** *Durch Adams Fall ist ganz verderbt*

*The 3rd of this triad is doubled at the unison (by alto and tenor voices). There-
fore, on the piano only three voices sound. With other instruments or voices the
full four parts would be heard.

D. Exercises in Locating and Identifying the Diatonic Triads

The exercises in this group provide essential practice in the important skill of locating triads within the diatonic tonality and identifying them quickly by Roman numeral, type, and letter name.

> INSTRUCTIONS
> Each exercise below is made up of triads extracted from a single tonality. Identify the tonality, supply its key signature, and label each triad by Roman numeral. Also indicate the type of triad (major, minor, or diminished) and write out the letter names of its notes.

exercise 61.

exercise 62.

exercise 63.

exercise 64.

exercise 65.

exercise 66.

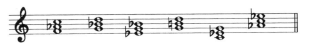

INSTRUCTIONS

The next group of exercises is somewhat more demanding. A series of bass notes is given. (1) Identify the key from the accidentals and supply the key signature. (2) Label each triad by Roman numeral. (3) Write out the letter names of the notes above each bass note. (4) Notate the upper voices in full, beginning from the soprano position indicated. The rules of voice leading should be observed, with special attention given to the stepwise progression of the soprano voice. The four steps are demonstrated below.

exercise 67.

exercise 68.

exercise 69.

exercise 70.

exercise 71.

exercise 72.

Chapter 3

THE HARMONIC PROCESS OF CHORD GENERATION: SIXTH CHORDS

> This principle of inversion is the core of all the diversity that characterizes harmony.
>
> Jean Phillipe Rameau, 1722

37. The Generative Role of the Consonant Triad

Because the consonant triad is the basic harmonic element in tonal music one might well expect to find only chords of that structure in compositions. Of course we know that this is not the case. The harmonic vocabulary of tonal music is highly diversified. Yet the influence of the triad pervades the tonal universe, for all chords are generated from it by three processes—harmonic, melodic, and rhythmic. In the present chapter the first of these, the harmonic process, is introduced.

38. Inversion of the Bass: the Harmonic Process of Chord Generation

In section 13, Chapter 1, the inversion of intervals was explained. It was stated that the inversion of an interval is possible because notes an 8ve apart are regarded as equivalent. When this harmonic principle is extended to the triad the result is *chord inversion.* By chord inversion is meant the placement of the bass an 8ve higher (or two 8ves, three 8ves, . . .), so that the chord note which was immediately above the bass becomes the new bass note. The next example illustrates the relation between interval inversion and chord inversion.

example 68.

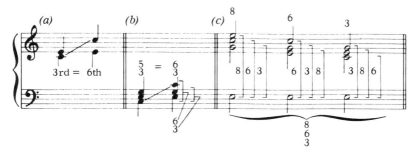

At (*a*) the lower note of the 3rd is inverted (placed an 8ve higher) so that a new interval is generated: the 3rd becomes a 6th. The two intervals are regarded as equivalent. At (*b*) the bass of a triad is inverted, leaving the former 3rd as a new bass note. By this means a new chord is generated which contains the same notes as the parent chord but in a different arrangement. This new chord comprises the intervals of a 6th and a 3rd above the bass and is called the chord of the 6th, or more simply the *6th chord,* after the interval that distinguishes it from its parent triad. Accordingly, it is figured 6, not $\frac{6}{3}$, the 3rd being understood in all cases. Example 68(*c*) shows the 6th chord in its three possible soprano positions: the position of the 8ve, the position of the 6th, and the position of the 3rd. As in all cases, the distribution of the upper parts does not affect the interval content of the chord. This is affected only by change of bass.

The 6th chord is regarded as equivalent to the $\frac{5}{3}$ from which it is generated. Under certain circumstances, however, it is not the harmonic equivalent of the parent triad, but has a melodic origin and function—circumstances that will be considered in subsequent chapters. For the present we shall regard the 6th chord as the counterpart of its parent triad and examine its various functions in relation to that chord.

39. The 6th Chord as Extension of the Parent Triad

The equivalence of the parent $\frac{5}{3}$ and its inversion, the $\frac{6}{3}$, is most evident when the two chords form a pair. This is illustrated in the next example.

example 69.

At (*a*) is shown a succession of four diatonic triads: I IV V I. At (*b*) each of these triads is followed by its 6th chord.

Example 69 illustrates an important function of inversion: an inverted chord often prevents or corrects parallel 5ths and 8ves without changing the harmony. The 5ths marked by diagonal lines at (*a*) are corrected by the 6th chord inserted at (*b*). Here and elsewhere the prohibition of parallel 5ths and 8ves serves indirectly to create a more elaborate melodic and rhythmic texture.

Example 69 shows the 6th chord as a suffix that extends the parent triad. The 6th chord may also extend the parent triad by serving as a prefix. Example 70 illustrates.

example 70.

40. Doubling of the Notes of the Consonant 6th Chord

The 3rd of the triad usually moves stepwise to a note of the next chord. When the triad is inverted, the 3rd becomes the bass note of the 6th chord. Therefore if the bass is doubled at the 8ve, parallel 8ves often will result. This relationship is illustrated at (a) and (b) in Example 71.

example 71.

(a)   (b) 8ve doubled   (c) 6th doubled   (d) 3rd doubled

The two other possible doublings are shown at (c) and (d). Both are satisfactory and the selection of one or the other depends upon the melodic and rhythmic details of a particular context.

Doubling of the bass of the 6th chord does not always result in parallel 8ves. In the passage below, the doubling notes are led in contrary stepwise motion to the next chord.

example 72.

A four-voice succession of 6th chords in parallel motion (called *parallel 6th chords*) requires a different doubling for each chord if stepwise voice leading without parallel 5ths and 8ves is to be obtained. This technique of *alternate doubling* is illustrated at (a) in the next example.

example 73.

(a) alternate doubling

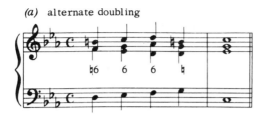

(b) 3 voices only — 6th in soprano

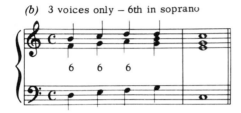

(c) 3rd in soprano creates parallel 5ths

If it is not essential to maintain four voices and if the 6th is in the soprano of each chord, one can shift to three voices temporarily, as shown at (*b*). This can be done only if the 6th is in the soprano. If the 3rd is in the soprano parallel 5ths are created between the two upper voices, and if the 8ve is in the soprano parallel 8ves between bass and soprano result.

41. The 6th Chord as Representative of Its Parent Triad

The 6th chord often occurs without its parent chord, and serves not as an extension but as a representative. In this capacity it fulfills much the same function as would the parent chord in the same context. The next example offers a comparison between parent $\frac{5}{3}$ and 6th chord in the same contexts.

example 74. Chorale: *Herr Jesu Christ, dich zu uns wend*

At (*a*) the melody is harmonized by $\frac{5}{3}$'s. This creates two problems: the repetitious bass in the first and third measures and the parallel 8ves between soprano and bass in the second measure. At (*b*), 6th chords are substituted for $\frac{5}{3}$'s at the three problematic points and the defects are thereby removed.

42. The 6th Chord as First Inversion of the Triad

Each of the three notes of the triad can serve as bass note. The triad as a $\frac{5}{3}$ is said to be in *fundamental position,* or *root position.* The 6th chord is often called the *first inversion* of the triad and symbolized by combining a Roman numeral with the Arabic figure 6, as in the following excerpt.

example 75. HAYDN: *Variations in F minor*

The Roman numerals in Example 75 indicate the fundamental notes of the parent triads. The Arabic figure 6 means that the chord is the first inversion of the triad whose fundamental note or root is designated by the Roman numeral. Thus the symbol for the second chord in the excerpt is read as "the first inversion of the triad on scale degree 5." Similarly, the symbol I^6 does not indicate a 6th chord constructed above scale degree 1, but rather the first inversion of the triad whose fundamental note is scale degree 1.

To sum up, Arabic figures show the vertical structure of the chord and indicate its voice leading requirements (especially in the case of dissonant chords, as will be shown); the Roman numerals show chord relations and harmonic progression in terms of the diatonic triads.

A word of warning is in order here: Not all 6th chords are inversions of some parent triad. This distinction is amplified in section 208.

43.   Dissonant Diatonic-6th Chords

The three dissonant diatonic triads, VII in major and minor and II in minor rarely occur in fundamental position in four voices. Usually they are represented by their 6th chords. In both modes the VII^6 often connects I with I^6 as shown below.

example 76.

At (a) we see the chord pair I I^6 in both major and minor. At (b) bass and soprano add a passing note which fills in the skip at (a), while the inner voices complete the chord, VII⁶. Characteristically, the voice leading is stepwise and the bass of the dissonant-6th chord is doubled at the 8ve. The 6th is not doubled. Since it is the leading note and has a fixed progression, doubling would result automatically in parallel 8ves or unisons.

In Example 76 it is important to notice that the final 6th chord in each case serves as an extension of its parent triad since it is connected to the parent triad by the intervening dissonant-6th chord. This is a simple instance of a basic aspect of tonal music: the formation of a larger unit through the coherent interaction of its components. In Example 76, each group of three chords serves to extend the tonic triad.

The II⁶ in minor often prepares the cadential V. The chord is shown in the same context but with different doublings in Example 77 below.

example 77.

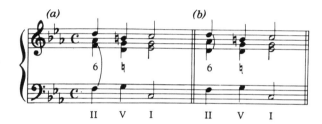

At (a) the bass is doubled. At (b) the 6th is doubled. The 3rd of this chord should not be doubled. Since it is scale degree 6 in minor it has a fixed progression downward by half step, and doubling would result automatically in parallel 8ves or unisons as in the case of the doubled leading note of VII⁶ remarked above.

44. Second Inversion of the Triad ($\frac{6}{4}$) as a Dissonance

It has been seen that inversion of the bass of the fundamental triad produces a 6th chord, called the first inversion. Unless the fundamental triad is a diminished triad, the 6th chord thus generated is a consonant chord which can either extend its parent chord, as shown in section 39, or represent it, as shown in section 41. In both instances the 6th chord is a consonant chord equivalent to the parent chord. However, when the inversion process is extended beyond the first inversion a chord equivalent to the parent chord is not produced. The reason for this is shown in the following illustration.

example 78.

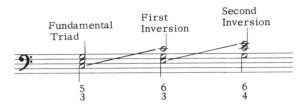

Example 78 shows that inversion of the bass of the 6th chord produces a chord that contains the intervals of a 6th and a 4th. Since the 4th is a dissonant interval this second inversion of the triad is a dissonant chord and therefore cannot be regarded as the extension or representative of the parent triad.

Unlike the parent triad and its first inversion, the $\frac{6}{4}$ is a dependent, unstable chord which depends for its meaning upon a triad other than the parent chord. This dependence is clearly evident in the case of the $\frac{6}{4}$ chord which often precedes V at the cadence, the *cadential* $\frac{6}{4}$.

example 79. Chorale: *Wer weiss wie nahe*

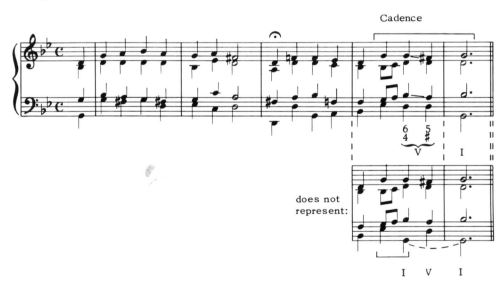

In Example 79 the cadential V is preceded by a $\frac{6}{4}$. The 6th and the 4th descend together stepwise to the 5th and 3rd of the V, as indicated by the figures and by the diagonal lines in the example. The $\frac{6}{4}$ embellishes and delays the V$\frac{5}{3}$ upon which it depends for its meaning. It does not represent the parent triad, I. This fact can be demonstrated by substituting the parent I for the $^6_4$ as shown in Example 79. The effect of the parent triad is not at all the same as that of the $^6_4$. It creates a discontinuity in the bass line (indicated by the bracket) and anticipates in an undesirable way the final I (indicated by the dotted line).

Only in one special instance does the $^6_4$ represent its theoretical parent chord: in the case of the "consonant" $^6_4$. This form of the $^6_4$ as well as other variants of the dependent or dissonant $^6_4$ are explained and illustrated in Chapter 11.

EXERCISES

A. List of Some Important Terms to Define and Memorize

Harmonic process
6th chord as extension
6th chord as representative
Dissonant diatonic-6th chords
Parent triad

Parallel 6th chords
Fundamental position
First inversion
Second inversion

B. Basic Keyboard and Aural Exercises

INSTRUCTIONS
These are the same as the instructions given for the preliminary exercises in Chapter 2:
Play each exercise at the keyboard. Then, before going on to the next, sing the exercise in the following ways, using the keyboard to check for accuracy not to accompany the voice.
1 Sing the entire bass.
2 Sing the entire soprano.
3 Beginning from the soprano note sing all the notes of each chord in descending order, close position. Use the neutral syllable "la."
4 Beginning from the bass note sing all the notes of each chord in ascending order, close position.
The exercises should be repeated until a certain degree of fluency is attained. With each repetition transpose the patterns to a different key and provide a different metric-rhythmic pattern. For singing, letter names should replace the neutral syllable, "la," when the exercises are repeated.

exercise 73. **Basic Chord Pattern 1 (see Exercise 49)**

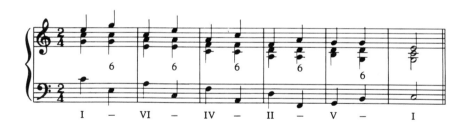

Here each chord of the basic pattern is followed by its first inversion. This greatly expands the basic succession. Arabic figures are shown between the staves, while Roman numerals which designate the position of the fundamental note in the diatonic scale are shown below the bass staff. The dash means that the preceding numeral still applies.

exercise 74. **Basic Chord Pattern 2 (see Exercise 50)**

In the preceding exercise the 6th chords served to extend the parent triad. Here they represent the parent triad: IV^6 stands in place of IV, III^6 stands in place of III, and so on.

At this point we add to the basic keyboard and aural exercises common cadential successions in which the cadential dominant is prepared by II or IV or by the first inversions of those triads. All should be committed to memory and, following the order of the circle of 5ths, played in every key.

exercise 75. **Cadential V prepared by II or II^6**

exercise 76.   Cadential V prepared by IV or IV⁶

IV   V   I   IV⁶   V   I

IV   V♮   I   IV⁶   V♮   I

C. Figured Bass Exercises

INSTRUCTIONS
These are to be played at the keyboard, notated in full, and sung according to the instructions given for the basic keyboard and aural exercises. In addition, each 6th chord marked by an asterisk should be labeled either as extension or representative of its parent triad.

exercise 77.   Chorale: *Schmücke dich, o liebe Seele*

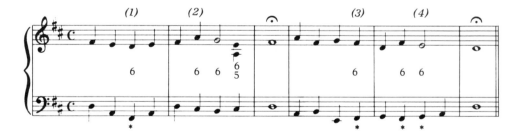

comments

1   The 6th (soprano), should be doubled here in order to avoid parallel 8ves in the connection to the following chord.
2   Impending parallel 8ves can be avoided by correct doubling of the first 6th chord.
3   Were the parent triad to be substituted for the 6th chord here, parallel 8ves and 5ths would automatically result in the connection from the preceding chord. Thus, the 6th chord serves as a voice leading corrective.
4   Change of harmony is required on the last beat.

exercise 78.   TELEMANN: *Money*

comments

1   The figures $\begin{smallmatrix}6\\4\\\sharp\end{smallmatrix}$ $\begin{smallmatrix}5\\\sharp\end{smallmatrix}$ indicate the exact horizontal succession of voices. The $\begin{smallmatrix}6\\4\end{smallmatrix}$ is discussed in section 44.

2   Each bass note in this measure and the two following is embellished by an auxiliary eighth note that does not belong to the harmony. These notes develop the harmony rhythmically and melodically but have no effect either upon the structure of the chords or upon their connection.

exercise 79.   Chorale: *Ich dank' dir, lieber Herre*

comments

1   The second eighth note belongs to the following harmony. This kind of embellishment is known therefore as an ***anticipation.***

2   The chord $\binom{5}{3}$ harmonizes the first of the two eighth notes. The second eighth note in soprano and bass is an unharmonized, unaccented passing note.

3   The figures here indicate the exact linear succession: the 4th above the bass moves to the raised 3rd above the bass.

exercise 80.   Chorale: *Singen wir aus Herzensgrund*

comments

1 Whenever the bass of a 6th chord moves to the bass of a $\frac{5}{3}$ by step, as here, one must take care to double a note other than the bass, otherwise parallel 8ves may result. Here it is best to double the 3rd at the unison.
2 The figures indicate the exact horizontal succession: the 5th above the bass moves to the 6th above the bass.

exercise 81. **Chorale:** *Herr, ich habe misgehandelt*

exercise 82.   Chorale: *Lobet den Herren*

exercise 83.   BASSANI: *Harmonia festiva*

exercise 84.   Chorale: *Gottes Sohn ist kommen*

Chapter 4

THE PROGRESSION
OF DIATONIC TRIADS

As I advance in the science of harmony
I become convinced that its absolute
principle resides in the relations between
its sounds, relations of tonality. These
result from a certain necessary order
from which the sounds derive their functions, their attractions, their antipathies,
and ultimately their laws of combination
and succession.

François Joseph Fétis, 1849

45. The Purpose of This Chapter

One writer, the early nineteenth-century theorist, Gottfried Weber, has asserted
that there are precisely 6888 possible harmonic progressions. Fortunately there is
no need to study that many in order to understand tonal music. They can be dealt
with in terms of general principles and applied in music of various styles.

By harmonic progression we do not refer to the voice leading techniques for
moving from one chord to another. Rather, we mean the selecting and ordering of
harmonies in such a way that they form coherent and effective units of several
chords. In a still larger context harmonic progression means the progression of
harmonies and harmonic units over the span of an entire composition. The reader
should remember that the same principles apply to both small and large contexts.

46.   Harmonic Progression and Tonality

The notion of harmonic progression is very closely bound up with the concept of *tonality* which emerged with fully developed tonal music. This concept embraces the main structural components of the tonal composition; within it are expressed the highly diversified events and multiple relationships which form a totality, a musical unity. This is not to say that all events within the tonal composition have harmonic significance. In subsequent chapters, notably 11 and 13, consideration will be given to those linear (contrapuntal) aspects of structure that do not have immediate harmonic significance.

The concept of harmonic progression can be approached directly from familiar and elemental materials, the scale and the triad. We begin with the triad.

47.   The Tonic Triad as Source of the First Principle of Chord Relation

Diatonic consonant chords form the harmonic basis of all tonal compositions. Among these chords the tonic triad is of primary importance. It contains the first principle of chord relation and progression, a principle based upon the triadic interval of the 5th. The 5th is of fundamental importance because it, and it alone, identifies the triad. This primary role is illustrated below.

example 80.

From the complete triad shown at (*a*) we extract the lower 3rd (*b*). As shown, this 3rd may associate itself either with the A minor triad or the C triad. It does not belong to either one exclusively. At (*c*) we extract the upper 3rd of the C major triad. Here again we see that it may belong to either one of two triads. However, at (*d*) we extract the 5th of the triad and see immediately that it is not ambiguous as is the 3rd. It belongs to one and only one triad the C triad, and identifies, or delimits that triad. The significance of the tonic and dominant triads now becomes clearer.

48.   Tonic and Dominant Triads: Primary Triads That Delimit the Key

Just as the 5th delimits the triad, so the cadential succession V I delimits the key. Example 81 summarizes, showing first the vertical 5th as it delimits the triad, then the horizontal bass and harmonic progression V I as it delimits the key.

example 81.

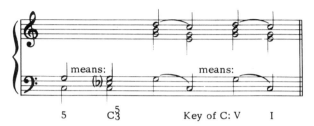

The triads I and V are called *primary triads* to indicate their primary function described above. Those on the remaining scale degrees are called *secondary triads.* Example 82 shows the two classes.

example 82.

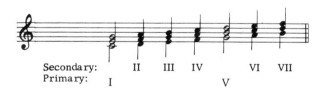

The remainder of this chapter is devoted to the ways in which these two classes of triads are related and to the ways in which they combine to form chord progressions.

49.   Diatonic Position and Progression by Bass 5th

The term progression suggests an orderly motion from one point to another. Thus, to describe a harmonic progression we must be able to give the positions of its beginning and ending chords. It also would be desirable to have a way of measuring harmonic distance. The primary triads and the 5th by which they relate to one another provide the initial means for fulfilling those requirements.

First, the location of each diatonic triad is described in terms of its distance from I as measured by the bass interval of the descending 5th. If we begin with the triad nearest to I by the interval of a 5th, namely V, we can easily determine the position of the remaining triads by continuing the process, that is, by adding the nearest triad to V by 5th, and so on. Example 83 illustrates.

example 83.

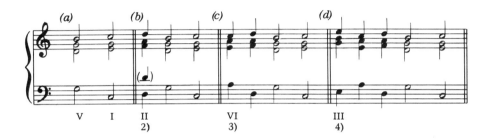

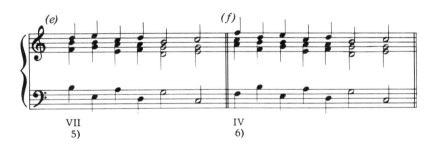

At (a) are the primary triads. V progresses to I by 5th. At (b) the triad which lies a 5th above V is added: II. (In order to keep the progression within the range of the bass clef we represent every other descending 5th by its inversion, the ascending 4th.) At (c) the triad which lies a 5th above II is added to the progression: VI. And so the process continues until all seven diatonic triads are combined in a harmonic progression, a progression which moves by successive bass 5ths. The number in parentheses below each secondary triad indicates the number of 5ths by which it is distant from I.

In Example 84 the same progression is given a metrical setting, with I serving as initial upbeat. This has the advantage of revealing the way in which the chords form a succession of pairs that culminate in the cadential pair, V I.

example 84.

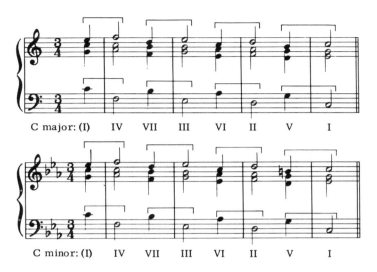

C major: (I)   IV   VII   III   VI   II   V   I

C minor: (I)   IV   VII   III   VI   II   V   I

50. The 2nd as Melodic Interval of Chord (Bass) Relationship

The 5th relationship, as explained above, is the most important for harmonic progression. All other intervals of progression are subordinate to it. Next in importance is the 2nd relationship exemplified by the chord pair IV V. The 5th relationship is exemplified by the chord pair V I.

example 85.

I   IV   V   I

Example 85 shows IV as a prefix to V. The interval of bass progression from chord to chord is the 2nd. We will characterize this stepwise interval of bass progression as melodic. We can then describe such stepwise progressions more specifically as auxiliary note or passing note formations. For instance, the bass of IV (F) here serves as a lower auxiliary note to the bass of V.

   When the triad on IV serves as a stepwise preparation of V as shown in Example 85 we will call it a *dominant preparation*. Similarly, VI often serves as a stepwise dominant preparation. An illustration follows.

example 86. BEETHOVEN: *Quartet in F major, Op. 59/1* (registers simplified)

51. The 3rd Relationship

Bass 3rd relationships between chords are always subordinate to other, stronger, relationships, either the 5th or the 2nd relationship. Example 87 demonstrates this.

example 87.

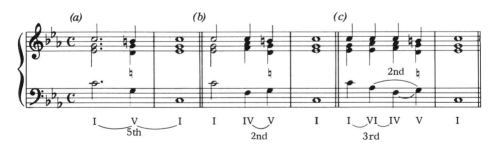

   At (*a*) we see the 5th relationship I V I. At (*b*) V is prepared by IV, a second relationship. At (*c*) VI is added to the chord succession, forming 3rd relationships with both I and IV.

   Of first importance, however, is its 2nd relationship with V as stepwise preparation. Thus, read from left to right Example 87 illustrates the relative values of the intervals of chord progression. The 5th is first in importance; next comes the 2nd; and finally the 3rd, which is always subordinate either to the 5th or to the 2nd, rhythmic and other conditions being equal.

Example 88 provides another short illustration of the three intervals of progression in combination.

example 88.

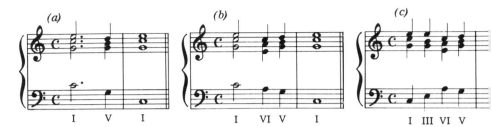

At (a) the interval of progression is the 5th. At (b) the dominant preparation VI adds the two other intervals of progression, forming a 3rd relationship with I and a 2nd relationship with V. In the complete progression the 5th remains as the main interval, with the 2nd next in importance, and the 3rd last. Thus VI and V form a chord pair, not VI and I. Similarly, at (c) III and VI form a pair related by the 5th, while the 3rd between III and I is of secondary importance.

52. Inversion of the Interval of Progression

In connection with Example 83 we remarked that the 5th relationship was represented by the inversion of the 5th, the 4th. Inversion does not alter the interval of progression. The inverted equivalents of 5th, 2nd, and 3rd relationships are summarized in Example 89.

example 89.

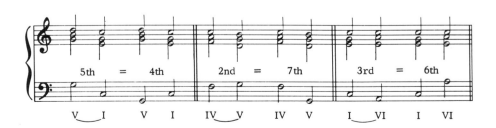

Example 89 also shows that the three intervals of progression (5th, 2nd, and 3rd) plus their inversions (4th, 7th, and 6th) comprise all the diatonic intervals except the 8ve and unison. The 8ve is an interval of progression only insofar as it is involved in the inversion process. Therefore, in order to complete our examination of consonant chord relationships and progression we must consider the function of 6th chords, which are produced by the inversion process.

53.   The Function of 6th Chords in Consonant Chord Progression

In Chapter 3 we examined the function of 6th chords as extensions or representatives of the parent triad. In longer harmonic units composed of several chords, such as those we are considering in the present chapter, 6th chords pose no new problems. In fact, only the representative 6th chord requires comment. Often the bass of the representative 6th chord moves by 2nd, whereas the bass of the parent chord would move by 5th in the same context.

The 6th chord thus combines the 2nd and 5th relationships. The 2nd relationship is actually given; the 5th relationship is implicit. Example 90 illustrates.

example 90.

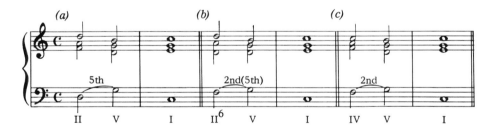

At (a) we see the progression II V I, which is based entirely on the 5th relationship. At (b) II[6] is inserted to represent the parent II. The bass now moves by 2nd and the chord serves as a stepwise dominant preparation similar to IV(c). Yet the underlying harmonic relationship is the 5th relationship indicated by the Roman numerals. In all cases these show the progression of the fundamental note of the triad.

In working out chord progressions one must often consider both relationships, the explicit 2nd of the bass and the implicit 5th of the fundamental.

Example 91 provides another illustration of II⁶ as dominant preparation.

example 91. HAYDN: *Symphony in G major* ("Oxford")

In this context 2nd and 5th relationships are balanced. There are, however, instances in which the melodic function of the first inversion far outweighs its relation to the parent chord. An example follows.

example 92. SCHUMANN: *Carnaval*

Clearly the melodic value of the I⁶ as upbeat to IV is primary here. Note that the bass moves in parallel 10ths with the upper voice toward the accented IV. If the parent I were substituted for I⁶, as at (*b*), the effect would not be at all the same. The parallel 10ths here provide an instance of the importance of linear intervallic patterns. (See section 220.)

54. The Functions of the Dissonant Diatonic Triads

In section 43 it was stated that the dissonant diatonic triads rarely occur in fundamental position. Most often they are represented by their first inversions. These
chords, VII in major and minor and II in minor, are used to connect consonant
chords, and although essential from the melodic standpoint they are secondary to
the consonant triads with regard to harmonic progression. This is perhaps most
convincingly demonstrated by the fact that a dissonant triad is never a goal of a
harmonic progression. (See section 58.)

55. Harmonization of Scale Degree 6 in Minor as Ascending Passing Note

Like the dissonant diatonic triads, the chord which usually harmonizes scale degree
6 in minor is only of local significance. Since it is essential for melodic reasons we
include it here as a diatonic consonance, but with the qualification that its use is
restricted to the harmonization of scale degree 6 in minor as an ascending passing
note. Example 93 shows that scale degree first in the soprano, then in the bass.
In both cases the chord which harmonizes the altered 6th degree is IV♮. The
Roman numeral is enclosed in parentheses to indicate that the chord is not equivalent to the regular IV in harmonic value. In this context it serves a linear function
to make consonant the first of the two passing notes that fill out the interval of
the 4th from G to C.

example 93.

56. The Secondary Dominant Triad as Chromatic Extension of V—I Relation

Thus far discussion and examples have been restricted to diatonic triads. There is,
however, a consonant chromatic triad of such common occurrence even in pre-
dominantly diatonic contexts that it should be considered at this point. This is the
secondary dominant triad. The following series of examples illustrates the structure
and function of this chord.

example 94.

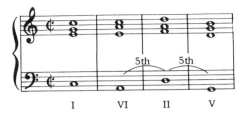

Example 94 shows a progression of four chords terminating on V. The last three chords are related by 5th. In the next example the bass remains the same, but the 3rd of the second chord has been raised, creating a chromatic passing note in the soprano.

example 95.

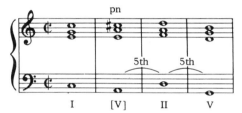

This altered, or chromatic, triad now relates to the following chord exactly as does dominant to tonic in minor. The chromatic passing note may be regarded as a transitory leading note, exemplifying the law of the half step (section 10). For these reasons it is called a secondary dominant triad and symbolized by [V]. It does not usurp the role of the main dominant triad in the key, the primary triad, but merely imitates its structure and function, and thus enhances the progression to the triad which it precedes—II in this instance. Example 96 presents the passage upon which Examples 94 and 95 are based.

example 96.   BEETHOVEN: *Prometheus Overture*

Allegro molto

Any consonant diatonic triad can be preceded by a secondary dominant triad. Below is an example of secondary dominant triads drawn from a seventeenth-century composition. The original is without bar lines. Brackets have been supplied to indicate the harmonic groups; key signature and accidentals have been modified to conform with modern practice.

example 97. HEINRICH SCHÜTZ: *Kleines Geistliches Konzert IX*

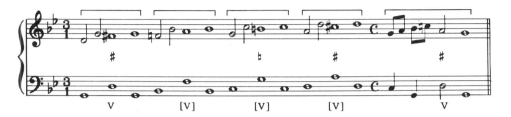

example 98. Chorale: *Das walt' Gott Vater und Gott Sohn*

Here VI is preceded by the first inversion of a secondary dominant triad, [V⁶], whose bass is a chromatic passing note that serves as a transitory leading note.

Secondary dominants (sometimes called "applied dominants") are so common in tonal music—and will be encountered so often in subsequent examples—that further illustrations at this point seem unnecessary.

57. Harmonic Direction

We have seen that consonant triads form chord pairs related by one of three intervals, the 5th, the 2nd, or the 3rd. In harmonic progression the most important of these three intervals is the 5th. Example 83 has illustrated how the position of each consonant triad in the key is measured in terms of 5ths distant from I. From these concepts of chord relationship, harmonic position, and chord progression, we derive the concept of harmonic direction: the orderly progression from one chord toward another chord—the harmonic goal. The factor of direction distinguishes harmonic progression from mere harmonic change. Progression toward a specific goal may involve several chords which form subgroups consisting of chord pairs, threes . . ., but the main elements of the progression are, first, the harmony which serves as point of departure and, second, the harmonic goal. The following example illustrates those two elements:

example 99.   BEETHOVEN: *Piano Sonata in G major, Op. 31/1*

The point of departure for the progression is I. The harmonic goal of the progression, V, is indicated here and elsewhere in the present volume by an arrow. After the statement of I in the first measure the composition unfolds only in the melodic dimension—through changes of soprano position—until the point marked by an asterisk. There VI serves as a cue to the direction of the progression toward V, the harmonic goal.

58.   Direction and the Harmonic Axis I V I

Essentially there are two harmonic directions: toward I and toward V. These primary diatonic triads form the *harmonic axis* of tonal music. Two models are presented below (one in major, one in minor) which show how the consonant diatonic triads function with respect to this axis. These models are designed to show the norms of diatonic progression succinctly so that they can be learned easily. They have many practical applications, for example, in selecting chords to harmonize melodies, in harmonizing basses, and of course in analyzing and composing chord successions.

example 100.   Model of Consonant Diatonic-Chord Progression in the Major Mode

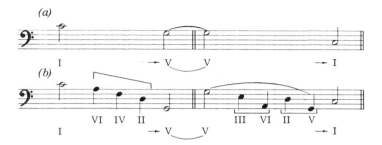

At (*a*) we see the harmonic axis formed by the progression I V I; at (*b*) the consonant diatonic triads (secondary triads) in relation to this axis. The first part of (*b*) shows VI, IV, and II, as they carry the progression from I to V. With the exception of VI none of these triads relates closely to I. Instead, they direct the progression toward V, and therefore are called *dominant preparations.* Each may move to V separately—VI and IV by 2nd, II by 5th—or all three may occur in the order shown.

The second part of Example 100 shows the progression from V to I. Here the secondary triads III, VI, and II implement the progression. In contrast to the secondary triads within the progression I V, which form a group of three chords, the triads here form chord pairs, as indicated by the brackets.

The model of progression in the minor mode follows.

example 101.   Model of Consonant Diatonic-Chord Progression in Minor Mode

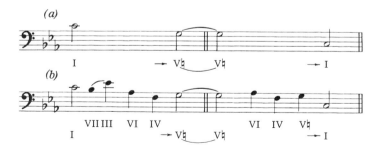

As noted earlier, the triad on the leading note is dissonant in both major and minor modes. Therefore it is excluded from the models. In the minor mode II

is also dissonant and therefore excluded. The remaining triads arrange themselves with respect to the harmonic axis as shown in Example 101. This model is similar to that of the major mode except for the more prominent role of III in the progression from I to V. And, since II is excluded, the progression from V to I in minor is shorter than that in major.

59.   Circular Progression

There are three main types of harmonic progression, all illustrated in the models: (1) *circular* progression; (2) *opening* progression; (3) *closing* progression. The first of these, circular progression, departs from a chord and has as its goal the same chord—for example, I I, or V V.

example 102.   SCHUBERT: *Waltz in E major, Op. 18a/1*

Here the harmony unfolds between two soprano positions of the tonic triad. At the beginning of the progression I is in the soprano position of the 5th; at the end of the progression it is in the soprano position of the 3rd. The I is both point of departure and goal. There is no other harmonic goal, since the I⁶ serves as an extension of I and the V has a subsidiary function, as indicated by its position in the metric-rhythmic pattern. From the standpoint of harmony therefore the progression is circular, self-contained.

60.   Circular Progression by Sequence

A special type of circular progression is illustrated by the example below, a somewhat shortened version of Basic Chord Pattern 2.

example 103.

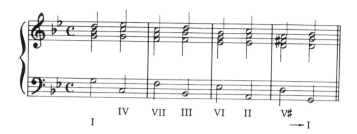

             IV   VII   III   VI   II   V♯
      I   → I

The progression begins and ends on the tonic triad and includes every diatonic triad but one, the dissonant VII. The triads are so arranged that their bass notes form an unbroken succession of descending 5ths. (Every other descending 5th is represented by its inversion, the ascending 4th.) A progression of this kind, which involves the repetition of a bass and chord pattern is called a *sequence.* (In Chapter 11, section 220 the intervals formed by the outer voices of such patterns are discussed.)

    Handel has used the sequence shown in Example 103 in a short keyboard composition:

example 104. Based on HANDEL's *Passacaglia* from *Keyboard Suite in G minor*

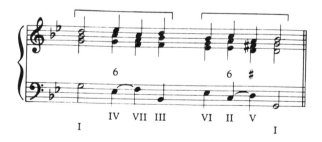

            IV VII III   VI II V
      I   I

Here the sequence is slightly modified. Both IV and II are inverted, so that in place of the uninterrupted bass progression of alternating 5ths and 4ths we hear the two groups marked by brackets. This division is made even clearer by the melodic pattern in the upper voice, which repeats after two measures:

example 105.   HANDEL: *Passacaglia* from *Keyboard Suite in G minor*

61.   Opening Progression

In contrast to a circular progression, an opening progression departs from one chord and has as its goal a different chord. The prime example of this type of progression is I V, the progression shown in Example 99 (Beethoven's *Op. 31/1*). A shorter illustration follows.

example 106.   SCHUMANN: *Folk Song* (*Album for the Young*)

The first change, from I to V⁶, forecasts the goal, but the progression is completed only with the final V (in fundamental position). A longer example of opening progression follows.

example 107.   BRAHMS: *Waldesnacht, Op. 62/3*

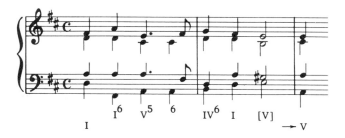

The harmonic goal of this progression, V, is approached via its secondary dominant triad. This serves to establish V firmly as the goal.

Opening and circular progressions combine in the next example.

example 108. Based on Chorale: *Auf meinen lieben Gott*

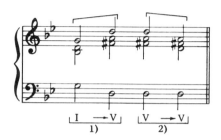

This passage consists of two progressions, only the main harmonies of which are shown in Example 108. The first moves from I to V, an opening progression. The second moves from V to V, a circular progression. Example 109 presents the two progressions in their entirety.

example 109. Chorale: *Auf meinen lieben Gott*

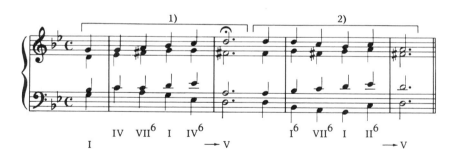

Single progressions of this kind are often called *phrases*. In the present volume the terms progression or harmonic unit usually are used instead of phrase because the latter term often is confusing to those who are accustomed to associate it with the vocal or instrumental phrase, a musical unit which may or may not correspond to the harmonic phrase.

62. Closing Progression

By closing progression is meant a progression that returns to I, usually from V.
Two examples are given below.

example 110.   Chorale: *O Ewigkeit, du Donnerwort* (reduction)

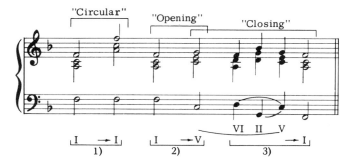

Example 110 is a synopsis of the full chorale setting. It contains three harmonic
units, the first a circular progression, the second an opening progression, the third
a closing progression from V to I. Thus all three types of progression are represented. In the closing progression the triads on VI and II behave as indicated in
the model, Example 100: as dominant preparations they direct the progression
toward the cadential V.

Progressions based on consonant chords can be expanded to any length. The
three basic progressions shown in Example 110 above are greatly expanded in the
complete setting of the chorale presented below.

example 111.   Chorale: *O Ewigkeit, du Donnerwort*

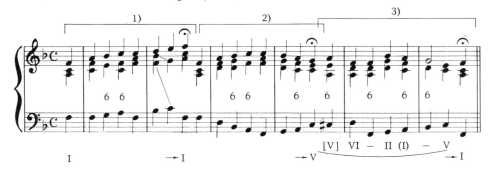

We draw attention particularly to the chords within the third unit, the closing
progression. The basic progression is VI II V I. Here, in the expanded progression,
VI is introduced by its secondary dominant triad and followed by its first inversion. The II is also followed by its first inversion—but not immediately. Inserted
between II and II⁶ is the bass passing note A. This A supports a I⁶. Since the I⁶

here neither extends nor represents the tonic triad, but has only a subordinate melodic function as a connection between the II and II^6, the Roman numeral I is enclosed in parentheses.

The next excerpt is more symmetrical than the chorale above. Again, a synopsis of the harmonic progression is given first.

example 112.

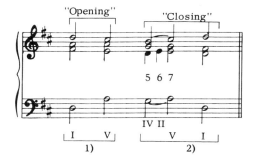

The first harmonic unit is an opening progression I V. The second is a closing progression, in which II^6 prepares the cadential V. The complete passage is given in the next example.

example 113. MOZART: *Symphony in D major, K.385* ("Haffner")

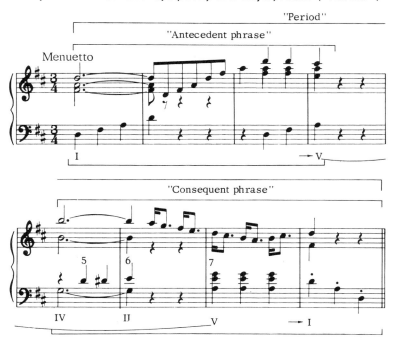

The complete closing progression includes IV as well as II. Observe that the change from IV to II involves a change of only one note: D to E, or in figures, 5 to 6.

A succession of two phrases such as that illustrated by Example 113 is often called a *period.* The first phrase of the period opens to the dominant and is called the *antecedent phrase,* while the following phrase is called the *consequent.* (These terms are used infrequently in the present volume.)

63. Harmonic Goals Other Than I or V

In the foregoing sections we have concentrated on harmonic progression as it is controlled by the harmonic axis I V I. Only I or V have been shown as harmonic goals. A consonant secondary triad can occur as a harmonic goal under one of the conditions described below:

1   When the secondary triad is an intermediate goal. For example, the dominant preparations II and IV are often intermediate harmonic goals of progressions which then continue toward V. An instance of this is quoted in Example 117 below.

2   When the secondary triad has been established as a *quasi-tonic.* Under this condition it then has its own secondary triads and controls a harmonic domain in the same way as the main tonic triad. This usually involves the process of modulation—the subject of Chapter 9.

3   When the secondary triad substitutes—as in the case of the substitution of VI for I. (See section 65.)

64. Harmonic Function

We have seen that the harmonic function of a chord is described in terms of its direction in relation to the two triads, I and V, that form the harmonic axis. For example, if it is preceded by I the function of VI is to direct the progression toward V. If VI then forms a chord pair with IV the direction toward the dominant is further confirmed. The normative harmonic function of a triad is not always confirmed, but the exceptions can easily be understood with the aid of the models of progression presented in Examples 100 and 101.

In harmonic progression, as in speech, there are often digressions, repetitions, interpolations, and ellipses. An understanding of these comes not from experience alone, but from experience combined with a sure knowledge of normative harmonic functions and the principles of chord relationship from which they derive.

Under certain circumstances linear intervallic patterns take precedence over harmonic functions, and, indeed, in these cases attempts to read harmonic progressions will lead to peculiar results. (See section 220.)

65. Substitution

An important aspect of harmonic function is the technique of *substitution*. By substitution is meant the exchange of one diatonic triad for another which has the same direction in relation to the harmonic axis. For example, the dominant preparations II, IV, and VI are interchangeable.

Substitution is not the same as the representation of a triad by its first inversion, although the two techniques are related. Substitution involves two different triads, for example, II and IV, whereas representation involves the same triad in two different forms, such as I and I⁶. An inversion may of course substitute for a triad other than its parent triad, as when II⁶ substitutes for IV at the cadence.

example 114.

(a) IV as dominant preparation   *(b)* II⁶ substitutes for IV

IV	V	I		II⁶	V	I

Although certain triads are interchangeable from the harmonic standpoint they may differ markedly from the melodic standpoint. Thus in Example 114 the soprano in the case of II⁶ is quite different from the soprano in the case of IV. Melodic and rhythmic requirements therefore determine the choice of chord when more than one is available for a particular harmonic function.

The general information on progression given above is applied below in brief descriptions of the normative functions of each diatonic triad. In each case differences between major and minor modes are considered. This summary also affords an opportunity to review the names customarily given to the diatonic triads. Although the present volume uses only a few of these the remaining terms are widely used and therefore the student should know them.

HARMONIC FUNCTIONS of the INDIVIDUAL DIATONIC TRIADS

66. I (Tonic)

The tonic triad has two principal harmonic functions. It serves as the point of departure for progression, notably at the beginning of the composition, and it serves as the ultimate goal of harmonic progression.

The equivalence of the tonic triads in major and minor is illustrated by the chromatic alteration of the cadential I in minor which forms the *tierce de picardie,* or Picardian Third. An example follows.

example 115. Chorale: *Von Gott will ich nicht lassen*

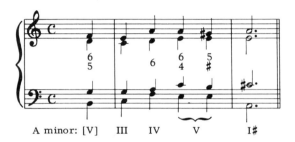

Tierce de picardie is the traditional name given to the raised 3rd of the minor triad at the final cadence, as in the example above.

Occasionally there occurs a chord which has the structure of I but not its function. An instance of this was remarked in connection with Example 111. In such cases the Roman numeral is enclosed in parentheses.

67. II (Supertonic) in the Major Mode

The term supertonic indicates the position of this triad *above* the tonic. Functionally, however, the supertonic triad has little relation to the tonic triad. By virtue of the 5th relationship II always functions as a dominant preparation.

In some cases II serves as an intermediate harmonic goal (see section 63). An example is given below.

example 116. MOZART: *Symphony in D major, K.504* ("Prague")

68. II in the Minor Mode

In minor the supertonic triad is diminished, a dissonant triad. We will see later that dissonant intervals require progression by 2nd. For this reason the II in minor rarely occurs in fundamental position as a $\frac{5}{3}$ progressing to V by 5th, as does II in major, unless it is part of a sequence as in Basic Chord Pattern 2. Usually it occurs in the first inversion.

II functions in minor just as it does in major: as a dominant preparation. A short example is provided below:

example 1-17. SCHUMANN: *Anfangs wollt' ich*

Because it is a dissonant triad and entirely dependent upon a consonant chord for its structural meaning, the supertonic triad in minor cannot be a harmonic goal as can the supertonic in major.

Indeed, the harmonic function of II is so firmly determined by the rules of harmonic syntax that, as shown in Example 118 at (a), it cannot serve as a passing chord between I and I^6, although the voice-leading is perfectly correct, without implying a progression to V. In the pretonal music of the Renaissance, of course, one finds successions such as those at (a), but in tonal music the dissonant 6th chord (or its equivalent) is the rule.

example 118.

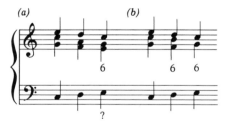

69. III (Mediant) in the Major Mode

The normative function of the mediant triad in major is indicated in the model, Example 100: it progresses to VI by 5th. It is important to notice that III does not serve as a dominant preparation. On the contrary, it occurs as a suffix to V. It also occurs as a suffix to I. Thus III is quite distant from both elements of the harmonic axis, and is related to them only through VI.

The mediant triad often occurs in a subordinate melodic role as a connective between I and IV:

example 119.   Chorale: *Nun lob', mein Seel', den Herren*

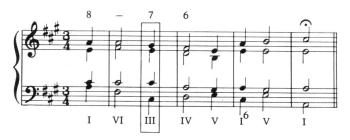

In this role III supports the soprano progression 8 7 6 (scale degrees), as shown here. Every consonant triad may have subordinate melodic functions of this kind, a fact that will become even more evident in the sections devoted to melodic structure, Chapter 7.

70.   III in the Minor Mode

The function of III in minor differs significantly from that of III in major. Whereas in major the mediant is relatively unimportant, in minor it is a quasi-primary triad. Its importance has already been indicated both in the model, Example 101, and also in the Handel *Passacaglia,* Example 104. The structural reasons for this more important role are to be found in the relationships which two other triads bear to III, relationships which derive from the structure of the natural minor scale. Example 120 illustrates these.

example 120.

At (*a*) we see the diatonic progression I IV VII III in minor. The last three chords easily group themselves in relation to III as a tonic—without chromatic alteration—so that III is heard as a harmonic goal. In short, IV in relation to C minor (I) becomes II in relation to III (E♭ major), while VII in relation to C minor (I) becomes V in relation to E♭ major (III). We see at (*b*) that an analogous situation is impossible in the major mode without extensive and disruptive chromatic alterations.

A short excerpt will illustrate the function of III in minor as a quasi-primary triad.

example 121.   Chorale: *Ach wie nichtig*

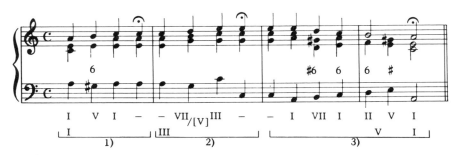

The first unit contains a circular progression; the second a progression to III via VII which serves as [V] of III. (The dual function of VII is indicated by the slant). The third unit contains a progression from III back to I via V. Example 122 below summarizes the passage in terms of harmonic goals.

example 122.

Here we see that the bass line arpeggiates the notes of the tonic triad, another indication of the control which the tonic triad maintains over the longer span of harmonic progression.

71.   IV (Subdominant) in Major and Minor

The triad on IV is called the subdominant because it occupies a position *below* the tonic triad analogous to that occupied by the dominant above:

example 123.

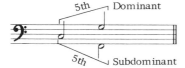

Its symmetrical position in relation to I and V led Rameau and many subsequent writers to rank the subdominant triad with the tonic and dominant triads. Thus one often reads of the *three* primary triads, I, IV, and V. This is a fallacious viewpoint since the IV usually functions as a dominant preparation, one of three such chords.

Sometimes the IV assumes a more independent role, as in the excerpt below.

example 124. SCHUBERT: *Death and the Maiden*

Here the IV and its first inversion stand between two statements of I. When the IV occurs apart from the V, as in this excerpt, its function is primarily melodic.

The IV sometimes occurs at the close of a composition, forming a cadential pair with I.

example 125. BRAHMS: *First Symphony*

In this context the IV I succession is called a *plagal* cadence. Actually, the plagal cadence rarely closes the composition, for it is usually preceded by a basic dominant-tonic ("authentic") cadence.

Earlier we saw the idiomatic use of the altered IV in minor to harmonize scale degree 6 as an ascending passing note (section 55). Still another subdominant idiom, this one in major, is illustrated below.

example 126. WOLF: *Benedeit die sel'ge Mutter*

Here IV^6 stands between two statements of V^6. It serves two functions here: its bass note embellishes the bass of V^6 and the chord as a whole substitutes for the tonic triad.

72. V (Dominant) in Major

V serves to establish the tonic triad. This function is particularly evident at the cadence. Apart from this cadential function, which is a local matter, V forms with I the harmonic axis that controls harmonic progression over the entire span of the composition. The full meaning of this will become apparent as we proceed. However, even in the present chapter we have found that a progression to V as harmonic goal, an "opening" progression, literally does open the way for further harmonic expansion. It is in this role that V is most cogently expressed as part of the harmonic axis. The cadential function, as we have said, is a purely local matter. There has been much confusion regarding these two distinct functions of V because many writers have not recognized that one has to do with detail, the other with harmonic development over the longer span of the composition. This confusion is evident in the persistent use of the term "half cadence" to describe the function of V as a harmonic goal. For instance, the V which stands at the end of the first harmonic unit of the Mozart passage quoted earlier (Example 113) would be described as a "half-cadence" by many writers, and presumably, so would the V in the second, fourth, and sixth measure of the following excerpt.

example 127. MOZART: *Quintet for Clarinet and Strings in A major, K.581*

Actually, the passage above is composed of four harmonic units, marked by brackets. The first three have V as goal; the fourth terminates on I. Thus, the passage consists of three statements of the opening progression I V, followed by the expected closing progression to I. There is only one cadence—in the final measure.

73. V in the Minor Mode

As explained earlier (section 29) the dominant triad has two forms in the minor mode. When it is the major triad which contains the leading note it functions just like the dominant triad in the major mode. However, when it is the minor triad which contains the natural 7th scale degree it is more independent of I, and often controls a large harmonic domain as a quasi-tonic.

As mentioned in section 69, every triad may have subordinate melodic functions. In the case of V in the minor mode, a characteristic subordinate melodic function is exemplified by the situation shown in Example 128.

example 128.

Here, although one might label the second chord V, it clearly has no harmonic function, but is the result of a descending passing note (scale degree 7) in the bass, paralleling the melodic descent in the soprano. (Compare Example 229.)

74. VI (Submediant)

The triad on VI is called the *submediant* because it occupies a position *below* the tonic triad analogous to that occupied by the mediant above the tonic triad. (See dominant and subdominant, Example 123.)

example 129.

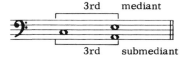

We have seen that VI serves as a dominant preparation both in major and in minor. Often it follows I immediately, providing the first cue to progression toward V. This is shown in the model, Example 100. In addition to this main function, VI has other roles. Of these the most important is its role as substitute for the tonic triad in major. An illustration follows.

example 130. Chorale: *Meine Seele erhebet den Herrn*

One would expect the tonic triad at the opening of the chorale. Instead, the VI is found in its place.

VI plays a prominent role altogether in this progression. In the second measure ,it is extended by means of its secondary dominant and in the third measure assumes its normative function as dominant preparation.

A special case of VI as substitute for I is the *deceptive cadence.* This is illustrated below.

example 131. MOZART: *Quintet for Clarinet and Strings in A major, K.581*

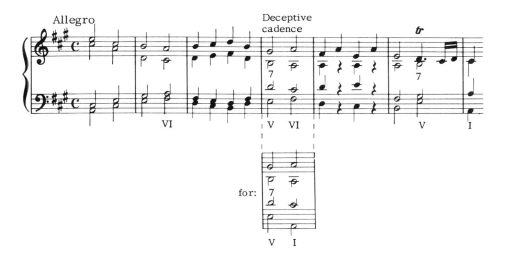

In the fourth measure one expects an authentic cadence which would close the first harmonic unit. Instead V progresses to VI, a motion called a deceptive cadence. This permits further extension of the dominant harmony. The cadential V occurs again after one measure, this time closing to I. By deceptive cadences progressions are not only extended but often are redirected toward a harmony other than I (or V).

75. VII (Leading-Note Triad) in Major

The VII is a dissonant triad both in major and in minor. Like II in minor, it occurs rarely in fundamental position. When represented by its first inversion it often stands between I and I⁶, as shown below.

example 132. Chorale: *Wer in dem Schutz des Hochsten*

The exclusively melodic function of VII⁶ is evident here. It connects two forms of the primary harmony. The same melodic function is illustrated in the next example.

example 133. Chorale: *Gott der Vater, wohn' uns bei*

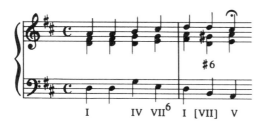

In Example 133 the VII⁶ stands between IV in the first measure and I. It harmonizes scale degree 7, the leading note, serving as a substitute for V. The second measure contains a chord of the same structure which functions as VII⁶ in relation to the goal harmony, V. In this context the chromatic VII⁶ substitutes for an inverted secondary dominant-7th chord (see section 109).

76. VII in the Natural Minor

As a major triad on unaltered or natural scale degree 7 in minor the VII functions as a secondary dominant triad in relation to the mediant. This was shown in Example 121. A further instance is quoted here:

example 134. BRAHMS: *Intermezzo in A minor, Op. 76/7*

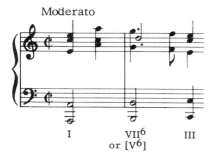

77. Summary of Functions of Diatonic Triads

In both large and small contexts the normative functions of the secondary diatonic triads and their first inversions are as follows:

DIATONIC LOCATION OF FUNDAMENTAL NOTE	NAME	FUNCTION(S) IN RELATION TO I AND V
II	*Supertonic*	Dominant preparation.
III (in major)	*Mediant*	Leads to dominant preparations IV, II⁶, or VI.
III (in minor)		Independent triad that often usurps role of tonic.
IV	*Subdominant*	Dominant preparation or melodic embellishment of tonic.
VI (in major)	*Submediant*	Dominant preparation or tonic substitute.
VI (in minor)		Dominant preparation.
VII (in major and harmonic minor)	*Leading-note triad*	Dominant substitute or melodic embellishment of tonic.
VII (in natural minor)	*Natural VII*	Secondary dominant in relation to the mediant triad.

EXERCISES

A. Some Important Terms to Define and Memorize

Harmonic progression

Interval of progression

Diatonic location (position)

Primary triads

Secondary triads

Dominant preparation

3rd relationship

Secondary dominant triad

Harmonic direction

Harmonic axis

Circular progression

Opening progression

Closing progression

Harmonic sequence

Phrase

Period

Harmonic function

Substitution

Subdominant

Submediant

B. Basic Keyboard and Aural Exercises

Before undertaking these exercises review those at the end of the previous chapter. The same procedure applies to these exercises, with additional instructions given below.

exercise 85. **Basic Chord Pattern 1**

Here the pattern is expanded by diatonic triads which serve as stepwise prefixes. It is interesting to observe that both I and V thus serve as embellishing chords.

INSTRUCTIONS
Fill in the inner voices and add the bass where missing.

$$I \quad (V) \quad VI \quad III \quad IV \quad (I) \quad II \quad V \quad I$$

exercise 86.

By means of the 6th chords the preceding pattern is expanded still further.

exercise 87.   **Basic Chord Pattern 2**

Here the 5ths' progression of the pattern is expanded by means of arpeggiation, which creates a succession of 3rds in each measure. In accord with the norms of progression the 3rds are secondary to the main progression which proceeds by 5ths.

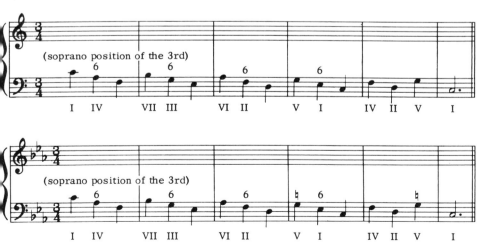

C. Figured Bass Exercises

These exercises provide additional and essential practice in locating and connecting chords. For the most part they contain only chords explained thus far. All unfamiliar chords as well as certain unfamiliar rhythmic situations are realized. The figured-bass exercises also provide excellent material for analysis. After playing and writing out the exercises in the usual manner identify each chord by Roman and Arabic numerals. Then determine the extent of each harmonic unit. Finally, characterize each progression as circular, opening, or closing.

exercise 88.   Chorale: *Was ist mein Stand, mein Glück*

comments

1   If the 3rd of the preceding 6th chord is doubled, a correct connection to this chord may be achieved by dividing the chord between the hands, that is, open spacing. In that case the left hand takes a B♭ 8ve, while the right hand takes F and D. In continuo playing this technique is called *divided accompaniment.*

exercise 89.   LOEILLET: *Solo for Flute and Continuo*

Allegro

comments

1   The 6th chord arises naturally here from the upward skip of the bass. It does not require a figure.

2   The dash here and elsewhere in the present volume indicates that the previous harmony remains in effect. That is, the voices above the bass do not change.

3   The harmonic unit which begins here contains a progression toward II as harmonic goal.

4   Here the situation is the reverse of that in measure 1: the $\frac{5}{3}$ arises as a result of the descending skip from the bass of the 6th chord. In order to have full harmony on the second beat an inner voice must replace the C♯ temporarily lost in the bass.

exercise 90.   Chorale: *Ach Gott, wie manches Herzeleid*

comments

1   The first progression is an opening progression. Its goal is the secondary dominant triad, [V] of V. In accord with the logic of harmonic progression, the harmonic goal of the subsequent unit is the V itself.

exercise 91.   HASSE: *Solo for Flute or Violin*

(1)

comments

1 Shift to three voices for these two 6th chords. Since one of the parallel 5ths which will result is not perfect they are not objectionable. If four-voice harmony is maintained, the notes must be divided equally between the hands.

D. Unfigured Outer Voices

At this point we introduce a new type of exercise: the realization of unfigured outer voices. The purpose of these exercises is to provide practice in the selection of appropriate chords under conditions of limited choice. These exercises constitute an important step toward the independent harmonization of upper voices and basses (Chapter 7).

> INSTRUCTIONS
> 1 Sing the upper voice. If the exercise consists of solo part and accompaniment sing both the solo line and the upper voice of the accompaniment.
> 2 Sing the bass line.
> 3 Play the outer voices. If the exercise consists of accompaniment and solo, play only the outer voices of the accompaniment.
> 4 Supply Arabic figures indicating your selection of chord. Only chords explained thus far may be used: diatonic triads—both consonant and dissonant—and secondary dominant triads and 6th chords.
> 5 Play and write the exercise as you would a figured-bass exercise.
> 6 Analyze the progressions from the standpoint of chord function, harmonic goals, as well as the harmonic function of the individual chord, the interval relationships which group the chords together, the harmonic direction of each group or larger unit, and the type of progression represented by each unit.

exercise 92. *Welsh Air*

exercise 93. JOHN WILSON: *From the fair Lavinian Shore*

exercise 94.   *Von Himmel kam der Engel*

exercise 95.   PURCELL: "Ah, How Pleasant 'Tis to Love" (solo voice and bass combined)

comments

1   Unharmonized bass passing note. Retain harmony from previous beat.
2   Unharmonized passing note in upper voice. Retain previous harmony.
3   The change of bass should fall on the second beat. Instead it is delayed by one
    eighth note, creating an unusual rhythm.

exercise 96.   Chorale: *Gott lebet noch*

exercise 97.   PURCELL: "I Attempt from Love's Sickness"

comments

1   This is a bass suspension chord, figured $\frac{5}{2}$. See section 184.

exercise 98.   **WILLIAM CROFT: "I Love the Lord"**

comments

1   The meter signature is to be interpreted as $\frac{4}{2}$.
2   The quarter note requires a chord.

Chapter 5

THE MELODIC PROCESS OF CHORD GENERATION: SEVENTH CHORDS

When we consider musical works we find that the triad is ever-present and that the interpolated dissonances have no other purpose than to effect the continuous variation of the triad.

Lorenz Mizler, 1739

78. Melodic Process Compared to the Harmonic

In tonal music all chords are generated from the triad by one of three processes, the harmonic, the melodic, and the rhythmic processes. The harmonic process, inversion, is applied to all triads, beginning with the tonic triad:

example 135.

Melodic (stepwise) progression of voices is not a factor in the harmonic process. The bass alone shifts to a higher 8ve, leaving the original 3rd of the chord as the new bass note.

In contrast to this, the melodic process of chord generation is characterized by stepwise progression, as its name indicates. Further, the harmonic process involves only one triad, whereas the melodic process involves two, I and V:

example 136.

Example 136 shows the chord pair V I. Stepwise and common-tone progression occurs in all voices above the bass except the soprano, which skips from scale degree 5 to scale degree 3. Stepwise progression in all voices above the bass is achieved when the skip is filled by scale degree 4 as a passing note:

example 137.

Earlier we defined a chord as a group of three or more notes which have the duration of a full metrical unit. Since the passing note, scale degree 4, in this case has the value of a full metrical unit it must be counted as a chord note. And since the interval which it forms with the bass is a 7th, a dissonant interval, it has also created a new kind of chord, called a *7th chord.*

This, then, is the melodic process by which the 7th chord was introduced into tonal music: the triad assimilated a passing dissonance. Since the triad involved is the dominant triad this particular kind of 7th chord (there are others) is called the *dominant 7th,* symbolized V^7. Let us examine its interval structure.

example 138.

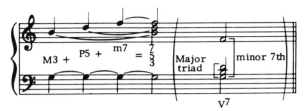

$$M3 + P5 + m7 = \begin{smallmatrix}7\\5\\3\end{smallmatrix}$$

Major triad   minor 7th

V^7

As illustrated in Example 138 above, the dominant 7th chord contains a major 3rd, a perfect 5th, and a minor 7th. In short, it consists of a major triad plus a minor 7th.

    The full figuring of 7th chords is not used in figured bass. The figure 7 alone implies the 3rd and usually the 5th as well. Both 3rd and 5th are represented if chromatically altered, however. And in certain cases where the 5th is obligatory the chord is figured $\frac{7}{5}$.

79. The V⁷ as Representative of a Class of Dissonant Chords

All chords that contain a dissonant interval are called *dissonant chords.* All dissonant chords that contain the intervals of a 7th, a 5th, and a 3rd are called 7th chords. Since 7th chords are derived directly from triads, the basic harmonies, they constitute the first and most important class of dissonant chords. And since the dominant 7th chord is derived from a primary triad it is the most important representative of the entire class of 7th chords. As we shall see, its behavior is characteristic of 7th chords in general.

80. Melodic Function: the V⁷ as Passing Chord

In section 64 harmonic function was explained. We now introduce the concept of melodic function. The melodic function of its soprano note determines the melodic function of the V⁷. If a passing note is in the soprano the chord is called a *passing chord.* If an auxiliary note is in the soprano the chord is called an *auxiliary chord.* Not all chords have strong melodic functions; some are stable consonant chords which have primarily harmonic significance. The 7th chord, however, always has a melodic function. If the 8ve is in the soprano—the only stationary note of the chord—we describe melodic function in terms of the motion of the dissonant note, wherever it may lie.

    The V⁷ in the next example is a passing chord.

example 139. BEETHOVEN: *First Symphony, Minuet and Trio*

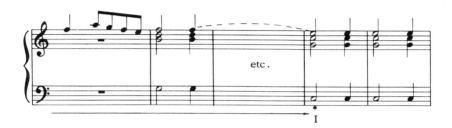

The first part of the trio ends on V in the soprano position of the 8ve. The next part begins with the passing 7th in the upper voice. This 7th is retained, with embellishments, for a total of eighteen measures before descending to the 3rd of the tonic triad. *Duration never alters chord function.* Example 139 is essentially the same melodic and harmonic pattern as that shown in Example 137.

81. Resolution of Dissonant Notes

When the dissonant note in Example 139, the 7th, finally progresses to the consonant 3rd of the tonic triad, we say that the dissonance is *resolved.* By resolution we mean therefore the obligatory progression of dissonant intervals to consonant intervals. Two rules govern the resolution of dissonance. Both are illustrated by the V^7:

1   The dissonant note must resolve. The direction of resolution is determined by the second rule:
2   The dissonant note always resolves by step (usually in descending direction) to the nearest consonant note. The law of the half step explained in section 10 applies here with particular force.

82.   Resolution of the Tritone

The V⁷ contains scale degrees 4 and 7, the two notes that form the dissonant diatonic interval of a tritone:

example 140.

Since both notes are governed by the law of the half step (in major) they resolve in contrary motion as shown in Example 140, either expanding to resolve on the 6th or contracting to resolve on the 3rd. In the minor mode, resolution of the tritone is the same as in major but it depends more upon the leading note since there is no half step between scale degrees 3 and 4.

It is important to recognize that scale degree 7 is not the same as the 7th of V⁷. It is for this reason that we say "7th" when we refer to the interval, and "scale degree 7" when we refer to the diatonic position of a note.

83.   The V⁷ as Auxiliary Chord

The next example illustrates the evolution of a V⁷ chord from an auxiliary note embellishment. Rhythm plays an important role in this case.

example 141.

Here a submetrical eighth note dissonance (*a*) is enlarged and assimilated as a chordal element (*b*).

Example 142 shows the same chord arising from an auxiliary note approached by skip.

example 142.

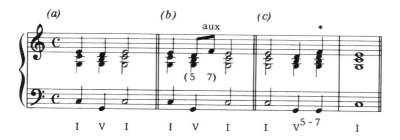

The figures 5-7 represent the change from the triad V to the dissonant-7th chord. The melodic role of the 7th is clearly illustrated in the following excerpt.

example 143. CHOPIN: *Berceuse*

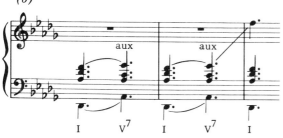

At the beginning of the composition the repeated auxiliary note figure in the accompaniment (F-G♭) prepares for the entrance of the soprano melody on F in the third measure. The reduction at (*b*) shows the relationship more directly.

The next excerpt illustrates the V⁷ as passing chord (twice) and as auxiliary chord.

example 144. BEETHOVEN: *Fifth Symphony,* Last Movement

Before we examine the V⁷ in other characteristic contexts we must consider certain important additional aspects of its structure and progression.

84. Soprano Positions of the V⁷

The most active soprano positions are those of the 7th and the 3rd. These are the notes which form the tritone, a dissonant, active interval that seeks resolution. The 8ve position occurs seldom since it is the least active melodic note, being simply a doubling of the bass.

85. Doubling of the Notes of the V⁷

Since the resolution of the 7th is fixed—it must descend by step—it cannot be doubled. Parallel 8ves would result:

example 145.

This rule applies to all dissonant notes. They cannot be doubled, except in unusual circumstances.

In four-part harmony the 5th of the V⁷ often is omitted and the bass is doubled. This doubling permits stepwise resolution to a complete tonic triad (Example 146*a*), whereas if no note is doubled, the chord resolves stepwise to an incomplete triad, a triad that lacks a 5th (Example 146*b*).

example 146.

The 3rd of V⁷ is never omitted, for it is essential to the dissonant interval of the tritone which characterizes the chord.

86.   Apparent Exceptions to the Rule That the 7th Always Descends

The 7th always resolves downward. Under certain conditions, however, it seems to ascend stepwise at the point of resolution. Three such situations are illustrated and explained in the next examples.

example 147.

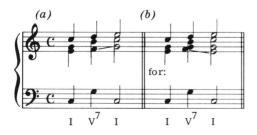

In the succession shown at (*a*) the 7th ascends to make the final triad complete. If it were to descend the final triad would lack a 5th. When the V⁷ is in five parts as at (*b*) both conditions are satisfied: the final triad is complete and the 7th resolves as it should. Another common apparent exception to the rule of descending resolution is illustrated by the following passages.

example 148.   J. S. BACH (?) : *Prelude for Organ*

$V^{7(8)}$ I

example 149.   BEETHOVEN: *Six Bagatelles for Piano, Op. 126/1*

Here in both cases the 7th is embellished by its upper auxiliary note. This embellishment forms an 8ve against the bass and may momentarily give the effect of having resolved the 7th. Actually it only temporarily displaces the 7th, which remains in effect to resolve downward as indicated by the arrow.

Still another melodic technique creates the illusion of ascending resolution in the next example.

example 150.

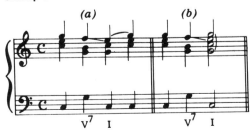

At (a) the 7th resolves downward normally to the 3rd of the tonic triad. The upper voice then changes to a different position, to the position of the 5th, as indicated by the slur. At (b) the resolution of the 7th and the shift of soprano position occur simultaneously: as the 7th resolves downward G replaces E as soprano note. This telescoping of two motions is indicated by the arrows. The technique illustrated here is called *overlapping* (after Schenker). A somewhat complicated instance is shown in Example 151. Notice that the left-hand part clarifies the underlying voice-leading.

example 151.   MOZART: *Piano Concerto in D minor, K.466,* Second Movement

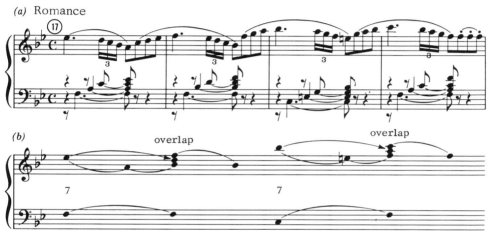

(a) Romance

(b)

87.   V^7 at the Cadence

Very often V^7 represents V at the cadence. The difference between the two chords lies in the fact that the 7th of V^7 tends to emphasize the 3rd of the final tonic triad. This is evident in the following example, where the resolving tritone points up both the 8ve and the 3rd of the I, and the 5th of I is omitted.

example 152.   BEETHOVEN: *Piano Sonata in B♭ major, Op. 22*

88.   The Skip Away from the Leading Note at the Cadence

The 3rd of V^7 is the leading note. Normally it resolves upward. However, if all the following conditions exist, the leading note does not resolve upward but instead skips down to the 5th of the I: (1) if the texture is limited to four parts; (2) if the V^7 is in the soprano position of the 5th; (3) if a complete final tonic triad is required. Example 153 illustrates this situation.

example 153.

V^7 I

Since the 5th is in the soprano and therefore cannot be omitted the leading note (3rd of the V^7) must skip down to take the 5th of the final I, while its normal note of resolution is taken by the upper voice.

89.   Secondary Dominant-7th Chord $[V^7]$

In section 56 the secondary dominant triad was introduced as a chromatic extension of V. The chromatic extension of V^7 is the secondary dominant-7th chord. This chord, symbolized $[V^7]$, serves the same function as the secondary dominant triad. The following excerpt contains two of these chords.

example 154.   BEETHOVEN: *Third Symphony*

The first $[V^7]$ serves as prefix to II. The second $[V^7]$ serves as prefix to IV. Any consonant diatonic triad may be embellished by a chord of this type.

90.   The Minor-7th Chord (m7)

In all, there are five types of 7th chord. The first type is the dominant 7th
explained previously. The second type is the minor 7th. II7 in the major mode
is the diatonic model for this chord. Its origin, illustrated below, resembles that
of the dominant-7th chord.

example 155.

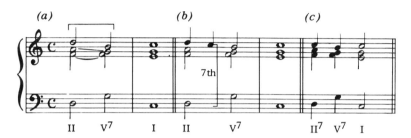

At (*a*) we see the triadic succession II V7. Alto and tenor move by step while
the soprano skips. At (*b*) the skip of a 3rd in the soprano is filled by a metrical
passing note which creates a 7th that is assimilated by the II. As in the case of
the V7, the addition of the 7th does not alter the direction of the II. Indeed, the
dissonant 7th only makes the direction toward V more explicit. We can extend
this observation to formulate a general principle that applies to all 7th chords:
Harmonically they function exactly as the diatonic triads from which they derive.

Like the V7 explained in section 83 the II7 can also originate from the
auxiliary note embellishment.

The intervals of the II7 are compared with those of the V7 in the next
example.

example 156.

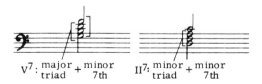

The V7 consists of a major triad plus a minor 7th, while the II7 consists of both
a minor triad and a minor 7th. Hence the name minor 7th is given to the latter
type. Note also that the minor-7th chord does not contain a tritone, as does the
V7, but like the 7th of V7, the 7th of II7 requires descending resolution.

91.   IV⁷ in Minor

The only minor-7th chord in the diatonic minor mode (harmonic form) is IV⁷. Like the diatonic triad from which it is derived, IV⁷ is often a dominant preparation. In that capacity every voice of the chord, including the bass, moves stepwise. Example 157 provides an illustration.

example 157.   SCHUMANN: *Auf einer Burg* (piano accompaniment only)

92.   The Half-Diminished-7th Chord

This third type of 7th chord is exemplified by II⁷ in the minor mode. Like II⁷ in major, it also serves as a dominant preparation. Example 158 shows that the *half-diminished-7th chord* originates from a passing metrical dissonance just as do the dominant-7th and minor-7th chords.

example 158.

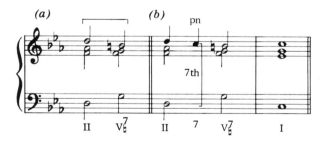

As we shall see, the *full diminished-7th chord* (º7) consists of a diminished triad plus a diminished 7th. The half-diminished 7th, symbolized ø7, also is based upon a diminished triad but its 7th is minor, not diminished. Hence the name of the chord. Example 159 shows the II⁷ at the beginning of an art song.

example 159. SCHUMANN: *Ich will meine Seele tauchen*

(a) Quietly

The harmonic synopsis at (*b*) shows the chord succession without the arpeggiation. It is based upon the triadic progression II V I.

A detailed picture of the typical resolution of II⁷ is provided by Example 160.

example 160.

As in all 7th chords, the dissonant 7th of the half-diminished chord resolves downward by step. The 3rd of the half-diminished usually remains to become the 7th of the V⁷, as shown here. A peculiarity of the half-diminished-7th chord, however, is the progression of the dissonant interval of the diminished 5th, the tritone. This interval does not behave as does the tritone of the dominant-7th-type chord. Instead, the 5th descends stepwise in parallel 3rds with the 7th, as shown in Example 160. Thus, in the half-diminished-7th chord the tritone does not operate as a dissonant interval.

The half-diminished-7th chord occurs in the major mode on scale step VII. The chord is not often an independent 7th chord, however, as is explained in section 112.

93. The Major-7th Chord (M^7)

The fourth type of 7th chord is exemplified by IV^7 in the major mode. Its melodic origin is shown below.

example 161.

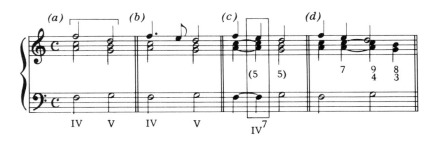

The dominant preparation IV becomes IV^7 when the submetrical passing note is enlarged and assimilated into the chord. This chord consists of a major triad plus a major 7th—hence its name.

In Example 161(c) it may be observed that when the major-7th chord resolves to V parallel 5ths occur between two of the upper voices. These can be prevented in several ways, one of which is shown at (d) where the 7th resolves but the progression of the parallel voice is delayed until the following beat. This technique forms a suspension chord (see Chapter 10).

94.   7th Chords in Sequence

A combination of melodic and rhythmic processes may affect a series of triads in such a way that a sequence of 7th chords is created, as shown by the series below.

example 162.

At (a) is seen the progression III VI II V I. Eighth passing notes at (b) increase the melodic content. At (c) the passing notes are enlarged and assimilated as chord elements, thus producing an uninterrupted series of 7th chords. An example of this, accompanied by a harmonic synopsis is given below.

example 163.   J.S. BACH: *Prelude in A♭ major, WTC I*

In such sequences of 7th chords the dissonant 7th resolves to an interval conso-nant with the bass. However, the chord of which the interval is a part is no longer a consonant chord.

95. Summary of the Diatonic-7th Chords

The diatonic-7th chords are summarized in Example 164. Of the five main types four have been explained, namely the dominant 7th (V⁷), the minor 7th (m⁷), the major 7th (M⁷), and the half-diminished 7th (°7).

example 164.

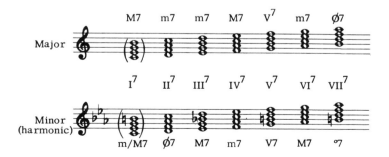

The fifth type of 7th chord, the diminished 7th, has a different structural origin and therefore is explained elsewhere (section 111). Since 7th chords based upon I in both major and minor are not independent 7th chords they are enclosed in parentheses in Example 164. (See section 174.) In these and in many other cases one must consider not only the vertical structure of the chord in isolation but also its linear or melodic context.

96. Summary of the Harmonic Functions of 7th Chords

Much more important than the distribution of the various 7th chords in the diatonic tonalities are their functions. The 7th chords, and indeed all dissonant chords, have two general harmonic functions: (1) they expand the harmonic content of a progression; (2) they make harmonic direction more specific. The 7th chords never replace the diatonic chords upon which progression is based. They make the direction of those basic harmonies more explicit and, in Mizler's words, "effect the continuous variation of the triad." Thus the progression of the 7th chord is always the same as that of the diatonic triad from which it derives. II is a dominant preparation; therefore, II^7 is also a dominant preparation. The cadential V progresses to I; therefore the cadential V^7 also progresses to I, and so on.

97. Summary of the Melodic Functions of 7th Chords

The 7th chords also serve the soprano or other melodic voice. The 7th itself is always either a passing note or an auxiliary note. It is never a stable note, no matter how long it may be prolonged.

98. Comparison of 7th Chords

The 7th chords resemble one another since they originate from the same melodic-rhythmic process. Their common origin is reflected in the fact that the dissonant note, the 7th, resolves downward by step in each case. However, the 7th chords differ in function, just as do the diatonic triads from which they derive. They also differ with respect to interval structure. Only the V^7 (and the diminished 7th, which is explained in Chapter 6) contain an operative tritone. The half-diminished 7th contains the tritone but the interval does not resolve like a dissonance.

EXERCISES

A. List of Some Important Terms to Define and Memorize

Melodic function (of a chord)

Resolution

Secondary dominant-7th chord

Minor-7th chord

Half-diminished-7th chord

Major-7th chord

Dominant-7th chord

Overlapping

B. Keyboard Exercises

exercise 99. Basic Chord Pattern 1
Expanded by secondary dominant-7th chords.

exercise 100. Basic Chord Pattern 2
Progression expanded by 7th chords.

C. Figured Outer Voices

INSTRUCTIONS

These exercises should be carried out in the same way as those at the end of the previous chapter. They should be realized at the keyboard and on paper, chord structure and function should be indicated, and the harmonic units and goals should be designated.

exercise 101.   Chorale: *Alle Menschen müssen sterben*

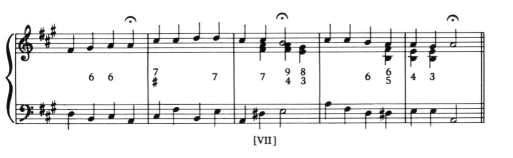

[VII]

exercise 102.   Chorale: *O Welt, ich muss dich lassen*

exercise 103.   Chorale: *Werde munter mein Gemüte*

exercise 104.   PEPUSCH: *English Cantata*

D. Unfigured Outer Voices

exercise 105.   Folk Song: *Barbara Allen*

exercise 106.   Chorale: *In dulci jubilo*

exercise 107.   HANDEL: *Sonata in G minor for Flute and Continuo*

This is an interlude between two fast movements. The harmonies should be read in G minor, in terms of their direction toward V. Thus, the interlude begins with VI and the first unit cadences on that harmony. The next unit is directed toward IV, which, like VI is a preparation for the dominant triad. This appears in the final measure of the excerpt, and leads to the tonic triad which begins the subsequent Allegro (not shown).

Chapter 6

THE INVERSIONS
OF THE SEVENTH CHORDS

There is within every chord a fundamental and natural order . . .; but the circumstances of a particular progression, of taste, of expression, of beautiful melody, of variety, of *rapprochement* with the harmony, often cause the composer to change that order by inverting the chords, and in consequence to change the disposition of the parts.

Jean Jacques Rousseau, 1768

99. General

There are three major classes of dissonant chord: 7th chords, suspension chords, and linear chords. Of these only the 7th chords are inverted.

Inversion of a 7th chord raises two important questions: (1) In what way does it relate to the parent 7th chord; that is, how does it represent the function of the parent chord? (2) Each inversion has what individual characteristics that render it particularly appropriate for a certain context? Both questions will be answered in the present chapter as we discuss the inversions of the main types of 7th chord, beginning with the inverted dominant 7th.

145

THE INVERSIONS OF V⁷

100. Structure and Function of Inversions in Relation to Parent Chord

By successive inversion of the bass (shown by the arrows in Example 165) each note of the 7th chord serves in turn as bass note.

example 165.

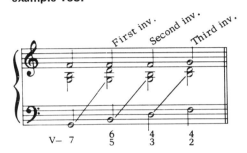

The first inversion has the original 3rd as bass note, the second the original 5th, the third the original 7th. Although the arrangement of the notes and thus the intervals of each inversion differ from those of the parent 7th chord, the inversions nevertheless have the same harmonic function as the chord from which they originate. This is shown in the next example.

example 166.

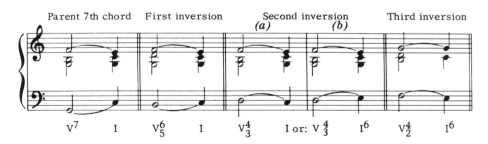

Example 166 shows that each inversion resolves either to I, as does the parent 7th chord, or to I⁶. Since an inversion usually has the same harmonic function as the parent 7th chord it often serves as an extension of that parent chord in much the same way that a 6th chord serves as an extension of its parent triad. Chord pairs formed in this way do not represent a change of harmony but, rather, different forms of the same harmony.

Despite the strong harmonic similarity between the parent 7th chord and its inversions the latter have individual melodic characteristics, and in some cases do not follow the pattern of resolution established by the parent chord. Before examining individual inversions let us consider two major aspects of their relationship to the parent chord.

First, the dissonant elements of the parent 7th chord not only are represented in each inversion, but they also resolve in the same way in each inversion. In the case of V^7 and its inversions the dissonant elements are the notes that form the tritone, that is, the 3rd and the 7th above the bass of the fundamental 7th. The 7th is dissonant against the bass, while the 3rd is dissonant against the 7th, an internal dissonance.

example 167.

Example 168 shows the resolution of the tritone in each inversion of the dominant-7th chord.

example 168.

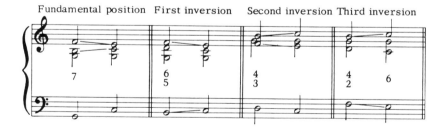

In each case the tritone resolves stepwise to the same notes of the tonic triad or its first inversion, in accord with the law of the half step.

The second major aspect of the relationship between the inversions and their parent 7th chord is this: All the notes of the inversion progress by step, whereas the parent chord normally combines stepwise progression in the upper voices with a skip in the bass.

We turn attention now to the individual characteristics of each inversion of the dominant-7th chord.

101. The First Inversion (V$_5^6$)

The complete figuring of the first inversion is $\begin{smallmatrix}6\\5\\3\end{smallmatrix}$.

example 169.

As indicated by the parentheses, only the figures $\begin{smallmatrix}6\\5\end{smallmatrix}$ are used unless the 3rd is altered chromatically. These figures refer to the two notes which represent the interval of the 7th in the parent chord. In Example 169 the note which represents the original 7th is shown as a black note.

The dissonant notes of the V$_5^6$ are the bass and the 5th. These form the tritone, as shown above. Accordingly, the bass resolves upward by half step; the 5th resolves downward by half step. Because of its characteristic stepwise progression an inverted 7th chord can be described most effectively with respect to the melodic roles of its outer voices. In the case of the V$_5^6$ the bass plays the most active melodic role, serving both as auxiliary and as passing note. Both functions are illustrated below.

102. The V$_5^6$ as Auxiliary Chord

The following example shows the V$_5^6$ between two consonant chords, I^6 and I. Since the bass note of the V$_5^6$ here is an incomplete lower auxiliary note (the leading note in the key) the chord is called an auxiliary V$_5^6$.

example 170. BEETHOVEN: *Fifth Symphony*

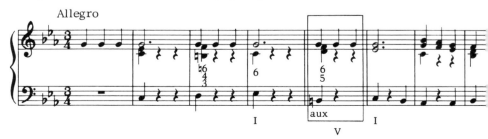

103. The V$^6_5$ as Passing Chord

When the V$^6_5$ features the bass as a passing note, it is called a passing V$^6_5$.

example 171. HAYDN: *Symphony in F♯ minor* ("Farewell")

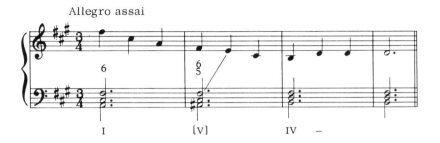

Here the bass is a chromatic passing note which supports a [V$^6_5$]. Moreover, the dissonant fifth enters as a passing note on the second quarter of the measure, as indicated by the diagonal line in Example 171 and as shown in the representation of the underlying voice-leading in Example 172.

example 172.

104. The Diminished Triad as Part of V$^6_5$

Very often the 5th of the $^6_5$ is stated horizontally, as in Example 171. In figured bass this kind of statement of the $^6_5$ may be represented by the linear figures 6 5, as demonstrated below.

example 173.

6   5 means: 6   6   not: 6   5
                                        5   3

The figures 6 5 indicate the exact linear succession in the upper voice. In addition, they imply that the 6th is to be held over to form a $^6_5$. They do not mean that the 6th chord progresses to $^5_3$, a diminished triad. In figured bass practice this retention of the 6th was understood. Thus both 5 and ♭5 in the following excerpt would be realized as $^6_5$'s.

example 174. BUXTEHUDE: *Trio Sonata in C minor*

6   6   6   5   ♭5

105. An Apparent Exception to the Rule about Tritone Resolution

Occasionally one finds the following progression of the $^6_5$.

example 175.

V$^6_5$ I   [V$^6_5$]   III

Here the dissonant 5th resolves upward instead of downward both in the V$^6_5$ and in the [V$^6_5$]. By this means, stepwise voice leading is obtained from strong to weak beat. If the dissonant note resolves normally there results a skip from strong to weak beat, which brings with it an undesirable accent on the weak beat:

example 176.

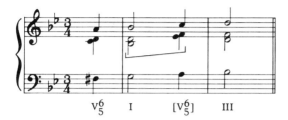

$$V_5^6 \quad I \quad [V_5^6] \quad III$$

The irregular progression of the dissonant 5th in Example 175 also may be explained as a transferred resolution: The note to which the dissonant 5th would normally resolve, B♭, is taken by another and more prominent voice (the soprano in this case) so that the stepwise resolution of the dissonance becomes superfluous. Clearly the doubling of B♭ in Example 176 lacks point and only disturbs the metric-rhythmic pattern, as suggested above.

106.   The Second Inversion (V_3^4)

The complete figuring of the second inversion is $\begin{smallmatrix}6\\4\\3\end{smallmatrix}$. Example 177 shows this chord in relation to the parent V^7 and the V_5^6.

example 177.

$$7 \qquad \begin{smallmatrix}6\\5\end{smallmatrix} \qquad \begin{smallmatrix}6\\4\\3\end{smallmatrix}$$

As in the case of the first inversion, the complete figuring is not used. Only the figures $\begin{smallmatrix}4\\3\end{smallmatrix}$, which represent the interval of the 7th in the parent chord, are required. The 6th is understood and always included, but is not figured unless altered chromatically.

The dissonant notes of the $\begin{smallmatrix}4\\3\end{smallmatrix}$ are the 6th and the 3rd. These notes form the tritone and resolve accordingly, the 6th upward by half step, the 3rd downward by half step. It may seem strange that two notes both consonant with the bass should behave like dissonances and require resolution. This is because they form the dissonant internal interval of the tritone which resolves in the inversions just as it does in the parent 7th chord.

107.   The V$_3^4$ as Auxiliary Chord

Like the $_5^6$ the $_3^4$ can serve as an auxiliary chord. Example 178 provides an opportunity to compare these two chords in a similar structural role.

example 178.   SCHUMANN: *Ich wandel'te unter den Bäumen*

Here we see the bass of the V$_3^4$ as upper auxiliary note to the bass of the tonic triad. The bass note of the V$_5^6$ which follows serves as lower auxiliary note to the bass of the same triad. Example 179 summarizes this relationship.

example 179.

Notice that the eighth-note B shown in Example 179 is a passing note in both outer voices; it does not constitute a return to B of the tonic triad. The latter occurs only on the downbeat of m. 3.

108.   The Passing V$^4_3$

The second inversion of the dominant-7th chord often has the passing function illustrated in the following excerpt.

example 180.   BEETHOVEN: *Sixth Symphony*

The bass of the V$^4_3$ here serves as descending passing note which connects I^6 with I. The tritone resolves normally.

In contrast, when the bass note of the V$^4_3$ is an ascending passing note the tritone does not resolve normally. Instead, the 3rd above the bass, which should descend (since it represents the 7th of the parent 7th chord) ascends, as shown in Example 181.

example 181.   German Folk Song: *Freut euch des Lebens*

This is an instance of transferred resolution (see section 92). Example 182 illustrates the technique by comparing the auxiliary $^4_3$ with the passing $^4_3$.

example 182.

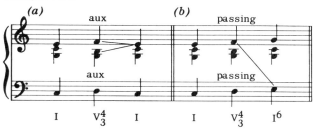

At (a) we see the auxiliary V_3^4. Both soprano and bass are auxiliary notes. The tritone resolves normally. At (b) both soprano and bass of the V_3^4 are passing notes. The resolution of the dissonant 3rd in the soprano is transferred to the bass.

Observe also that the outer voices of the passing $_3^4$ move in a pattern of ascending parallel 10ths. These fluent intervals carry the progression upward, over-riding the tendency of the dissonant 3rd to resolve downward.

109.   VII⁶ as a Substitute for V_3^4

The dissonant diatonic-6th chord, VII⁶, closely resembles the V_3^4, and in fact is often substituted for it. Example 183 illustrates their association.

example 183.

Here the two chords are shown in the same context. The VII⁶ differs from the V_3^4 by only one note. It lacks the 4th.

In a strict four-voice texture, if the bass is doubled by the soprano, the VII⁶ is required as a substitute for the V_3^4. (In order to have the V_3^4 another part would have to be added, making a total of five voices.)

example 184.

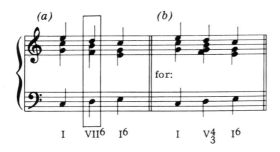

An illustration of the VII⁶ in its role as obligatory substitute for V_3^4 is provided by Example 185.

example 185.   BEETHOVEN: *Piano Sonata in C major, Op. 2/3*

F major: VII$_\flat^6$

Before leaving the VII^6 we note that it has a chromatic counterpart, just as V has as its chromatic counterpart the secondary dominant chord. This chord is marked [VII^6]. In figured basses it is easily recognized by the alterations which the 6th and sometimes the 3rd require. Example 186 shows [VII^6] of V in comparison with [V$_3^4$] of the same triad.

example 186.

110.   The Third Inversion (V$_2^4$)

The complete figuring of the third inversion is $\frac{6}{4}_2$.

example 187.

Unless, however, the 6th is altered only the figures $\frac{4}{2}$ are used. Actually, only the figure 2 is necessary, but when speaking of this chord we say $\frac{4}{2}$ in order to avoid confusion with the Roman numeral II.

The bass itself is now dissonant and must resolve downward, normally to I^6, as shown in Example 187. The descending resolution tendency of the bass of this inversion is so strong that it can overcome even the descending resolution tendency of the 7th of the parent V^7. An instance is quoted below.

example 188.   BEETHOVEN: *Piano Sonata in E major, Op. 109*

An example of the usual resolution of V_2^4 and $[V_2^4]$ follows:

example 189. HANDEL: *Concerto grosso in G minor*

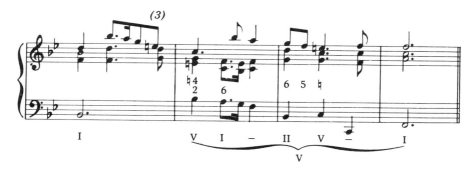

This excerpt is presented in some detail in order to demonstrate the functions of an inverted dominant-7th chord in relation to the basic consonant structure.

1   At this point IV, a dominant preparation, is introduced by its secondary dominant 7th in the third inversion. What appear to be parallel 5ths between two of the upper voices actually are not. At this point the soprano suddenly skips down to an inner voice, and the inner voice, in turn, takes the note to which the soprano would have moved in the normative stepwise voice leading shown below the example.

2   The V_2^4 chord here is somewhat concealed by the submetrical passing notes in the soprano. The eighth note which falls on the beat does not belong to the harmony at all, but is an accented passing note, as shown by the reduction.

3   The E♮ here belongs to the following harmony. The entire passage consists of two harmonic units. The first contains an opening progression from I to V. The second unit contains another opening progression which moves even more strongly to the dominant. The last part of this progression is a modulation, a special kind of progression which is the subject of Chapter 9. Thus all the chords within the last three measures are shown in relation to V as a quasi-tonic.

The function of the three inverted dominant-7th chords is constant. In each case they serve as stepwise prefixes to more essential diatonic harmonies.

THE DIMINISHED-7th CHORD

111. The Diminished-7th Chord: an Altered Inversion of V⁷

In Chapter 5, section 90, it was stated that there are five types of 7th chords. Only four of these were explained in that chapter. We come now to the fifth type.

Consonant chords are often connected by dissonant chords called *diminished-7th chords* (°7). Unlike the 7th chords explained in Chapter 5, which are independent 7th chords derived from triads, the diminished-7th chord is an entirely dependent chord derived from an inverted dominant-7th chord. Its origin in the diatonic minor mode is illustrated below.

example 190.

At (*a*) we see V$\frac{6}{5}$, whose bass note is the leading note. At (*b*) the 6th in the soprano is embellished by a metrical auxiliary note which forms a diminished 7th with the bass. The chord thus created takes its name from that characteristic interval.

Sometimes we regard the chord as a 7th chord on the leading-note triad, as shown at (*c*). This may be convenient if it occurs without preparation by V$\frac{6}{5}$ as at (*c*), but one should bear in mind that the leading-note triad usually occurs in fundamental position only in sequences and therefore is not apt to have generated the diminished-7th chord.

Inversions of the diminished-7th chord derive from the second and third inversions of the dominant-7th chord:

example 191.

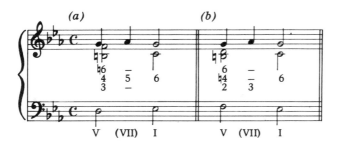

Example 191 points up another important characteristic of the diminished-7th chord: It differs from the inverted dominant-7th chord by only one note. This difference is reflected in the figures. The figures for the diminished-7th chord are always one inversion lower than those of the chord from which it derives. Thus in Example 191 the diminished-7th chord at (a) is figured $\frac{6}{5}$, while the preceding dominant-7th chord is figured $\frac{4}{3}$.

For purposes of practical application it is important to remember that the diminished-7th chord is derived from an inverted dominant-7th chord by a change of only one note. Two other characteristics are important for the same reason. First, the diminished 7th shares no notes with the chord of resolution. Second, every note of the diminished 7th resolves stepwise. These characteristics guide us if we wish to convert an inverted secondary dominant-7th chord into a diminished-7th chord. The two may be regarded as interchangeable; a consonant chord or chord pair may be embellished by either one.

To illustrate, let us assume we wish to provide a IV[6] chord with a diminished-7th chord ([o]7) as prefix. We begin by considering the possible secondary dominant-7ths, as shown in Example 192.

example 192.

Either [V$\frac{4}{3}$] or [V$\frac{4}{2}$] serves as prefix to IV[6]. Next, we apply our knowledge of the special voice-leading characteristic of the [o]7: stepwise resolution of all voices. Since only one note (G) in each inverted secondary dominant-7th chord does not progress by step, if we raise that note by a half step we derive the diminished-7th chords shown in Example 193.

example 193.

The lack of common tones between the °7 and the chord of resolution also provides a rule for correct notation: The °7 share no notes of the same letter name with the chord to which it resolves. Thus in Example 193 it would be incorrect to notate the A♭ as G♯, since the note G is in the chord of resolution.

We emphasize that the °7 derives only from inverted dominant-7th chords. The parent V⁷ cannot be replaced by a °7 without changing its direction entirely.

The reader may have observed that in Example 193 neither diminished-7th chord actually contains the interval of a diminished 7th. Only the diminished-7th chord derived from the dominant ⁶₅ contains that characteristic interval. Quite apart from the spelling of the notes, however, every diminished-7th chord consists of a series of minor thirds above the bass note. Therefore, because the notes of the °7 chord are equidistant and because each is a four-note chord there are only three °7 chords:

example 194.

In four-part harmony all notes of the °7 must be present. No note is doubled. This, as well as other characteristics of the °7 described above, can be seen in the following examples.

example 195.   BEETHOVEN: *Piano Sonata in C minor, Op. 13*

In Example 195 we find the V prepared by a diminished-7th chord. To appreciate the special effect of the latter chord, consider how the passage would sound if a secondary dominant-7th chord replaced it, as in Example 196.

example 196.

We have come to associate the diminished-7th chord with a feeling of greater intensity. The following excerpt shows even more clearly the difference between its effect and that of the secondary dominant-7th chord.

example 197.   BEETHOVEN: *Piano Sonata in C minor, Op. 10/1*

Allegro molto e con brio

Here we see that the passing V_3^4 in measure 4 becomes a diminished-7th chord (VII$_5^6$) in the following measure. This involves a change of only one note: G is replaced by A♭. The diminished-7th chord is prolonged for almost four measures, finally resolving to I⁶ at the end of the passage, as indicated by the arrow.

The diminished-7th chord can also occur as a linear chord without dominant implications. This mode of occurrence is explained in Chapter 11, section 219.

112. The Half-Diminished-7th Chord in Major (VII^7)

Like the VII^7 in minor, VII^7 in major is derived from V$^6_5$.

example 198.

Example 198 shows first the succession V$^6_5$ I. The metrical auxiliary note is included at (b), forming a minor 7th with the bass. At (c) the 7th chord is shown without preparation by V$^6_5$. This chord is sometimes identified as VII^7, a half-diminished chord which resolves to I and which substitutes (rarely) for V$^6_5$. Actually it is used sparingly in compositions, although it does occur often in the idiom shown below.

example 199.

Here the half-diminished-7th chord connects IV and V. Its passing function resembles that of a secondary dominant-7th chord and therefore the Roman numeral VII is enclosed in brackets. Another example of the same idiom follows.

example 200. BRAHMS: *Variations on a Theme by Haydn, Op. 56b*

In this excerpt the VII^7 stands between II^6 and the cadential $^6_4$, again serving as a passing chord much like a [V$^6_5$].

Like the triad VII, the VII^7 progresses by 5th only in sequences.

THE INVERSIONS OF THE MINOR-7th CHORD

113. General

Again we take as model of the minor-7th chord the II^7 in the major mode. Successive inversion of the bass of this chord produces the following array of four chords:

example 201.

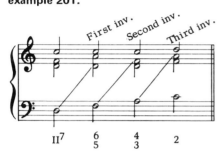

The figures for inverted 7th chords are the same regardless of the type of parent 7th chord from which the inversions derive. As in all cases, figures indicate only the general interval content of the chord. The exact size of each interval is determined by the chord's position in the diatonic tonality or by chromatic alterations if they occur.

The resolutions of the three inversions of the II^7 are summarized in Example 202:

example 202.

The parent chord, II^7, progresses to V or to V^7. Each of the first two inversions also resolves to V or V^7. The third inversion resolves to V^6.

Unlike V^7, II^7 does not contain the tritone. This is a major difference between the two types. As a consequence the only note which requires resolution is the 7th of the parent chord and the note that represents the 7th in each inversion. As indicated by the diagonal lines in Example 202, the 7th descends in parallel motion with the 5th. This pattern is continued in each inversion. We now survey the typical behavior of each inversion.

114. The First Inversion (II^6_5)

Measured upward from the bass the II^6_5 contains only consonant intervals. The chord does not function as a consonance, however, for it still contains the 7th of the parent chord, and therefore requires resolution. The 5th is the dissonant note in this inversion.

The following excerpt illustrates the two most common functions of II^6_5.

example 203. MOZART: *The Magic Flute* (First Quintet)

The first harmonic unit contains a progression directed toward I. The cadence, however, is deceptive: VI replaces the expected tonic triad. The second harmonic unit begins in the same way as the first, but this time the progression to I is completed. Within the first unit II$^6_5$ serves as a combination passing-auxiliary chord between I^6 and V: the bass of II$^6_5$ is a passing note, its upper voice an auxiliary note. At the deceptive cadence II prepares the dominant. Its bass functions as a lower auxiliary note to the bass of V. Within the second four-measure unit the first II$^6_5$ again serves as a passing-auxiliary chord. It also prepares the V, replacing the II used in the cadence of the first unit. In this connection, note that the first cadence contains only consonant chords. The composer reserves the dissonant equivalents of these consonant chords for the heightened effect of the second cadence.

When II^7 progresses to V^7 the 3rd of II^7 is retained as a common tone which becomes the 7th of V^7.

example 204.

The 3rd of the parent chord becomes the bass of the first inversion. Thus, when the common tone is retained, as shown in Example 204, the succession II$^6_5$ V$^4_2$ results.

example 205.

The next example illustrates the II$^6_5$ as an intermediate harmonic goal.

example 206. BEETHOVEN: *Minuet in E♭ major*

Here II⅗ stands at the end of the first harmonic unit. Its dissonant character suggests that it is only an intermediate goal, however, and this is confirmed by the subsequent unit, which begins on V⁷. Thus the function of II⅗ is the usual one: it prepares the V⁷. In melodic terms the bass note of the II⅗ here is an ascending passing note which connects I⁶ with V⁷, just as in Example 203.

115. The Second Inversion (II⁴₃)

The II⁴₃ occurs infrequently. As a passing chord leading to V it is usually replaced by [V⁴₃]:

example 207.

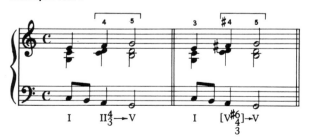

The reason for this substitution is melodic: The [V⁴₃] contains the raised scale degree 4 (♯4) which carries the melodic progression upward more effectively than does the natural scale degree 4. This again is an instance of the law of the half step.

When the bass of the II$\frac{4}{3}$ is an ascending passing note, as in the following example, the 3rd (which represents the 7th of the parent chord) must progress irregularly.

example 208.

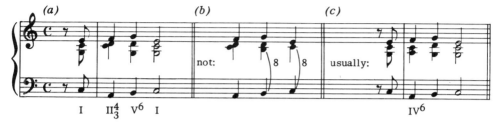

I   II$\frac{4}{3}$ V^6 I   IV^6

At (*a*) the dissonant note (the 3rd) must skip down rather than resolve downward by step, for if it were to resolve stepwise the bass of V^6 would be doubled, as shown at (*b*), and parallel 8ves would result between V^6 and the I. The bass progression shown here (scale degrees 6-7-8) is more often harmonized by IV^6 V^6 I (*c*). This succession permits stepwise voice leading without impending parallels.

116.   The Third Inversion (II$\frac{4}{2}$)

Like V$\frac{4}{2}$ the progression of the II$\frac{4}{2}$ is fixed since the dissonant note is in the bass. Thus the third inversion prepares V^6 or V$\frac{6}{5}$, as shown in the next example.

example 209.   MENDELSSOHN: *An die Entfernte* (voice and accompaniment combined)

[V^7]   II   II$\frac{4}{2}$ V$\frac{6}{5}$ V^7 I

THE INVERSIONS OF THE HALF-DIMINISHED-7th (II⁷) CHORD

117. General

The half-diminished-7th chord and its inversions function in much the same way as do the minor-7th chord and its inversions. Indeed, if we compare the II⁷ in a major key with the II⁷ in its parallel minor key, we find that they differ by only one note. The inversions of the half-diminished are summarized below.

example 210.

Like the minor 7th, the half-diminished 7th contains two voices which descend in parallel motion: the dissonant 7th and the 5th. The resolutions of the half-diminished 7th and its inversions are easily remembered if this fact is borne in mind.

118. The First Inversion (II⁶₅)

Example 211 illustrates the normative function of II⁶₅ as a dominant preparation.

example 211. CHOPIN: *Nocturne in C minor, Op. 48/1*

This progression is made up of two chord groups. The first comprises the first two measures, centering upon I. The second group begins with the two dominant preparations, VI and II$\frac{6}{5}$, then leads through the V^7 to the final I, closing the progression.

119. The Second Inversion (II$\frac{4}{3}$)

In section 115, we explained certain of the difficulties involved in the use of the minor $\frac{4}{3}$. The half-diminished $\frac{4}{3}$ is even more restricted, although it does occur more frequently than the minor $\frac{4}{3}$. The bass of the half-diminished $\frac{4}{3}$ can only descend.

example 212.

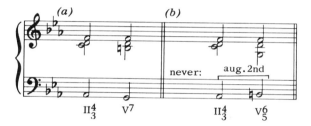

The bass never ascends, as shown in Example 210. This is because the interval of the augmented 2nd is formed between the bass notes of II$\frac{4}{3}$ and V$\frac{6}{5}$, an interval that requires special treatment in order to be accommodated to a melodic progression, whether in the bass or in the upper voice.

120. The Third Inversion (II$\frac{4}{2}$)

The opening of Haydn's "Farewell" Symphony illustrates the II$\frac{4}{2}$.

example 213.   HAYDN: *Symphony in F♯ minor* ("Farewell")

Observe the way in which the dissonant bass of the $II\frac{4}{2}$ propels the harmony toward $V\frac{6}{5}$. The passage quoted consists of a circular progression, the first statement of the tonic triad at the beginning of the movement.

121.   Inversions of the Major-7th Chord (IV^7)

Apart from sequences, the major-7th chord with descending resolution occurs infrequently. Its function as a dominant preparation is limited by the law of the half step which applies to the 7th of the chord itself in this case and dictates the ascending resolution of the 7th shown at (a) below rather than the descending resolution shown at (b) which is required for progression to the dominant.

example 214.

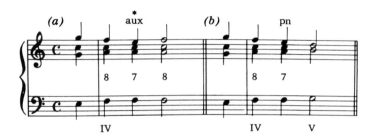

For this reason the idiomatic use of the half-diminished-7th chord [VII^7] explained in section 112 is preferred over IV^7 in such melodic contexts.

    Although the fundamental position of the IV^7 is not often used the first and third inversions occur frequently. Example 215 illustrates a typical context for the first inversion:

example 215.

The following excerpt contains IV_5^6 in a somewhat more elaborate setting.

example 216.   CHOPIN: *Fantaisie in F minor, Op. 49*

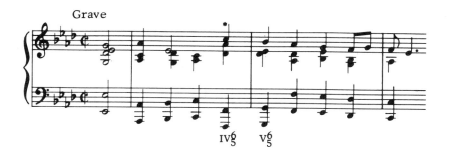

The third inversion of the major-7th chord, IV_2^4, commonly arises as the result of a passing note in the bass.

example 217.

Neither the major-7th chord nor its inversions have the same binding harmonic effect as do the other 7th chords. In many cases the functions of this chord are most efficiently and correctly explained entirely in melodic terms. For this reason we exclude it from the following summary.

122.   Summary of the 7th Chords and Their Inversions

Example 218 summarizes the four main types of 7th chords.

example 218.

Dominant 7th
V⁷ – I

Diminished 7th
(°7)
Substitute for
inversions of
V⁷ or [V⁷]

Minor 7th
(m7)
II⁷ – V⁷

Half-
diminished 7th
(ø7)
II⁷ – V⁷

EXERCISES

A. List of Some Important Terms to Define and Memorize

Transferred resolution

Passing $\frac{4}{3}$

Exchange of voices

Diminished-7th chord

Internal dissonance

Obligatory VII[6]

B. Basic Keyboard Exercises

Each inverted 7th chord is played and sung in close position as the first chord of a pair. The chord is then played in the various soprano positions and the outer voices are sung as shown. The chords may also be arpeggiated from the soprano downward, as before, but this of course does not indicate the inversion. Here the main effort should be directed toward recognition of the inverted 7th chords and their contexts. Arpeggiation from the bass upward reveals the inversion, while singing of the outer voices shows the soprano position. Only the inversions of the V^7 are shown here. They provide a model for the inversions of the other 7th chords, which should be worked out fully in the same way.

exercise 108. Basic Chord Pattern 1 in major

In the exercises at the end of the previous chapter, secondary dominant-7th chords were inserted before every other chord of this pattern in order to expand the progression. Here inverted secondary dominant-7th chords are inserted for the same purpose. They differ from the parent 7th chords in that they create a far more active bass line.

exercise 109.   Basic Chord Pattern 1 in minor

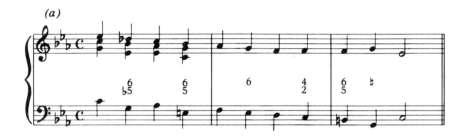

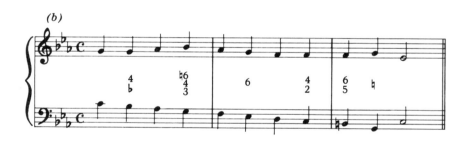

exercise 110.   **Basic Chord Pattern 2 in major**

At the end of the previous chapter the triads of the basic pattern were changed into 7th chords. Here those 7th chords are replaced by their inversions.

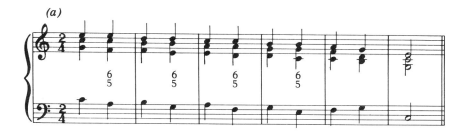

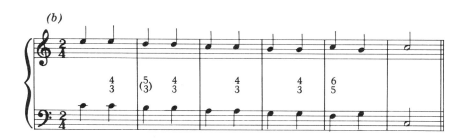

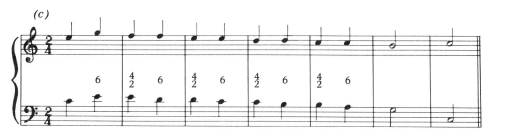

exercise 111.   Basic Chord Pattern 2 in minor

(a)

(b)

(c)

exercise 112.   Cadences which include II$^6_5$

exercise 113.

C. Figured Basses

INSTRUCTIONS

The exercises should be utilized fully, as follows:

1 *Sing* soprano and bass lines from beginning to end before realizing the figures. After realization sing the chords in arpeggiation both from the bass upward and from the soprano downward.

2 *Play* the realization both as it is being made and when it is completed. Those with limited ability at the keyboard should strive to achieve a steady tempo, no matter how slow. Try to think ahead and prepare for the next chord. Anticipate the change of harmony. If possible perform the accompanied vocal or instrumental pieces. In cases where there are no words the line can be sung on the neutral syllables "la" or "loo."

3 *Write out* the realization in all cases. With further experience it should be possible to write the exercises away from the keyboard, always trying to imagine the sound as completely as possible. The keyboard can then be used to check. The singing of soprano and bass and the arpeggiation from bass and from soprano are valuable aids towards the development of this skill.

4 Describe the structure of each chord and its harmonic and melodic functions.

The inversions of the 7th chords can be located easily at the keyboard by using the following procedure:

1 In close position, left hand, the $\frac{6}{5}$ is a triad plus a 2nd on top:

2 In close position, left hand, the $\frac{4}{3}$ is a 6th chord plus a 2nd above the middle note:

3 In close position, left hand, the $\frac{4}{2}$ is a triad added one step above the bass note:

exercise 114.   Chorale: *Herzlich tut mich verlangen*

exercise 115.   Chorale: *Herr, ich habe misgehandelt*

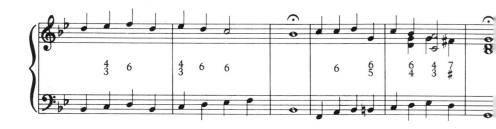

exercise 116.   Chorale: *O Gott, du frommer Gott*

exercise 117.   Chorale: *Schwing dich auf zu deinem Gott*

exercise 118.   BASSANI: *Harmonia festiva (Lucida aurora)*

D.   Unfigured Outer Voices

exercise 119.   LOEILLET: *Sonata for Flute and Continuo*

exercise 120.   **Chorale:** *O Welt, sieh hier dein Leben*

exercise 121.   JEREMIAH CLARKE: "An Hymn for Good Friday"

exercise 122.   JEREMIAH CLARKE: "An Hymn for Christmas Day"

E. Four-Voice Chorale Settings

At this point we introduce a different type of exercise, the harmonization of a chorale melody for performance by mixed voices. During the tonal period many composers contributed their talents to the enrichment of this genre. Of all the chorale harmonizations those by J. S. Bach are not only the best known but also universally regarded as the finest. However, they are so highly developed melodically and harmonically that they do not function well as introductory examples and therefore we use a less complex harmonization to demonstrate the procedure, a chorale setting by Bach's contemporary, Graun.

The first part of a chorale arranged for four voices is presented below.

Chorale: *O Haupt voll Blut und Wunden.*
Harmonization by J. H. Graun.

This setting is similar to a keyboard setting in all essential respects. The spacing of the chords is of course different. However, all the rules of voice leading and all the principles of harmonic progression continue to apply. One additional condition must be observed: the normal vocal range of each part is not to be exceeded. This practical consideration is especially important if the harmonizations are to be sung in class—and this is strongly recommended. Effective vocal ranges for an average group of mixed, untrained voices are as follows:

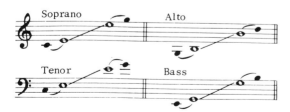

The small notes indicate practical limits while the large notes show the limits for comfortable singing.

In the above example the individual voices are indicated by stem direction. This is the traditional method. In the four-voice chorale the soprano is always notated with stems pointing upward, alto with stems pointing downward, tenor with stems upward, and bass with stems downward. This notational device makes clear the progression of each voice and also serves to point up the various combinations and oppositions of voices.

We begin with two exercises in distributing the harmony for four voices. The procedure is as follows. Figured outer voices are given—in this case the second phrase of the chorale above.

STEP 1. Fill in the harmony in the usual keyboard style, taking note of voice-leading problems such as impending parallelisms or awkward skips.

STEP 2. Redistribute the inner voices where necessary to make them lie within the ranges given above. Bear in mind the following:

1   Some of the voice-leading problems encountered in the keyboard version may be solved by the more open spacing of the vocal version.

However, beware of new problems which may arise when the voices are redistributed.

2   Certain progressions which are quite satisfactory in the keyboard setting do not lend themselves to the vocal arrangement at all. In such cases a different harmonization must be used for the vocal setting. This problem does not arise in our illustration since the harmonization is intended for vocal arrangement.

3   Avoid prolonged crossing of adjacent voices. This is not necessarily bad— indeed, it is often helpful, even essential. However, extended crossing is objectionable since the voices involved thereby lose their characteristic functions and registers.

4   If possible maintain stepwise progression of the individual voices. Use skips only where necessary for reasons of range, to avoid a parallelism, or for other legitimate reasons. As we have seen, skips represent melodic development and therefore they must not be used haphazardly.

5   The vertical interval between two adjacent voices should not exceed an 8ve. This is for reasons of sonority and texture. However, an exception to the rule is the interval between tenor and bass, which often exceeds the 8ve limit.

Graun's setting of this phrase is given below:

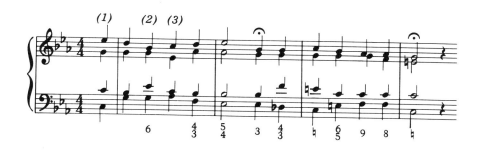

comments

1   It is evident that the redistribution of the voices with respect to the keyboard arrangement mainly involves the tenor. The opening chord here is in open position, in comparison to its close position below the soprano in the keyboard arrangement.

2   The tenor skip to E♭ is necessary since it is the only voice available to take the 6th of the chord. What would happen if the alto skipped down to E♭ while the tenor remained on B♭?

3   The alto skips to avoid impending parallel 8ves with the bass.

exercise 123.   Chorale: *Nun ruhen alle'Wälder.* Figures by J. C. Kühnau

comments

1   The alto skips to another note of the harmony in order to avoid impending 8ves with the bass.
2   Compare the harmonization of this phrase with that of the second phrase.

exercise 124.   Chorale: *Ach, lass dich jetzt finden komm*
Author of figures unknown (from Rinck Manuscript Collection, Yale Music Library).

comments

1   The $\frac{4}{2}$ serves here as a lower auxiliary note chord. It is not an authentic 7th
     chord but a chord which is entirely linear in origin. Therefore it belongs to the
     class of dissonant chords explained in Chapter 11.
     The entire chorale consists of three phrases. The harmonic plan is symmetrical:
     the two outer phrases contain circular progressions, while the central phrase
     opens to V.
     These four-voice chorale exercises represent an important step toward original
     composition. Their advantages are many. They reveal more clearly than do the
     keyboard arrangements the motion of the individual voices and consequently
     enable us to see the possibilities for developing voices separately and in combi-
     nation. In Chapter 14 those possibilities are examined more systematically.

Chapter 7

THE SOPRANO VOICE
AND
HARMONIC PROGRESSION

> The true goal of music—its proper enter-
> prise—is melody. All the arts of harmony
> have as their ultimate purpose only beau-
> tiful melody. Therefore the question of
> which is the more significant, melody or
> harmony, is futile. Beyond doubt, the
> means is subordinate to the end.
>
> Johann Philipp Kirnberger, 1771

123. The Special Importance of the Soprano

Of the three voices above the bass the uppermost, the soprano, is most important. There are two main reasons for this: (1) the succession of intervals which the soprano forms with the bass outlines and delimits the harmonic progression, and (2) the soprano voice almost always carries the themes and motives that charac- terize a particular composition and that serve both to unify and diversify it.

124. The Technical Meaning of the Term "Voice"

By "voice" we mean the succession of notes performed by a single human voice or single-line instrument. This voice may be quite complex. It may even carry several melodic elements simultaneously. The next two sections present certain fundamental facts about the structure of the soprano voice in tonal music. While these facts also apply to the other voices, they are most clearly evident in the soprano. Many will seem familiar from Chapter 1, for in a sense this is a review and extension of material presented there.

125. Basic Melodic Progression

Every tonal melody contains stepwise motions and may also contain skips. Stepwise progression, however, is primary. It characterizes many simple melodies, for example, the chorale tune given below.

example 219.   Chorale: *Jesu, Leiden, Pein, und Tod*

Basic melodic progression therefore is defined as progression by 2nd. To be sure, we often use the term melodic somewhat loosely to designate any succession of notes, regardless of the intervals they form. Nonetheless, in the technical sense basic melodic progression is identical with stepwise progression. The term "line," or "melodic line," refers specifically to the stepwise characteristic of melody. This definition of melody is implicit in earlier sections of the present volume, especially in Chapter 4 (section 50 and elsewhere) and in Chapter 5, where the two fundamental melodic functions, the auxiliary note and the passing note, were shown as chord-generating elements in the evolution of the harmonic language.

126. Scale and Triad: Melody and Harmony

In Chapter 1 the scale was described as a complete stepwise ordering of the notes of the diatonic key. Accordingly, the diatonic scale can be regarded as a kind of ideal melody. The tonic triad, on the other hand, represents harmony and the harmonic intervals, 3rd, 5th, and 8ve.

It is sometimes said that melody exists in the horizontal succession of notes, while harmony exists in the vertical simultaneity of notes (chords). This is false. Vertical and horizontal dimensions constantly interact. We have seen that an entire class of chords, the 7th chords, emerges when melodic elements, passing or auxiliary notes, are incorporated into the vertical grouping we call a chord. Further, we have found that the harmonic (triadic) intervals often are stated in the horizontal dimension. Thus, we distinguish between melody and harmony solely on the basis of intervals. The 2nd and its inversion, the 7th, are the melodic intervals. All other simple intervals are harmonic.

127.   Metrical and Submetrical Elements

Like the ideal melody, the diatonic scale, the basic stepwise melodic line is made up of notes which form harmonic intervals and notes which connect and extend those intervals. For instance, the first phrase of the chorale tune quoted above consists of the intervals of the tonic triad filled in by passing notes. An analysis of that fragment is shown below. The harmonic intervals are extracted and shown at (*b*).

example 220.   Chorale: *Jesu, Leiden, Pein und Tod*

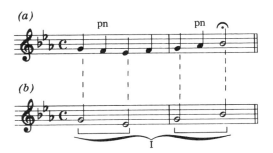

In this case the passing notes have the duration of the metrical unit, the quarter note, and therefore are called metrical passing notes. More complicated melodies may contain submetrical as well as metrical durations. Example 221 below illustrates the combination.

example 221.   BACH: *Chorale Variations* on *Sei gegrüsset, Jesu gütig*

The original form of the melody is given at (a). In the variation shown at (b) the second note is embellished by submetrical notes. Chapter 12 is devoted in part to a detailed consideration of such submetrical notes. Their use comprises a highly important aspect of compositional technique. The present chapter, however, is concerned only with metrical melodic notes since they alone normally have harmonic value.

The metrical auxiliary note and passing note have just been illustrated. The *metrical arpeggiation,* which characterizes many melodies, is a special case which requires more detailed explanation.

128.   Metrical Arpeggiation

Many soprano voices contain skips in addition to stepwise progression. Example 222 illustrates the meaning of the metrical skip, of arpeggiation, in relation to the basic stepwise pattern.

example 222.   Chorale: *Wie schön leuchtet der Morgenstern*

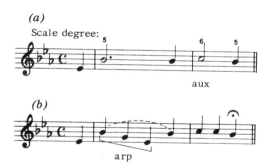

At (a) following the initial skip we see the basic stepwise pattern: scale degree 5 followed by a metrical auxiliary note, scale degree 6. At (b) scale degree 5 is embellished further by an arpeggiation which descends through the tonic triad. This arpeggiation is subordinate to the main stepwise progression, and therefore the dotted line shows that scale degree 5 continues, after having been interrupted by the arpeggiation.

The concept of basic stepwise progression is a traditional part of music theory, although many late nineteenth-century and early twentieth-century theorists apparently were unaware of it. In the eighteenth century J. D. Heinichen provided a very clear illustration which deserves to be quoted here.

example 223.   HEINICHEN: Analysis of a recitative passage. From *Der General-bass in der Composition* (1728)

(a)

(b)

Heinichen first presents the recitative as shown at (*a*). He then demonstrates the correctness of its voice leading by showing the underlying continuity of the soprano voice (*b*). The combination of stepwise succession in the soprano with bass line he calls the "fundamental notes." Reductions such as those shown at (*b*) were first used extensively and systematically by Heinrich Schenker, the eminent twentieth-century theorist, to illuminate complicated and sophisticated processes in art music of the tonal period. Some of the basic aspects of those processes are dealt with in Chapter 13 of the present volume.

129.   Arpeggiation as Compound Melody

If the individual melodic strands of an arpeggiation are developed in such a way that each has its own continuity and rhythmic identity the result is *compound melody.* This type of melodic development is illustrated in the next excerpt. The example shows step by step how the compound melody of the final version arises.

example 224.   TELEMANN: *Fantasy*

At (*a*) we find the familiar harmonic progression I II$^4_2$ V$^6_5$ I. Over this the soprano line descends from scale degree 5 to scale degree 3. Scale degree 5 is expanded by a metrical auxiliary note, scale degree 6.

At (*b*) the two upper lines are inverted: the alto is placed above the soprano. At (*c*) (the complete version as Telemann wrote it) these two lines are activated rhythmically and expressed as a single voice. This, then, is compound melody: the expression by a single voice of more than one melodic progression.

It is extremely important to note that each melodic line at (*c*) progresses just as it did at (*a*) and (*b*). That is, scale degree 5 in the soprano moves via scale degree 6 to scale degree 4, while the alto progresses from scale degree 1 to 2 and back again. Because these connections are expressed by a single voice in the final version (*c*) they are not continuous as shown at (*a*) and (*b*). The dotted lines at (*c*) show the actual progression, which is temporarily interrupted by the skips from one line to another. Note that the melody in the second measure of (*c*) does not contain G♯. The melodic focus is on the lower of the two lines. However, it is present in the accompaniment and returns as an active melodic note in the third measure.

Harmonically controlled melodic progression, as illustrated here, is a traditional concept in music theory, although the degree to which melody possesses independence from harmony or actually influences harmony has been debated extensively. J. P. Rameau represents one extreme position when he writes: ". . . melody is only a consequence of harmony." J. Mattheson represents the other extreme position when he writes: "In opposition to [Rameau's concept] I place melody at the very foundation of the entire art of composition." To a great extent both men were confused by the definitions of harmony and melody as isolated aspects of structure. It is in order to avoid this that we focus upon the coordination of melody and harmony, upon their combined role in tonal composition.

The concept of compound melody is of the utmost importance to analysis and composition. It enables one to understand more complicated melodic structures and to compose melodies of greater subtlety and interest. In the past, major teachers of composition have been aware of this fact. For example, Kirnberger took great care to explain the concept. He described what we have called compound melody as a "single voice which is constructed in such a way that it carries its own harmony with it and sounds like a two- or three-part composition . . ." He illustrates as follows:

example 225.   KIRNBERGER: *Die Kunst des reinen Satzes* (1771)

Kirnberger says that the voice shown at (a) sounds almost like the two-line setting at (b). In this way he demonstrates the continuity of each voice which "to the untutored" may not be readily apparent at (a) alone. He goes on to illustrate what we might call a three-line melody:

example 226.   KIRNBERGER: *Die Kunst des reinen Satzes in der Musik*

Again he provides a vertical condensation (*b*) to show the continuity of each individual line and its course within the harmonic progression.

Compound melody is not restricted to any style within the tonal period. Every developed tonal composition utilizes the technique. In some cases it is more evident than in others, as in the following two excerpts.

example 227.   MOZART: *Piano Sonata in A minor, K.310*

Here the compound structure is made apparent when the component lines suggested in the first measure are notated in full in the second. Similar verification of compound structure is provided by the next excerpt.

example 228.   BRAHMS: *Intermezzo in B♭ major, Op. 76/4*

The opening "melody" of the piece is shown at (*a*). Clearly Brahms regards this as a compound structure, for when the same melody returns later in the piece (*b*) the upper of the two lines is actually sustained.

Extreme instances of compound melodic structure are provided by Bach's compositions for solo cello and solo violin. In the excerpt shown in Example 229 the melody (*a*) is actually a complete three-voice texture, as shown at (*b*).

example 229.   BACH: *Suite in G major for Solo Cello, Menuet II*

130. The Transient Skip

Not every arpeggiation or partial arpeggiation represents compound melody. Very often it may be entirely a local event, a skip from one line to another and an immediate return. This kind of arpeggiation, which we have called a *transient skip,* does not influence melodic structure over a longer span, as does compound melody. An example follows.

example 230. Chorale: *Meine Seele erhebet den Herrn*

The soprano of this phrase is essentially a stepwise progression. The skip to E (bracketed) does not establish compound melody but is merely a temporary motion to another harmony note.

The transient skip is sometimes filled in by a passing note, as here:

example 231. BACH: *Chorale Variations* on *Sei gegrüsset, Jesu gütig*

At (a) is. the basic chorale melody. When this is compared with (b), an embellished version, we see that scale degree 3 in the second measure is followed by a transient skip down to scale degree 1. This skip is filled in by a passing eighth note.

131. Nonconsecutive Melodic Relations

In the previous examples we have seen that melodic notes need not be in immediate succession in order to be related. In the Telemann *Fantasy* (Example 224c) the notes of each stepwise line in the soprano voice were not always in immediate succession, yet their relatedness was made clear by the voice leading within the harmonic progression. This fact is of great importance to melodic structure and has practical value in the harmonizing of a given melody, the composing of a soprano voice, and many other musical tasks.

132. Displacement of a Line from Its Normal Position

Before leaving these general characteristics of melodic structure to deal with specific types of melodic progression we should observe the frequent displacement of a main line of compound melody from its normal position above the other line or lines. This was shown in the Telemann *Fantasy* (Example 224c), where the main line, which descends from scale degree 5 to scale degree 3 over the span of the entire phrase, lies below a static, secondary line.

HARMONIZATION OF COMMON TYPES OF STEPWISE SOPRANO PROGRESSION

133. Melodic Groups and Melodic Goals

A discussion of melodic progression presupposes the existence of melodic goals and melodic groups. Therefore let us begin by considering the factors that delimit a melodic group. A melodic group is defined by the metric-rhythmic pattern and by harmonic progression. When a harmonic goal is reached the melodic goal coincides with it. However, the harmonic goal may differ from the melodic goal in an important respect. For example, the harmonic goal may represent closure, while the melodic goal may be such that the melody remains "open," active, demanding further progression. Our next example illustrates this.

example 232. Chorale: *Allein Gott in der Höh' sei Ehr*

Here the bass and harmony execute a circular progression which closes on the tonic triad. The soprano, however, ends on an active note, the 3rd of the triad. This means that the composition is not completed, for although the harmony closes, the melody does not.

134. Types of Melodic Progression

The ultimate goal of a melodic line is always one of the stable notes of the diatonic scale (1, 3, 5, or 8), just as the ultimate harmonic goal is always one of the chords of the harmonic axis. Melodic progressions to, from, and around these stable notes may be characterized as "opening," "closing," and "circular," just as we characterize harmonic progressions with respect to the harmonic axis. In addition, we find a general type of melodic progression which traverses a triadic interval in descending direction. Each type is taken up separately in the following sections.

135. Circular Melodic Progression

The auxiliary-note embellishment is typical of circular progression, although intervals larger than the 2nd may also be traversed in a circular pattern. Standard harmonizations of the diatonic upper-auxiliary notes are summarized in the next example.

example 233.

The standard harmonizations of the upper auxiliary note are the same in major and minor. At the end of Example 233(b) is a reminder that raised scale degree 6 is only a passing note, never an auxiliary note. Examples which illustrate two of the above patterns are given below.

example 234.   HAYDN: *Chorale St. Antoni*

example 235.   SCHUMANN: *Viennese Carnival Jest*

Standard harmonizations of the diatonic lower-auxiliary note are summarized in the next example.

example 236.

In the major there are only two diatonic lower-auxiliary note formations: 8-7-8 and 3-2-3. By the law of the half step, scale degree 4 is bound to scale degree 3 and does not serve well as lower auxiliary note to 5. (In the rare instances when 4 does serve as lower auxiliary to 5 it is harmonized by IV⁶.)

In the minor each note of the tonic triad has available a lower auxiliary note. This is because scale degree 4 is a whole step away from both 3 and 5 and thus is not bound to either one by the law of the half step.

136. Opening Melodic Progression

The ascending progression from scale degree 1 to scale degree 3 typifies the opening progression: The line ascends from a stable note through a passing note to the active scale degree 3, thus opening a melodic interval (the 3rd) for further progression. A model chorale tune is presented in Example 237.

example 237.   Chorale: *Wer Gott vertraut*

The standard harmonization of the melodic progression 1 2 3 is shown in the next example.

example 238.

The passing note, scale degree 2, is harmonized by V (as in Example 237) or by V⁶. A more elaborate setting, using V⁶, is shown below.

example 239.   LOEILLET: *Solo Sonata for Flute and Thorough-Bass*

The basic stepwise progression of the soprano voice is indicated both by the stems pointing upward and by the scale degree numbers above the staff. The remaining notes in the soprano voice are submetrical embellishments: auxiliary notes and arpeggiations. The bass is embellished by transient skips.

The passing note, scale degree 4, in the ascending progression 3 4 5 in major is harmonized either by V$^4_3$ or by IV^6.

example 240.

The V$^4_3$ in this situation has been described as the "passing" $^4_3$ (see section 108). It enables scale degree 4 to escape the law of the half step by moving the outer voices in parallel 10ths. The IV^6 achieves the same result by providing a "neutral" consonant setting for scale degree 4. An illustration of the latter harmonization is provided below.

example 241.   BACH: *Concerto in C major for 2 Harpsichords* (reduction)

It is important to note that IV⁶ does not lead to V in this context, but to I⁶. When V harmonizes scale degree 5 as melodic goal, the passing scale degree 4 is raised chromatically and harmonized by a [VII⁶] of V, as shown below.

example 242.

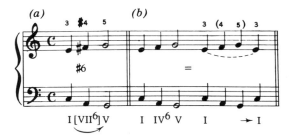

By raising scale degree 4 the half step occurs between ♯4 and 5, and in accord with the law of the half step ♯4 ascends. Without this chromatic alteration of scale degree 4 neither the melodic not the harmonic goal is reached in an effective way. V may not sound like a harmonic goal. Instead, the progression may sound as though it should continue toward scale degree 3 over I, as shown at Example 242(*b*).

In the minor mode scale degree 4 presents no special problem since, as remarked earlier, it stands equidistant from both 3 and 5. The following is a characteristic opening progression in the minor mode.

example 243.   Chorale: *Auf meinen lieben Gott*

Here the soprano ascends directly to scale degree 5 while the bass carries an opening harmonic progression, I V. Often the melodic opening from 1 to 5 in minor is coordinated with a harmonic progression from I to III, as shown in our next example.

example 244.   Chorale: *Ach wie nichtig*

The ascent to scale degree 5 is achieved in two groups. Scale degrees 1 2 3 are under the direct control of I. In the second group, however, passing scale degree 4 is harmonized by [V] of III so that at the end of the group the melodic goal, scale degree 5, coincides with the harmonic goal, III.

137.   Descending Melodic Progressions within Triadic Intervals

Thus far we have considered two types of melodic progression: (1) circular progressions involving auxiliary note embellishments of stable diatonic notes and (2) opening progressions, progressions which ascend through the triadic intervals of 3rd and 5th to the active notes of the triad.

There is a third type of progression, which descends through a triadic interval or its inversion but does not close on scale degrees 2 or 1. Two examples are given below.

example 245.   Chorale: *Ach Gott und Herr*

Here the soprano traverses the upper 4th of the major scale.

Another common descending progression of this type is shown in Example 246:

example 246.

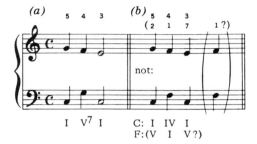

This progression descends from scale degree 5 to scale degree 3. The passing note, scale degree 4, is harmonized by V^7. In major keys it is rarely harmonized by IV, as shown at (*b*), because of the ambiguous 5th relation between I and IV, indicated in parentheses. This limitation applies only when scale degree 3 is the end of the melodic motion, as here.

Observe that neither of the above progressions has the effect of an opening progression, such as one finds at the beginning of a composition. Rather, they suggest progression toward closure. The next section deals with that type of progression.

138. Closing Progressions

Lines that end on scale degree 1 are called closing progressions. Usually such lines descend from the 5th or 3rd of the scale, as below:

example 247.   Chorale: *Jesu, meine Freude*

Closure to scale degree 1 is effected either by the soprano progression 2 1 (as in Example 247) or by the progression 7 8, shown below.

example 248.

Over the cadential succession V I the soprano progresses from 7 to 8 while the inner voice descends from 2 to 1. The typical closing soprano progression descends. Much less often does the line ascend to the final degree progression 7 8, as in Example 248 and below.

example 249.   Chorale: *Valet will ich dir geben*

139. Partial Closure

When a line descends to scale degree 2 over V we say that the progression is a partial closure. Both melody and harmony are directed strongly toward a cadence, yet the progression is not fulfilled. This partial closure is similar to a semicolon in effect. To illustrate we use the second phrase of the chorale whose first phrase served earlier to demonstrate opening progression (Example 243).

example 250.   Chorale: *Auf meinen lieben Gott*

The next example shows a partial closure followed by a closing progression, the normal sequence of progressions.

example 251.   Chorale: *Mach's mit mir, Gott, nach deiner Güt'*

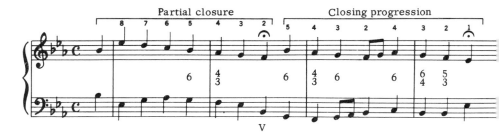

The partial closure should not be confused with the more general descending progression within a triadic interval as described in section 137. None of the latter type end on scale degree 2 and therefore do not suggest closure.

140. Melodic Sequence

A melody that features immediate repetition of a pattern at different pitch levels is called *sequential.* An example of such a melody is quoted below.

example 252.   MARCELLO: *Concerto for Oboe*

To say that a melody is sequential does not indicate the type of progression it represents. This can be done only after one has determined its direction, the interval it traverses, and its melodic goal. In Example 252 the sequential melody of the oboe is a series of ascending arpeggiations, each ending on the note which represents the basic stepwise line. This line, which is carried more obviously by the soprano of the continuo, contains two progressions: first, a circular progression that centers upon scale degree 5, then a progression which descends from scale degree 5 to scale degree 3. The two are summarized in Example 253.

example 253.

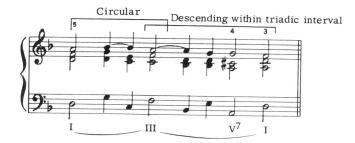

Example 253 also shows that the melodic progressions coordinate with two distinct harmonic progressions, the first an opening progression from I to III, the second a closing progression from III through V[7] to I.

A more comprehensive treatment of sequences is given in section 220, Linear Intervallic Patterns.

141.   Harmonization of the Diatonic Major Scale

Several of the types of progression explained above are represented in the harmonization of the diatonic scales. The scale harmonizations provide valuable guides to harmonization in general and should be memorized.

example 254.   Harmonization of the Diatonic Major Scale

example 255. Harmonization of the Diatonic Minor Scale (melodic)

THE HARMONIZATION PROCEDURE

142. The Principle of Harmonic Definition

When we supply chords for a given soprano voice, it is recognized that a soprano voice alone can have several meanings, depending upon the way it is harmonized or "set." A demonstration of this fact follows.

example 256. SCHUBERT: *Die Nebensonnen*

Example 256 presents the melody without its chordal support. Assuming from the signature that the key is A major we read the upper voice as the degree succession 3-2-(3)-4-3-2-1. The 3 in parentheses is a passing note which connects scale degree 2 with scale degree 4, an upper auxiliary note. Schubert's first setting of the melody is in accord with this reading.

example 257.

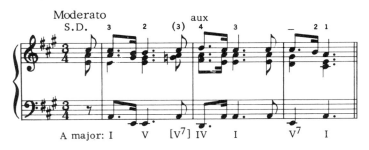

However, the second setting, which occurs a few measures later in the song, gives quite a different structural meaning to the upper voice.

example 258.

Here the soprano is set as the degree succession 5-4-(5)-6-5-4-3 in the key of the relative minor or submediant (VI). The two different interpretations of the same soprano voice are summarized in Example 259:

example 259.

The 3rd is shown first as a linear succession C♯-B-A, then as the vertical 3rd A-C♯. Schubert first interprets this 3rd as the lower 3rd of the A major triad (I), then as the upper 3rd of the F♯ minor triad (VI).

These two different interpretations of the same melody reflect the operation of a fundamental harmonic principle, *the principle of harmonic definition,* which is stated as follows: The structural meaning of the soprano voice is always defined by the bass and harmony. An additional demonstration of this principle is given below.

example 260.   Chorale: *Nun ruhen alle Wälder*

We assume from the key signature that the key of this melody is B♭ major and therefore read the succession as scale degrees 3-1-2-3-5-4-3. The melodic progression is circular, focusing upon scale degree 3. The harmonic setting shown in Example 261 confirms this reading of the soprano voice.

example 261.   Chorale: *Nun ruhen alle Wälder.* Bach's setting

Like the melodic progression, the harmonic progression is circular, beginning and ending on I. Further on in the chorale Bach has set the same soprano line in a different way:

example 262.

There the line is heard in terms of the "relative minor" (VI) as the degree succession 5-3-4-5-7-6-5. This is essentially the same harmonic reinterpretation as that used by Schubert above where the soprano line was heard first in relation to I, then in relation to VI. Both instances demonstrate the principle of harmonic definition. From this fundamental principle we can derive two criteria for the selection of appropriate chords to harmonize a given soprano voice:

1   The chord succession must support the melodic function of each note of the melodic succession and make clear its direction.

2   At the same time, each chord must have a specific and logical function in the harmonic progression. This applies to the main consonant chords which underlie the progression as well as to those chords which have secondary functions. Consider, for example, the following settings of scale degree 2 as a passing note.

example 263.

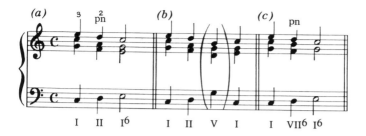

At (a) II has been selected to support the descending passing note D. This chord is incorrect because it suggests the further harmonic progression shown at (b). In a specific sense it is too strong harmonically to serve as a passing chord in this small context. It functions as a dominant preparation but is not followed by a dominant.

An appropriate passing chord for this situation is shown at (c): VII[6], the dissonant 6th chord which so often has that melodic function.

The second criterion listed above is based upon harmonic function. This criterion may sometimes take precedence over the first, which has to do with the melodic functions of the soprano notes. In such cases the standard harmonization patterns must yield to the requirements of harmonic progression. As an instance of this, consider the standard setting of the circular progression 3-2-3-4-3 as shown at Example 264(a):

example 264.

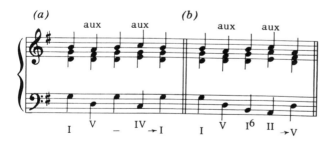

When the harmonic progression is directed toward V, as at (b) the standard harmonization is forsaken for one which prepares the goal more effectively. At (b) the deviation from the standard progression occurs with the I[6], the chord which introduces the dominant preparation II. Example 270 presents the passage from which this progression was drawn.

example 265.   BEETHOVEN: *Concerto for Piano and Orchestra in G major, Op. 58*

We turn now to the step-by-step procedure for harmonizing a soprano voice.

143.   The Six Steps in Soprano Harmonization

The main purpose of the harmonization procedure outlined below is to provide for organized and intelligent applications of the principles of harmonic progression as they relate to the progression of the soprano voice. The ear and aural intuition are to be used at all times, of course, but the "picking out" of chords at the piano will teach nothing. True, this method may occasionally yield passable results with elementary material, but eventually it will lead only to frustration. The procedure outlined below is designed to guide the student toward logical and productive method that will prove effective regardless of the complexity of the material. To demonstrate the procedure we begin with the initial phrase of a familiar chorale melody:

example 266.   Chorale: *Herr, wie du willst*

STEP 1. Analyze the melody for:

    a. degree succession (basic stepwise line).

example 267.

    b. metrical embellishments (submetrical embellishments are harmonized only in special circumstances).

example 268.

    c. types of melodic progression.

example 269.

    d. subgroups within the progression, particularly sequences.

example 270.

STEP 2. Sketch in the bass and symbols for the *minimal harmonization.*

example 271.

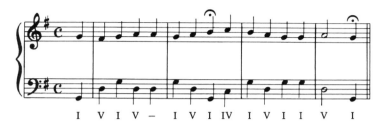

The minimal harmonization employs only diatonic triads in fundamental position, plus V^7, and VII^6. Wherever possible use the standard harmonizations. At this stage we are not concerned about 5ths and 8ves, but only about chord selection in terms of harmonic function.

The importance of the minimal harmonization cannot be overestimated. From this firm basic structure one can proceed in an orderly fashion to construct more elaborate settings. Often the minimal harmonization will contain parallel 5ths and 8ves and sound somewhat dull. Nevertheless, it is of great value in achieving an effective final harmonization. Kirnberger has stressed the value of such a basic harmonization in the following words: "A complete composition must be constructed in such a way that when all dissonances are eliminated the remainder is harmonically coherent. Therefore as an essential part of the art of composition one must know how to support a melody with consonant harmonies alone."

STEP 3. Invert the minimal harmonies in order to correct parallel 5ths and 8ves, improve the melodic structure of the bass, achieve a better counterpoint between the outer voices, and in order to render the metric-rhythmic pattern more coherent and effective.

example 272.

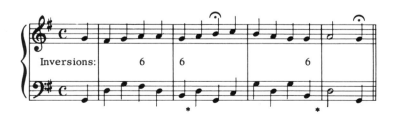

STEP 4. Use secondary triads as substitutes for primary triads if they improve the progression.

example 273.

Diatonic substitutions: VII   VI   II

In Example 273 three substitutions have been made. The first and last fulfill the need for stepwise bass progression indicated in Example 272 by asterisks. The second substitution (VI for I) prevents the tonic chord from arriving in an accented position too early and thus arresting the forward motion of the progression.

STEP 5. Where the context is appropriate replace triads with 7th chords and inverted 7th chords. [V] and [V^7] may also be introduced.

example 274.

STEP 6. Complete the harmonization sketched out at Step 5 by working out all the details of voice leading, just as in a figured bass with given soprano.

example 275.

The procedure thus consists of the six steps summarized below. The student should memorize them and follow them consistently until he has gained sufficient experience to enable him to condense the procedure.

SUMMARY OF STEPS IN THE HARMONIZATION PROCEDURE

1 Analyze the melody.
2 Minimal harmonization (triads in fundamental position, V^7, VII^6).
3 Invert minimal harmonies.
4 Substitute triads.
5 Add 7th and inverted 7th chords.
6 Notate in full.

In Chapters 10 and 11 two new classes of chords will be presented, completing the vocabulary. In the outline above, these may be introduced quite naturally at Step 5.

144. Sample Harmonizations

We now apply the procedure to several soprano voices, each of which features a different type of metrical embellishment. The first features a form of the auxiliary note.

example 276.   Given soprano: *Austrian Folk Song*

example 277.   Step 1: Analysis

example 278. Step 2: Minimal harmonization

Our minimal harmonization here is defective at two points (marked by brackets) where the bass and harmony are repeated across the bar line. A repetition of this kind has an adverse effect upon the metric-rhythmic pattern, since change of measure should be marked by change of harmony. Inversion of the chords involved is not a satisfactory solution since they remain closely related to the parent chords they follow. A satisfactory solution can be obtained by introducing one substitute and by supplying one primary triad with a prefix. However, we have delayed this until Step 4, where it belongs. Thus at Step 3 (Example 279) we use only two inversions. Although not essential to the harmonization these render the bass line more fluent melodically.

example 279. Step 3: Invert minimal harmonies

Observe particularly the effect of IV⁶ in the first measure of Example 279 as compared with the parent IV in the first measure of Example 278. The parent chord provides too much harmonic accent for the incomplete upper auxiliary note. It tends to hinder the unfolding of the soprano voice. In large part this is due to the counterpoint of the outer voices, which emphasizes the 8ve B♭.

example 280. Step 4: Substitute triads

By substituting VI for I and preparing V by II[6] we have removed the repetition over the bar line mentioned above.

example 281.   Step 5: Add 7th and inverted 7th chords

7ths and secondary dominants: [V]   VI

The only 7th chord introduced here is the cadential V[7]. However, the secondary dominant triad is used to good advantage in the second measure. It serves to link the two melodic groups together strongly and, in addition, corrects the impending parallelisms between I and VI which are evident in Example 280.

example 282.   Step 6: Notate in full

I   IV   V   [V]   VI   II   V   I

Another step-by-step harmonization follows. Here the given soprano combines passing and auxiliary notes.

example 283.   Given soprano: Chorale, *Schmücke dich, o liebe Seele*

example 284.   Step 1: Analysis

example 285. Step 2: Minimal harmonization

I   V   I   V   I − V   I   I − IV I   V   I   V   I

Two aspects of the minimal harmonization should be noted. First, the bass line is extremely repetitious and greatly restricted by the tonic and dominant harmonies. This defect can be remedied easily in the subsequent steps. Second, we use the V⁷ here in the minimal harmonization for the first time. (The V⁷ and VII⁶ are the only dissonant chords admitted to the minimal harmonization.) As shown above in Example 246, IV is unsatisfactory as a harmonic setting for scale degree 4 when that degree serves as a descending passing note. V^7, V^6_5, or V^4_3 are standard.

example 286. Step 3: Invert minimal harmonies

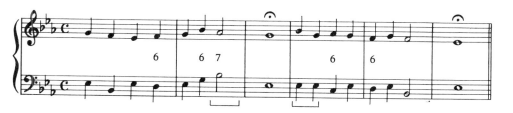

Inversion improves the bass line but does not remove all the other defects. With the aid of substitute harmonies and prefixes the static points indicated by brackets in Example 285 can be corrected at the next step.

example 287. Step 4: Substitute triads

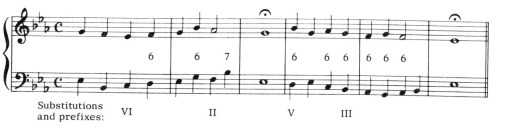

Substitutions
and prefixes: VI   II   V   III

In the second measure II serves as prefix to V^7 so that the soprano note A♭ is harmonized by two chords. III^6 has been substituted for I in the fourth measure. The substitute chord does not progress in the same way as the original. This can be tested by playing the succession III^6-V^6 and noting the effect of discontinuity. The bass succession which follows logically from III^6 forms a counterpoint of parallel 6ths with the soprano (with only one exception), a very fluent progression of imperfect consonances which leads to the two perfect cadential intervals, 5th and 8ve.

example 288.   Steps 5 and 6: Add 7th and inverted 7th chords. Notate in full

The next soprano features an ascending arpeggiation.

example 289.   Given soprano: Chorale: *Sollt ich meinem Gott nicht singen*

example 290.   Step-1: Analysis

Arpeggiation, especially complete arpeggiation as in this case, provides the most obvious clue to harmonization. Here is seen the complete tonic triad unfolded in an ascending arpeggiation. The melodic progression as a whole is circular, beginning and ending on scale degree 1. Within the over-all progression are two sub-groups, the first the arpeggiation, the second the auxiliary note pattern 8 ♯7 8.

example 291. Step 2: Minimal harmonization

example 292. Step 3: Invert minimal harmonies

The single inversion here improves the bass progression somewhat. But again, substitutes and prefixes are required to provide harmonic development (Step 4).

example 293. Step 4: Substitute triads

Only the dominant preparation IV is added here. This improves the bass of the second measure, but the first measure remains static since it is bound to the tonic triad and its first inversion.

example 294. Steps 5 and 6: Add 7th and inverted 7th chords. Notate in full

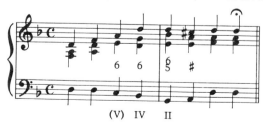

Here II_5^6 replaces IV as dominant preparation. In consequence, IV can be used one beat sooner. We continue "thinking backwards" and fill in the bass 3rd, D-B♭, with the passing note C. This C forms a 6th with the soprano A, suggesting a passing 6th chord or possibly a $_2^4$. We choose the 6th chord since it effects a stronger change to correspond with the secondary metrical accent. Now the bass and harmony of the first measure have a feeling of movement which matches to some extent the strong ascending arpeggiation of the soprano.

The next soprano, the English song, *Thou soft flowing Avon,* also features arpeggiation, both complete and partial.

example 295. Step 1: Analysis

Example 295 shows that the basic stepwise line is interrupted often by skips down to a lower voice, the voice which is stated on the initial upbeat. The short group which begins in the fourth measure and which centers on scale degree 1 actually belongs in the lower register, as shown by the small noteheads in parentheses.

example 296. Step 2: Minimal harmonization

The minimal harmonization presents no special problems since the analysis showed clearly the melodic function of each note in the given soprano. It made clear, for example, that the A♭ in the third measure is a descending passing note, not an auxiliary note, and therefore is to be harmonized by V⁷.

example 297. Step 3: Invert minimal harmonies

Compare the counterpoint of the outer voices in the third measure here with that in the third measure of Example 295. VII⁶ here is a substitute for a passing V⁴₃.

This particular melody does not lend itself to substitute triads; therefore we omit Step 4 and proceed to the final stage of the harmonization, combining Steps 5 and 6 as before.

example 298. Steps 5 and 6: Add 7th and inverted 7th chords. Notate in full

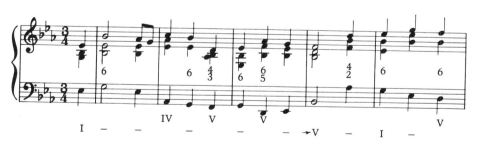

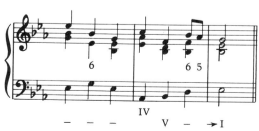

145. Common Mistakes in Harmonizing Melodies

Before proceeding to the exercises in harmonization, it may be helpful to list some of the pitfalls. As remarked above, chords "sound wrong" for specific reasons. Of course it is important to know that a particular chord is incorrect, but that alone is insufficient. One must understand why. The reason often has to do with a conflict between harmonic and melodic function. An instance of this has already been seen in the II which was used as a passing chord (Example 263). As a general rule one should take special care when using chords which have a strong harmonic direction, particularly when they are in fundamental position: for example, the triads which form the harmonic axis, I and V, and V^7. These chords must be distributed strategically in the total progression. They should not be made to serve secondary melodic functions which other harmonies could serve more effectively.

A summary of the main requirements for correct harmonization follows:

1 *Chord selection.* The chord must be selected with regard to its function in the harmonic progression as a whole and with regard to its definition of the soprano note as a point of departure, melodic goal or metrical embellishment. Some chords quite correctly have a purely local effect; others form the basic progression of the passage. Some chords are essentially passing chords, others auxiliary chords. Confuse the two and the harmony sounds wrong.

If selected with regard to the requirements of the particular progression, substitute chords can serve many valuable melodic and rhythmic functions. One must remember, however, that a substitute chord, especially a triad, may have a direction which differs greatly from that of the original chord. For example, if VI is substituted for I it is apt to direct the progression toward V, which may or may not be desirable in a given context.

Both inversions and substitute chords must be used with restraint. If they serve no purpose they should not replace the original chord.

In no event are chords to be selected for each melodic note as though it existed in isolation. This inevitably leads to poor harmony. If the harmonization procedure outlined above is followed this will not occur.

2 *Chord structure.* The triad must be complete in four parts. In the case of 7th chords (but not their inversions) the 5th may be omitted and the 8ve doubled.

3 *Chord connection* (voice leading). Parallel 5ths and 8ves are to be avoided. All dissonant notes must be correctly resolved. Stepwise voice leading is the norm.

Several of the common types of mistake are collected together in Example 299. The mistakes are lettered to correspond to the observations that follow.

example 299.   Chorale: *Ach Gott vom Himmel sieh darin*

(a)   Chord incomplete. Here the I also gives a feeling of cadence. A substitute, VI, would be far better. (Also parallel 8ves between outer voices.)

(b)   Repetition over the bar line obscures metrical pattern.

(c)   Parallel 8ves between outer voices.

(d)   Wrong harmonic goal. From this point on the harmonic progression lacks specific direction. There is a tendency, though not well defined, to progress to III, but this is contradicted by the final cadence.

(e)   Either this chord should be a D_3^5 or the preceding chord should be a ♯6. As they are they do not form a pair.

(f)   Again the chords do not form a pair. The dissonant-6th chord should serve as a passing chord or auxiliary chord and lead to a B-minor triad in first or second inversion, not to the G-major triad as here.

(g)   This chord does not follow from the preceding chord at all. The problem here is one of coherent harmonic progression.

(h)   The function of the D_3^5 here on the downbeat is quite unclear.

(i)   The sudden occurrence of the V of B minor is jarring. There is no preparation whatsoever for this important harmony. Also note that the 3rd has not been raised, which makes it impossible for the chord to function properly as a dominant.

A correct setting of this chorale, by Kirnberger, is given in Example 300.

example 300.   Chorale: *Ach Gott vom Himmel, sieh darin.* Setting by Kirnberger

Observe particularly the way in which closure is avoided at the fourth note in the melody—by substitution of VI for I. Also observe the way in which the final two melodic groups, which are identical, are set. The first is not permitted to anticipate the cadential progression of the second.

EXERCISES

A. List of Some Important Terms to Define and Memorize

Voice

Basic melodic progression

Metrical arpeggiation

Compound melody

Transient skip

Circular melodic progression

Partial closure

Melodic sequence

Counterpoint of the outer voices

Principle of rhythmic grouping

Principle of metrical placement

Harmonization procedure

Minimal harmonization

Principle of harmonic definition

B. Basic Keyboard and Aural Exercises

INSTRUCTIONS

These alternate scale harmonizations should be played and sung following the usual procedure. In addition, they are to be transposed to at least three major and minor keys with a change of metric-rhythmic pattern for each new key.

exercise 125.

exercise 126.

C. Soprano Voices to Be Harmonized

INSTRUCTIONS

Harmonize, showing fully each step of the harmonization procedure.

exercise 127. **Chorale:** *Herr, straf' mich nicht in deinem Zorn*

226

exercise 128.   Chorale: *Wie nach einer Wasserquelle*

exercise 129.   Chorale: *Warum sollt' ich mich nicht grämen*

exercise 130.   Chorale: *Eins ist Not!*

exercise 131.   Chorale: *Singen wir aus Herzens Grund*

INSTRUCTIONS

Analyze these harmonizations in terms of the harmonization procedure. Realize for vocal performance.

exercise 132.   Chorale: *Gleich wie ein Hirsch eilt*

exercise 133.   Chorale: *Ach Herr mein Gott straf mich doch nicht*

exercise 134. French Folk Song: *Le Jeune Berger qui m'engage*

Moderato

exercise 135. German Folk Song: *Winters Abschied*

Quietly

exercise 136. French Folk Song: *Laire lan, laire lan laire*

Allegro

exercise 137. Chorale: *Nun sich der Tag geendet hat*

exercise 138. Chorale: *Seelenbräutigam*

exercise 139. *French Air*

Not too slow

exercise 140. French Song: *Margot sur la brune*

Chapter 8

COMPOSING
A SOPRANO VOICE
AND HARMONIZING
A BASS

Thorough bass teaches us to reduce to
its simple, original, natural, and derived
chords, every composition—for whatever
instrument it may be written, and however florid the melody, accompaniment,
or embellishments. It reveals the whole
wonderful construction of a work of
art. . . .

Johann Georg Albrechtsberger, 1790

The preceding chapter dealt with harmonic structure from the standpoint of the
soprano voice and its harmonic implications. Part of the present chapter is given
over to the complementary procedure: the realization of the harmonic and melodic implications of a bass. Essential to this compositional technique is the ability
to construct a coherent and effective soprano voice. Therefore the first part of
the chapter is devoted to explaining a procedure by which one may develop
that ability.

There are two methods of composing a soprano. First, it may be composed
before the harmony but with careful consideration of its harmonic implications.
This is the method often employed by the gifted and experienced composer.
Second, the soprano may be derived from a given harmonic succession. In this case
it is controlled by the bass and harmony from the outset. That is to say, the course
of the soprano is limited by the voice leading of the harmonic progression. The
first method, for all its virtues, presupposes a background of experience which the

230

reader of these pages may not possess. The second method, outlined below, offers him a secure approach to the multiple problems of melodic structure.

146. The Procedure for Composing a Soprano Voice

We begin with the harmonic progression given in Example 301.

example 301. After HANDEL: *Chaconne for Clavier*

Since the soprano voice is to be based upon a stepwise progression, controlled by voice leading, we must decide which of the harmonic strands will serve most effectively. Therefore we proceed systematically to construct a stepwise progression beginning with each soprano position of the initial chord in turn (Step 1).

example 302. Stepwise line from the 8ve Position

Here the soprano begins in the position of the 8ve and is led stepwise note against note of the bass. When there is a choice of stepwise progression the line is led to the active rather than to the static melodic note, since the soprano carries the sensitive notes of the harmony, those notes that provide melodic impetus in the progression. The active quality of a note therefore is determined by the interval which it forms with the bass and by its function in the chord. In general, the accented 8ve with the bass is avoided during the course of the phrase, especially when the 8ve is to be the goal. And in general the line takes the dissonant note of the harmony in preference to the consonant note. If the line does not follow these precepts it soon will begin to move along a more static strand of the harmony and consequently will not give the effect of direction and impetus which one expects of tonal melody. The first melodic group in Example 302 is good in these respects. It opens without interruption to scale degree 5. At the beginning of the third measure, where two stepwise progressions are possible, the progression to the active scale degree 3 is chosen rather than the progression back to scale degree 1, which would form an 8ve with the bass. The second melodic group in Example 302 is less satisfactory. It is circular, centering upon scale degree 5, and appears to resist all efforts of the harmonic progression to move it toward a closure. We may discover a better line for this group as we consider the other possibilities.

example 303.   Stepwise line from the Soprano Position of the 3rd

Example 303 is included here only for the sake of systematic procedure. It is evident that with the exception of the first note the line is the same as that in the previous example, Example 302, but since the line here does not open from scale degree 1, as in Example 302, its effect is somewhat different. Let us examine the next possibility.

example 304.   Stepwise line from the Soprano Position of the 5th

In an effort to break away from scale degree 5 the line has been led to E in the third measure. E, in turn, moves stepwise to scale degree 7 (the leading note) as the melodic goal of the first group. The leading note then resolves to scale degree 8, which dominates the second group. Taken as a unit, the two groups execute a closing progression which ascends from scale degree 5 to scale degree 1. Between the groups there is no contrast of progression nor is there much activity within either group. We have now completed Step 1. Step 2 is described below.

STEP 2: Select the best stepwise line. If no suitable stepwise line is available apply the technique of compound melody.

Since in each instance above, the stepwise line of the second group was very static we must apply the technique of compound melody to that part if we are to maintain an active and interesting progression. Example 305 illustrates an effective solution for the total line.

example 305.

The first group carries the ascent to scale degree 5 as in Example 302. This is a very satisfactory progression. The second group begins with the skip to F♯ in the fourth measure. The voice then ceases to progress stepwise, and moves instead by a series of descending skips. If we compare these skips with the stepwise progressions examined above we see that in each case the skip avoids a repetition. Thus in the sixth measure the soprano skips to E rather than retain G, the common note. Repetition is not necessarily "bad." However, in this short group it seems to be disadvantageous, since in every instance it leads to a circular progression which is at odds with the harmonic progression.

Often the basic stepwise progression must be abandoned, as in the second melodic group above. Indeed, this is highly advantageous in many situations—for example, if the stepwise line has become centered upon a single note, as above, or if it begins to descend toward closure before the harmonic progression has completed itself. A situation of this kind is demonstrated below.

example 306. BACH: *Sieben geistliche Oden*

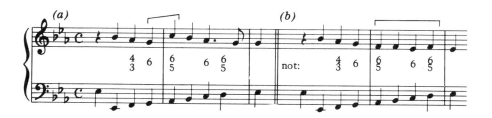

The composer does not follow stepwise progression all the way to the end in the upper voice here, but skips away at the point indicated by the bracket. The reason for this skip becomes clear when we consider the consequence of continued stepwise progression shown at (b). There the stepwise soprano line descends to scale degree 2 (F) and centers upon that note until the close on scale degree 1. This very dull line sounds like an inner voice. It does not interact in an effective way with the ascending bass line, as does Bach's line at (a).

Adherence to stepwise progression is obligatory under only one condition, a familiar one: A voice cannot skip away from a dissonant note, leaving it unresolved. Thus, the skip bracketed in the next example is incorrect.

example 307.

The F♯ in the fourth measure should have resolved upward to G in accord with its function as leading note in the scale and its tritone relation to the bass and harmony. Although certain other kinds of skips are not "forbidden" they may be considered poor from the standpoint of melodic coherence and orderly development. Faulty skips are indicated by asterisks in the next example.

example 308.

In the third measure a skip is made to an inactive note of the harmony whereas the voice should have followed the stepwise progression through the dissonant altered note C♯. The notes of the second group lack coherence, mainly because the skip from E to A destroys stepwise continuity and has no clear purpose at that point.

On the other hand, skips properly used are essential to good melody. No amount of metrical or submetrical embellishment will improve the following step-wise succession!

example 309.

We continue now to Step 3.

STEP 3: Add metrical arpeggiations wherever they enhance the progression of the basic line.

Example 310 illustrates two embellishments by metrical arpeggiation. Observe that the skips do not displace the basic progression selected in Example 310. The small notes above the bass may be played by the left hand while the right hand plays the soprano alone—a more convenient arrangement for the keyboard.

example 310.

The soprano voice shown at (a) is the basic structure selected earlier (Example 305). At (b) this basic structure is expanded by means of skips within the harmony. With the exception of the skip in the third measure these are descending skips. In every measure of (b) the note which represents the basic structure occurs in the same metrical position as it did in (a). Example 310(c) offers a more refined treatment of metrical arpeggiation. There, more weight is given to the embellishment. For example, in the second measure the arpeggiated note D takes two beats of the three-beat measure. It is important to realize that this in no way affects the basic structure. D remains an embellishment; it does not usurp the function of the note A, which carries the main stepwise progression. Observe that the skip in the seventh measure ascends, in contrast to the preceding skips, and that it also reverses the rhythmic pattern of the preceding measures. By such means the melody achieves variety and interest.

Although submetrical embellishments are reserved for special treatment in a later chapter, two have been introduced in the fourth measure of Example 310(c): the passing note E and the skip D.

147. Common Mistakes in Metrical Arpeggiations

Arpeggiations are activated chordal intervals; they obey the laws of voice leading. One cannot introduce as an arpeggiated note a note which would be incorrect in an unembellished chord succession. The doubling and voice leading expressed by an arpeggiation must conform precisely to that of the underlying chord succession in its pristine state. This principle was set forth in section 129 in the explanation of compound melody. It is illustrated again here using the fourth and fifth measures of the progression studied in the previous section.

example 311.

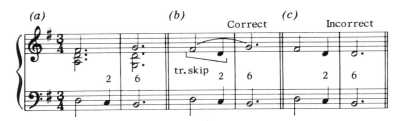

At (a) the chords are shown in full four parts; the voice leading is fully expressed. At (b) the soprano skips down over the change of bass. However, the previous note, F♯, remains in effect since it is still in the harmony. Moreover, it still requires resolution in the line where it originally occurred. Accordingly, the treatment of the skip as shown at (*b*) is absolutely correct, whereas that shown at (*c*) is entirely incorrect. In the latter case the F# is abandoned; it remains unresolved in the line where it originally occurred. The effect is one of discontinuity, for a melodic progression was prepared but unfulfilled. In sum, the techniques of arpeggiation do not permit lines to skip about haphazardly within the harmony. They must be applied with regard for the requirements of voice leading. If those requirements are disregarded, skips may also express parallel 5ths and 8ves as in the following example which is based upon the second part of our progression above.

example 312.

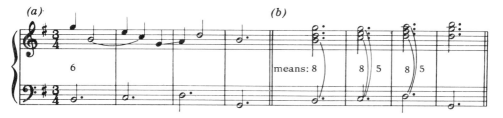

In the first measure the doubling of the bass (B) is incorrect since it inevitably gives rise to parallel 8ves. The succession G A from the second to the third measure likewise is incorrect, since it creates even a more obvious parallelism.

HARMONIZING A BASS

As the counterpart of harmonizing a soprano, harmonizing a bass is an important part of compositional technique. The unfigured outer voices in previous chapters provide a background of experience for the more detailed explanation of procedure which follows. The purpose of the exercises in unfigured outer voices was mainly practice in recognizing contexts for particular chords. The unfigured basses at the end of this chapter go beyond this. They afford valuable practice in constructing harmonic progressions and in composing the fundamental soprano voice which is indispensable to effective tonal music.

Like the standard harmonization of the soprano scales given in Chapter 7 the following standard harmonizations of the bass scales serve as guides. They are subject to modification depending upon metric-rhythmic pattern and other factors in specific contexts.

148. Standard Harmonizations of the Diatonic Scales in the Bass

Bass-scale harmonizations are not to be confused with the norms of harmonic progression given in Examples 100 and 101. The latter represent more general principles not shown in the bass-scale harmonizations. The bass-scale harmonizations afford a guide to the treatment of short successions within a larger progression. For example, if one were about to realize an unfigured bass consisting of scale degrees 1-2-3, the standard harmonization would show how this succession is often treated in tonal compositions. Whether the standard harmonization is in fact suitable for the particular passage would depend upon the nature of the progression as a whole, its point of departure, goal, metric-rhythmic pattern, and so on.

example 313. Harmonization of the Major Scale in the Bass

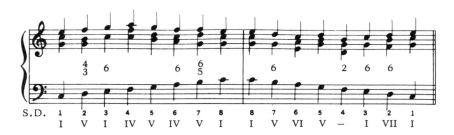

The standard scale harmonization thus provides a convenient repertoire of patterns. It is particularly useful in relationship to the problematic upper 4th of the scale, both in major and minor. Almost invariably this is harmonized as shown in Example 313. The following excerpt is typical.

example 314. MOZART: *Die Zauberflöte*

The ascending minor scale resembles that of the ascending major scale.

example 315.   Harmonization of the minor scale in the bass

Note, however, that the descending fourth of the minor scale requires a somewhat different harmonization than that of the major—for reasons of voice-leading parallelisms.

149.   Procedure for Harmonizing an Unfigured Bass

A specimen unfigured bass is given in Example 316:

example 316.   HAYDN

Adagio

As in the procedure for harmonizing a given soprano voice we shall now consider the step-by-step transformation of this given part into a complete musical setting.

example 317. Step 1: Identify the harmonic groups and goals

We bring to bear on this task the principles of progression as summarized in Examples 100 and 101, the standard bass-scale harmonizations given above, and the various exercises carried out thus far. It is often helpful, though not absolutely essential, to number the scale-degree succession first, as in Example 317. One should then bracket the harmonic groups, label the type of progression, and supply Roman numerals to indicate the basic consonant chords. With the goals and types of progression clearly defined, attention can be given to the details of the harmony, to secondary harmonic and melodic functions.

example 318. Step 2: Identify secondary harmonic and melodic functions and select appropriate chords

Here we read scale degree 5 in the first measure as the bass note of V connecting two statements of I. In relation to the soprano voice, which will be worked out below, this V probably serves as a passing or auxiliary chord. In the second measure, E (scale degree 7) is interpreted as an extension of the dominant harmony and labeled, accordingly, V6. Both in the third and fourth measures Bb is an auxiliary note to scale degree 5, harmonized by V. In the third measure it is important to notice that the bass note A serves as an auxiliary note between the two Bbs and is harmonized by the consonant 6th chord (I6).

example 319. Step 3: Write out the harmony in full, taking care to construct a good basic soprano line

The actual melody of the composition from which this bass was extracted is quite elaborate and contains a number of submetrical embellishments. What we have here in Example 319, although relatively complete, is still only an outline of the actual work. Beyond this point substitute chords and 7th chords could be introduced, the melody could be supplied with metrical embellishments, and so on. However, the bass has served its purpose and we move on to apply the same procedure to two additional basses. As before, the steps are illustrated fully in musical notation and verbal explanation is minimized.

example 320. HANDEL. Step 1: Identify the harmonic groups and goals

In completing the next step the standard scale harmonization will be helpful.

example 321. Step 2: Identify secondary harmonic and melodic functions and select appropriate chords

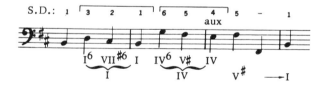

The first descending pattern (bracketed) can be harmonized with the standard chords shown in the descending minor-scale harmonization (Example 315). The standard setting can also be used for the second stepwise descending pattern, with the exception of the last note, scale degree 4. In the descending harmonization, scale degree 4 is obviously a descending passing note and is harmonized by V^4_2. Here, however, scale degree 4 is an auxiliary note to scale degree 5. This suggests that it is the bass of one of the dominant preparations; the most obvious choice is IV. The two descending patterns thus center upon I and IV respectively, and the over-all progression is the familiar I IV V I.

example 322. Step 3: Write out the harmony in full, taking care to construct a good basic soprano line

The last bass for demonstration of the procedure is given below.

example 323. CORELLI. Step 1: Identify the harmonic groups and goals

example 324. Step 2: Identify secondary harmonic and melodic functions and select appropriate chords

The secondary bass notes here could be harmonized entirely in the standard way, except for scale degree 6 in the third measure, which represents a deceptive cadence on VI. For the sake of melodic variation II^6 and II$^6_5$ have been substituted for IV in the fourth and sixth measures.

example 325. Step 3: Write out the harmony in full, taking care to construct a good soprano line

EXERCISES

A. Memorization of Basic Materials

Memorize the standard harmonizations of the diatonic scales in the bass, Examples 313 and 315. Play in all keys, following order of the circle of 5ths.

Memorize the step-by-step procedure for composing a soprano voice over a given harmonic progression.

Memorize the step-by-step procedure for realizing an unfigured bass.

B. Basic Keyboard and Aural Exercises

INSTRUCTIONS

Play and sing in the usual manner. Compare these harmonizations with the standard harmonizations. Compose different sopranos for the first two exercises.

exercise 141.   The major scale in the bass harmonized by diatonic consonances plus VII^6 and passing $\frac{6}{4}$

exercise 142.   The minor scale in the bass harmonized by diatonic consonances plus VII^6 and II^6

C.   Figured Basses

INSTRUCTIONS
To be realized in four voices, with special attention to the soprano.

exercise 143.   **HANDEL**

exercise 144.   **BOYCE**

exercise 145.   **MATTEI**

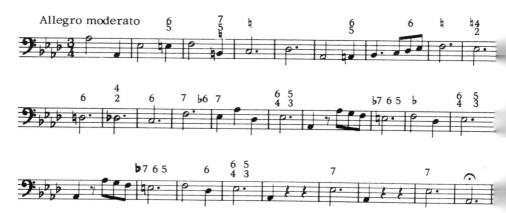

exercise 146. **PERGOLESI**

Allegro assai

D. Unfigured Basses

INSTRUCTIONS
To be realized in four voices, with special attention to the soprano. Show all steps in the solution of the exercise.

exercise 147. **PERGOLESI**

Adagio

exercise 148. **CORELLI**

Grave

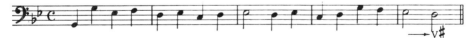

exercise 149. **PURCELL**

Moderato

exercise 150. **HAYDN**

Chapter 9

MODULATORY PROGRESSION

Modulation is the essential part of the art. Without it there is little effect, consequently little music; for a piece derives its true beauty not from the large number of fixed modes which it embraces but rather from the subtle fabric of its modulation.

Charles-Henri Blainville, 1767

150. Modulation as a Primary Means of Harmonic Extension

In earlier chapters two important means of harmonic development were examined: the harmonic, and the melodic processes of chord generation. By these fundamental means the harmonic content of tonal music was greatly expanded. The present chapter explores still another technique, one that permits extension beyond the harmonic unit controlled directly by the tonic triad. This technique is called modulation, or better, modulatory progression. So important is modulatory progression to tonal music that without the development and refinement of this technique it is doubtful whether such extended and unified tonal works as Beethoven's *Eroica Symphony* would have come into existence.

The essentials of the technique are shown in the following chorale setting.

example 326. Chorale: *Ach was soll ich Sünder machen.* (Setting after J. S. Bach)

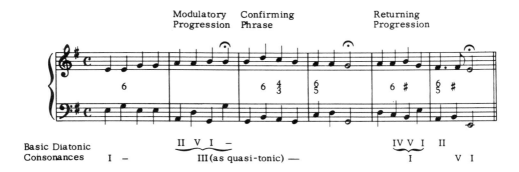

The first measure presents the tonic harmony. In the second it may be observed that the progression is directed very strongly toward III. As shown by the Roman numerals and brace the harmonies of that measure group themselves around III as though it were a tonic. When a triad begins to function like a tonic, as in this case, we shall call it a *quasi-tonic.* The function of III as a quasi-tonic triad is confirmed by the circular progression of the next harmonic unit. The temporary nature of this quasi-tonic then becomes evident, for the progression of the third phrase is directed back to the main tonic once more. When, as here, a diatonic triad becomes a quasi-tonic, the progression which establishes it in this semi-autonomous role is called a *modulatory* progression.

By means of modulatory progression a diatonic consonance is stabilized so that it assumes a degree of independence from the tonic. The process of modulation thus affords a means of harmonic development, a way of extending beyond the direct control of the tonic triad to create longer musical statements which are unified and coherent despite apparent diversity.

The basis of unity and coherence is this: A triad temporarily stabilized by modulation (quasi-tonic) nevertheless retains its characteristic function in relation to the harmonic axis. That is, it behaves in exactly the same way as when it occurs in a small context under the direct control of I. Neither duration nor quasi-tonic function affect the identity and ultimate direction of a diatonic triad. This is evident in Example 326, where the succession of basic consonances I III I V I over the span of the three phrases is exactly the kind of succession one might also find as a brief circular progression within a single unit. It is in this sense that we understand harmony in the larger dimension indicated by F. W. Marpurg when he wrote: "Harmony differs from chord as whole differs from part." In subsequent sections we will see that longer tonal compositions are nothing more nor less than stretched-out successions of consonant triads which behave according to the norms described in Chapter 4. Modulation therefore should be regarded as ordered harmonic extension, not as "change of key for the sake of variety," as some authors would have us believe.

The process of modulation is a remarkable part of the tonal system. Its logic is an extension of the logic of tonality. For this reason "free" modulation, or arbitrary modulation does not exist in art music. Modulation of this kind occurs only in music patched together for commercial purposes and in other poorly composed music. In fine music modulatory techniques operate entirely within the concept of tonality as the sum of harmonic, melodic, and rhythmic events regulated by a single tonic-dominant relationship: the harmonic axis of triadic music.

Modulations are of two general types: diatonic and chromatic. When the modulatory progression has as its goal a diatonic triad in the main tonality we say that the modulation is diatonic. When the goal of a modulatory progression is a triad which does not belong to the diatonic tonality, but which is based upon a chromatic degree, the modulation is called chromatic. This chapter is concerned only with diatonic modulation. The resources of chromatic modulation are discussed in Chapter 16.

151. Minimal Conditions Required for Modulation

Modulatory progression requires certain minimal harmonic, melodic, and metric-rhythmic conditions. These are outlined below, beginning with the harmonic conditions.

The minimal chords required for modulation are three in number: (1) the *quasi-tonic triad,* a consonant diatonic triad (2) the *modulating dominant,* which defines the goal harmony as a quasi-tonic (3) the *pivot chord,* the chord that prepares the modulating dominant and that serves as a link with the main tonality. In the following example the three chords are numbered to correspond with the above order.

example 327.   Chorale: *Ach was soll ich Sünder machen*

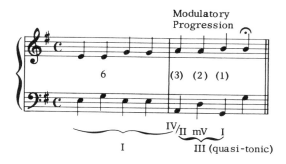

The functions of the modulating dominant and the quasi-tonic are familiar: They imitate the main dominant and tonic. The pivot chord, however, requires explanation. In Example 327, the pivot chord serves both as IV in relation to the main tonic (E minor) and as II in relation to the quasi-tonic (III, or G major). It thus serves as a chord of transition, as a signal for a change of harmonic focus. Its double function is indicated by the slanted line, so that we read the symbol IV/II as "IV becoming II."

To point up the special role of the pivot chord, Example 328 illustrates the direction which the pivot chord in question might have taken had it not served as a modulatory agent.

example 328.

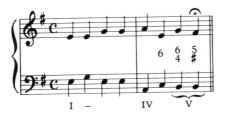

Here IV serves as dominant preparation of V. No modulation occurs since V is not preceded by chords which establish it as a quasi-tonic.

Before leaving the subject of the pivot chord an important fact must be noted: The pivot chord is always a dominant preparation, always either II, IV, or VI in relation to the quasi-tonic.

Minimal melodic conditions for modulation are as follows: the modulating melody either must contain a recognizable segment of the scale which belongs to the quasi-tonic or it must contain the leading note in a strategic position. Consider the following example:

example 329.   Chorale: *Das neugeborne Kindelein*

The second phrase indicates a modulation to the minor dominant triad. Two clues are provided by the melody: the progression D E F, which suggests scale degrees 1 2 3 in the key of the minor dominant (D minor) and the chromatic note, C♯, which is the leading note in that key.

With regard to metrical-rhythmic pattern the modulatory progression is the same as any other progression. The quasi-tonic triad falls on a metrically accented beat. The modulating dominant receives a metrical accent, and the pivot chord is almost always given a prominent position in the pattern, either by metrical or by rhythmical accent. Especially crucial is the case of modulation to V. In that case the modulating dominant, not the quasi-tonic, must be accented if V is to be maximally stabilized (section 158).

152. The Logic of Modulation

As we stated before, the logic of modulation is an extension of the logic of tonality. Many books on harmony give the impression that all modulations are equally feasible. This is erroneous. The selection of a particular diatonic triad as a goal of modulatory progression is made in accord with the norms of diatonic progression (Examples 100 and 101). Thus, V is the most frequent goal of modulation. In minor, III also is a common goal. And in a series of modulations from one secondary triad to another, the order and direction of the goal harmonies also is that given in the schematic norms. A modulation to IV is followed by a modulation to II, a modulation to VI followed by a modulation to II or to IV, and so on. In short, progression in the larger dimension is still controlled by the main harmonic axis despite the local control exerted by the quasi-tonics.

In accord with the logic of tonality certain diatonic modulations appear to be more "natural" than others. Natural modulations are those for which all or some of the minimal harmonic elements are available without chromatic alteration. A prime example is the modulation from I to III in minor, in which the modulating dominant and the three dominant preparations (VI, IV, and II) are available without alteration. This is the only completely natural modulation.

example 330.

I/VI VI/IV IV/II

153. The Returning Progression

Thus far modulation has been discussed in terms of progression away from I toward another triad. Once this triad has been established as a quasi-tonic it may be extended for some time. Ultimately, however, the harmonic focus returns to the main harmonic axis. The passage that effects the return will be referred to here as the *returning progression.* Invariably the returning progression is directed toward V of the main tonality, or toward a dominant preparation, but not toward I. Once V is reached I follows naturally.

154. Limitations upon Diatonic Modulation

The main limitation placed upon diatonic modulation is imposed by the very foundation of the tonal system: the harmonic axis. Modulatory progression must be carried out in such a way that the harmonic axis remains intact, for if its identity is destroyed or weakened the entire tonal structure becomes incoherent in terms of the system's premises. Specifically, this means that in instances where either the pivot chord or the modulating dominant are altered versions of either I or V, the particular modulation is less advantageous structurally, less accessible. And one case in which the primal function of the tonic itself is threatened—the modulation from I to IV in major—must be regarded as highly problematic.

An additional limitation is placed upon certain modulations if the essential pivot chord is not a diatonic triad in the main tonality. This means that the pivot chord, itself a dominant preparation, must be prepared in some way. Further difficulties arise when chromatic conflicts occur at the point of transition or when parallelisms are impending. The operation of these limiting factors is clearly evident in highly developed tonal music, and accordingly a number of examples will be cited as we survey modulation from I to each of the other diatonic triads. Since the structural differences between major and minor are especially pronounced with respect to modulation the modes will be examined separately, beginning with the major.

MODULATIONS IN MAJOR

155. Modulation from I to II in Major

The harmonies involved in the modulation from I to II and in the return are represented in Example 331.

example 331.

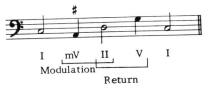

This modulation occurs rarely, probably because it is very difficult to stabilize II. It will be recalled that this chord relates by 5th to the V and therefore tends strongly to return to the harmonic axis rather than to pursue an independent career. In addition, none of the three possible pivotal chords is diatonic. These are summarized in the next example.

example 332.

An instance of modulation from I to II in major is quoted below.

example 333. SCHUBERT: *Das Wirtshaus* (Voice and accompaniment condensed)

Although the modulatory progression is complete, the II is not confirmed by the subsequent phrase. Instead, there is an immediate return to I. Example 334 is a synopsis of the passage, showing the main harmonic changes.

example 334.

Schubert uses the altered V (C minor triad) in place of a diatonic pivot in the modulation to II (see section 264). The return to V is made via IV.

156. Modulation from I to III in Major

With the exception of the pivot chord the minimal chords for this modulation and for the return are shown below.

example 335.

The three pivot chords are shown in the next example.

example 336.

Modulation from I to III in major occurs less frequently in compositions. Although III is accessible by diatonic pivot chord it is remote from V of the harmonic axis and therefore two or more harmonic steps are required for the return. In an instance of this modulation, Brahms circumvents the problem of return by abandoning III and beginning again on I without dominant progression:

example 337.   BRAHMS: *Waltz in B major, Op. 39/1*

157.   Modulation from I to IV in Major

Of all diatonic modulations the modulation from I to IV in major is the most problematic (c.f. section 71).

example 338.

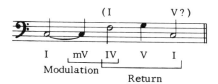

The reason for this is that when the tonic triad itself serves as modulating dominant the IV assumes the primal role and the tonality shifts to a different axis. In no other modulation is the functional identity of the tonic triad threatened in this way. For this reason the IV is rarely stabilized by modulation. True, IV often is used in opposition to I, for example in the trios of many minuets and in rondo forms, where marked harmonic contrast is desired. However, in such cases IV is stated directly; the change of harmonic focus is not prepared by modulatory progression.

Let us consider the pivot chord possibilities.

example 339.

We note here that II is a poor pivot chord since it is an altered form of V in the main tonality.

An instance of modulation from I to IV is quoted below.

example 340.　BEETHOVEN: *Eighth Symphony* (*Minuet and Trio*)

By no means is this a strong modulation to IV. Indeed, since there is no pivot chord and since the metrical accent is given to the 7th chord the entire passage might well be regarded as an extension of the chord pair [V⁷] IV. Observe that II and V⁷ effect the return to I. A more convincing modulation to IV is contained in the following chorale opening.

example 341. Chorale: *Nun preiset alle.* (Setting after Bach)

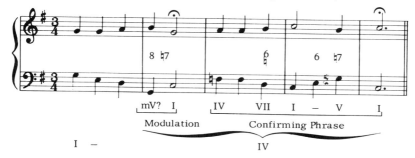

In this instance not the modulation but the confirming phrase establishes the IV as a quasi-tonic. The modulatory progression is too brief and also lacks a pivot chord.

158.   Modulation from I to V in Major

Since V is part of the harmonic axis it is only natural for it to be the most frequent goal of modulatory progression. Yet, in the major mode V is not easily stabilized as a quasi-tonic since it retains its tendency to yield to the gravitational pull of the tonic itself. This is evident in the following chorale setting.

example 342. Chorale: *Valet will ich dir geben* (Bach's setting)

In the third phrase there occurs a modulation to V. However, even the subsequent confirming phrase does not erase the persistent tendency of V to sound like the dominant of E♭. It lacks the independence of a quasi-tonic such as III in minor.

The following summary shows that V is very accessible by diatonic pivot chords.

example 343.

VI/II mV   I/IV mV   III/VI mV

159. Modulation from I to VI in Major

Here the modulating dominant does not conflict in any way with the harmonic axis, and the return to V is easily accomplished, often via II in order to avoid impending parallelisms between VI and V in direct succession or to reinforce the returning progression by the 5th relation, II V. The harmonic plan of the modulation and return is shown below.

example 344.

I   VI   V   I
└ Modulation ┘└ Return ┘

Example 345 summarizes the pivot chords:

example 345.

VII/II mV   II/IV mV   IV/VI mV

In this modulation all the pivot chords are diatonic. Since the dissonant triad VII is so restricted, it rarely serves as a pivot chord; consequently only two of these are practicable.

An example of a returning progression from VI to I follows.

example 346. BEETHOVEN: *Rondo for Piano, Op. 51/2*

Here VI progresses directly to the returning dominant, which is represented by its first inversion in order to avoid the parallelisms inherent in the succession.

A more radical and abrupt return from VI is made in the following composition.

example 347. SCHUBERT: *Waltz, Op. 27/12*

This excerpt begins with a cadence on VI which confirms that triad as a quasi-tonic. Still under the control of VI there follows the succession IV V$_3^4$ I^6 V. Then instead of returning to the quasi-tonic VI the next phrase begins on the returning V^7 and closes on I.

MODULATIONS IN MINOR

160.   Modulation from I to III in Minor

Since there are only four consonant diatonic triads in minor there are only that many diatonic modulations. We begin with the modulation from I to III, which is the only completely natural modulation, since both modulating dominant and all three pivot chords are diatonic. Example 348 summarizes the latter:

example 348.

Here in one instance the tonic chord itself serves as pivot (I/VI). Observe its use in the following modulatory progression.

example 349.   Chorale: *Was sorgst du ängstlich für dein Leben*

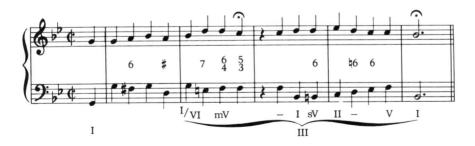

This modulatory progression spans two phrases. The first phrase carries the progression as far as the modulating dominant; the second completes the motion to III.

The following modulation to III uses the pivot IV/II. In this case the IV is replaced by the seventh chord, IV$_5^6$.

example 350. MOZART: *Symphony in G minor, K.550*

Like III in major, III in minor is remote from V of the harmonic axis. It must return to V via one of the dominant preparations. The chorale harmonization below demonstrates one way in which this can be done.

example 351. Chorale: *Herr, ich habe misgehandelt*

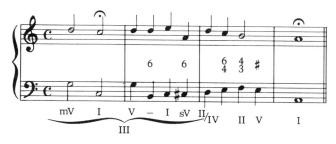

Observe that the pivot II/IV is preceded by its own secondary dominant. This suggests the possibility that modulations may be further prolonged by embellishing the pivot, which is indeed the case in many extended compositions.

161. Modulation from I to IV in Minor

In the modulation from I to IV in minor no diatonic pivot chords are available. Further, the modulating dominant is an altered version of I. Although the problem of shifting the harmonic axis does not exist here to the same extent as it does in major (see section 157), since the minor I does not contain the leading note, composers intuitively have been cautious about this modulation.

example 352.

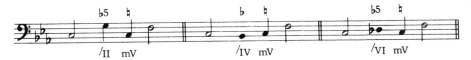

Thus, IV is approached often from V or from VI by modulation but it is rarely approached from I directly. Beethoven preferred to avoid the altered tonic triad altogether in a famous passage from the *Eroica Symphony*. There in the modulatory introduction to the fugato, which centers on IV, he approaches IV via three diminished-7th chords, as shown in the following reduction:

example 353.

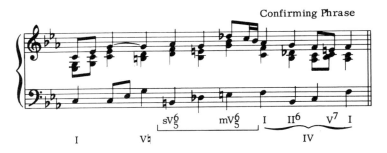

The dominant equivalents of the °7's are represented below the staff in Example 353. This shows more clearly that the modulating V_5^6 is preceded by its secondary dominant-7th chord, in the first inversion. (The unusual succession of two inverted 7th chords has to do with melodic development of the bass.) The passage is quoted in full below.

example 354. BEETHOVEN: *Eroica Symphony,* Second Movement

162. Modulation from I to V in Minor

In the minor mode the dominant triad as quasi-tonic is almost invariably the minor dominant, not the dominant which contains the leading note. Example 355 summarizes the pivot chords for this modulation.

example 355.

The first pivot is not diatonic (/II). The last, although diatonic, is apt to function like III, the quasi-primary triad which tends to be a goal of modulatory progression itself. Therefore the most effective pivot is I/IV. An example follows.

example 356.   CHOPIN: *Mazurka in A minor, Op. 7/2*

Vivo

I   V⁷   I

Modulatory Progression

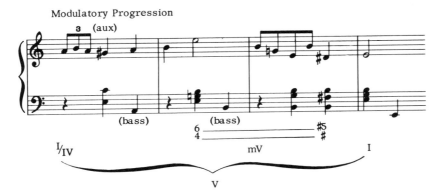

$^I/_{IV}$ mV   I

V

Since the minor dominant does not contain the leading note and therefore does not suggest immediate return to the tonic it is far more stable as a quasi-tonic than is the dominant in major.

The return from the minor dominnat requires only the raising of the 3rd of that triad so as to gain the leading note. Often this chromatic change is made simultaneously with arrival at the goal, as in the following excerpt.

example 357.   HANDEL: *Courante in E minor*

V#   —

163. Modulation from I to VI in Minor

VI in minor is difficult to stabilize. There are two reasons for this. First, it has a subdominant relationship to III and therefore tends to be drawn into the domain of that quasi-primary triad. Second, it affords direct access to V by half step and therefore even more strongly tends to fulfill its role as dominant preparation. These relationships are shown in Example 358:

example 358.

Examination of the pivot possibilities reveals further difficulties in the modulation from I to VI in minor.

example 359.

Of the three possible pivot chords, two relate strongly to quasi-tonics other than VI (VII relates to III as dominant; IV relates to V as dominant preparation). For all these reasons modulatory progression to VI occurs infrequently in the minor mode.

We may find that VI often controls a large section or movement of a work, but like IV in major, it is rarely established as a quasi-tonic by modulation in that role. Example 360 proves the rule by an exception drawn from the works of a composer famous for unorthodox techniques.

example 360. SCHUBERT: *Piano Sonata in A minor, Op. 164,* First Movement

The chromatic harmonies preceding the establishment of VI as a quasi-tonic are not labeled since they represent techniques of harmonic development discussed in a later chapter (Chapter 16). Their general effect here is to completely dissolve the harmonic axis so that by the time VI is reached it assumes a stability which it would not otherwise have in a more normative diatonic context.

    We have now examined all the diatonic modulations in both modes, indicating their special problems and advantages in harmonic extension. The following sections are devoted to other aspects of modulation.

164.   Modulation by Sequence

The sequence is often used as a modulatory means for achieving a rapid change of tonal focus. The basic elements of the modulation remain—pivot chord and modulating dominant—but they are embedded in the sequential progression. Consider the following.

example 361.

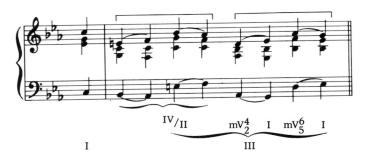

The next example presents the complete passage from which this sequence is drawn.

example 362.   BEETHOVEN: *Piano Sonata in C minor, Op. 13*

In the following example, a reduction of a more elaborate passage, the soprano voice clearly belongs to the scale of the goal triad, A minor (V), and thus prepares the change of harmony.

example 363.   BACH: *Fugue in D minor* (reduction)

A sequence is very flexible. It can be bent in several directions. For instance, the sequence in Example 363 could be returned to the tonic if only the soprano of the fifth chord were changed to B♭, as here:

example 364.

A sequence can be used for a returning progression also. In this capacity it often avoids parallelisms or other structural problems. An instance of sequence used for returning progression is quoted below.

example 365. BACH: *Prelude in E minor*

A full four-part version of the foregoing passage is given in Example 366. Submetrical embellishments and metrical passing notes have been eliminated in order to show the underlying sequential progression clearly.

example 366.

The harmonies in this modulatory sequence appear to have no functional relation to the harmonic goal. Indeed, they seem to be directed toward a G-major triad (III), which, indeed, the progression would reach if it were continued through one more chord pair. The basis of progression here is imitation. Each chord pair (bracketed) prepares each subsequent chord pair, until the final chord pair is defined as the cadential succession in the main tonality.

Although sequences are very flexible and often useful, particularly when a change must be made quickly—as in fugal expositions—they are at the same time quite weak from the standpoint of clear harmonic direction. A more general discussion of such sequences is given in section 220.

165. Modulatory Series

Modulations often occur in series. In the following example the modulatory series is based upon the chord succession I III IV V⁷ I. Both III and IV are goals of modulatory progressions.

example 367. CHOPIN: *Ballade in F minor, Op. 52* (harmonic structure and basic voice leading only)

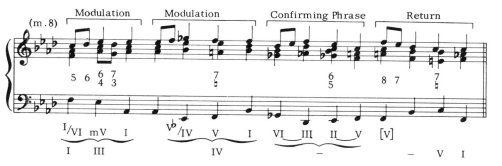

166. Interlocking Modulations

Interlocking occurs when the modulatory phrase ends on the modulating dominant and when the quasi-tonic which follows at the beginning of the next phrase is also a pivot chord in a new modulation.

example 368. Chorale: *Ach, bleib mit deiner Gnade*

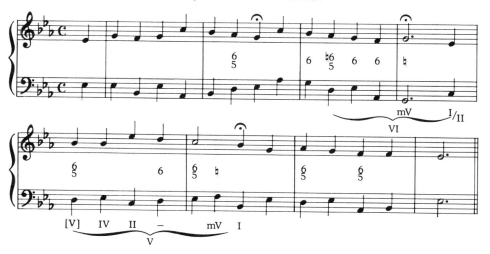

With interlocking modulation the goal harmony is not strongly stated and the effect is one of accelerated progression. Quite a different effect is achieved by the technique of *incomplete* modulation explained below.

167. Incomplete Modulation

Although C. P. E. Bach, Mozart, and Haydn used it, the technique of incomplete, or implied, modulation belongs primarily to nineteenth-century music after Beethoven. Abundant examples are found in the works of Chopin and Brahms, and almost any page of a Wagner score provides at least one illustration. An excerpt from Brahms is quoted here.

example 369.   BRAHMS: *Waltz, Op. 39/9*

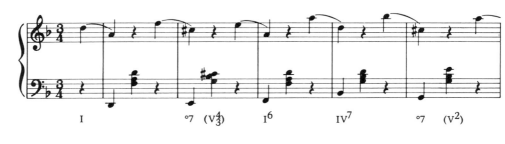

The progression is directed strongly toward IV. The modulating dominant stands at the end of the unit and IV is expected on the downbeat of the next measure. Instead, there is a return to the main tonic and the progression begins anew. The implied harmonic goal, IV, is never reached, despite the convincing preparation.

   An instance of incomplete modulation to a more remote triad is the following.

example 370. CHOPIN: *Nocturne in F major, Op. 15/1*

In this case III is prepared as the goal of a modulatory progression. The modulating dominant stands at the end of the phrase, as in the Brahms example above. However, the goal harmony is never stated. Instead, there is a return to I via V⁷. Observe that the modulatory progression does not contain a pivot chord, although the VI in the fourth measure suggests that at that point the harmony is moving in the direction of III.

168. Harmonic Extension without Modulation

Before closing this chapter on modulation it is essential to point out again that harmony often is extended compositionally without modulation. Many works, particularly shorter and more stylized forms (waltzes, minuets, scherzi, . . .) contain sections controlled by secondary triads which are not stabilized by modulation. An example follows.

example 371.   BEETHOVEN: *Piano Sonata, Op. 10/3,* Menuetto (reduction)

Example 371 summarizes the harmonic structure of this movement which comprises eighty-one measures. The Minuet consists of three harmonic units. The first of these is controlled by I. The second contains a modulatory sequence directed toward V. The third restates I. The Trio is approached directly, without modulation. Its controlling harmony is IV. Near the end of the Trio there occurs a progression that returns to V⁷. This in turn leads back to I and the repetition of the Minuet. The important thing to observe here is that the subdominant harmony of the Trio was not defined as a quasi-tonic by modulation. In this case and in a great many others we witness harmonic extension away from the harmonic axis, but extension that does not involve the process of modulation. These harmonies, which control long sections of compositions but are not stabilized by modulation, are often the very harmonies that are problematic with respect to the harmonic axis, as in the case of IV above, or which for other reasons are difficult to stabilize. Another instance is VI in minor (section 163). It is featured in the Mozart work represented below, a work which is remarkable for harmonic development, both in large dimension and in detail.

example 372.   MOZART: *Rondo in A minor for Piano, K.511* (reduction)

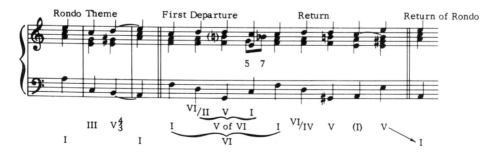

As indicated, Example 372 is a reduction. Certain important features have been omitted altogether, such as the elaborate chromatic section following the modulation to V of VI in the First Departure. However, the outline does have the advantage of showing the large-scale harmonic organization of the piece and the function of VI. This harmony is approached directly, without modulation. It then stabilizes its own dominant by modulation before returning to the main dominant.

Still another means of extension is illustrated in the next example, a harmonic sketch of the complete piece.

example 373.   HANDEL: *Courante from Suite in F minor*

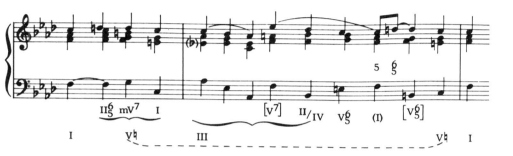

The statement of I is followed by a modulatory progression which prepares the natural V as harmonic goal. Simultaneously with arrival at V the 3rd of the triad is raised, enabling V to return immediately to I. However, V does not resolve; the next harmonic unit begins directly with III. After III has been stated and confirmed by its dominant the progression is directed back to V once more. This chord arrives at the end of the unit, after the progression has bypassed I (in parentheses). The completion of the connection V I occurs at the beginning of the third unit, a repetition of the first unit. Harmonic excursions of this kind are not unusual. They constitute important means of compositional extension along with modulation.

EXERCISES

A. List of Some Important Terms to Define and Memorize

Modulation

Quasi-tonic

Modulating dominant

Pivot chord

Natural modulation

Returning progression

Modulating sequence

Modulatory series

Interlocking modulations

Incomplete modulation

B. Basic Keyboard and Aural Exercises

INSTRUCTIONS

Play and sing the following modulations in the usual way. Transpose each one to a different key, following the order of the circle of 5ths. In each case the best initial soprano position is indicated in parentheses.

Major mode (after Mattei):

exercise 151. **From I to II in major**

exercise 152. **From I to III in major**

exercise 153. **From I to IV in major**

exercise 154. **From I to V in major**

exercise 155.   From I to VI in major

Minor mode (after Albrechtsberger):

exercise 156.   From I to III in minor

exercise 157.   From I to IV in minor

exercise 158.   From I to V in minor

exercise 159.   From I to VI in minor

C. Unfigured Outer Voices

INSTRUCTIONS
Realize in four parts at the keyboard and on paper. Identify all chords by Roman
numeral. Label all modulations, using the symbols introduced in this chapter.

exercise 160. **Chorale**

exercise 161. **LULLY:** *Alceste*

exercise 162. **Chorale**

D. Soprano Voices to Harmonize

The soprano usually contains clues to the goal of modulation. It may unfold the scale or a portion of the scale that belongs to the quasi-tonic, for example the descending 5th from scale degree 5 to scale degree 1, or the ascending 4th from scale degree 5 to scale degree 8—both strong indicators of the new quasi-tonic note. In the ascending motion just mentioned the soprano incorporates the new leading note. Consider the following chorale melody.

Here shortly after the beginning of the second phrase the F# provides a strong clue to the modulatory progression toward V. If the subsequent notes are read as scale degrees in the G major scale, the scale of V, we find that they form a pattern which closes on scale degree 1. Observe particularly the pivotal melodic note 3/6. This corresponds to the pivot chord in the harmonic progression. A minimal harmonization for this chorale melody is sketched out below.

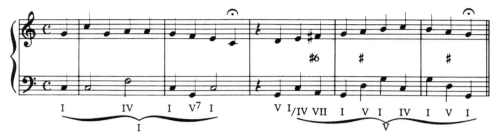

Once the pivotal harmonic and melodic points have been identified the remainder of the progression can be harmonized with the aid of the standard harmonization patterns, bearing in mind that these are now applied to the scale of the quasi-tonic. For example, A in the fourth measure is not scale degree 6 in relation to the C major triad (I), but scale degree 2 in relation to the G major triad (V). The minimal harmonization's faults are corrected in the next version:

*Corrections.

The soprano voice sometimes does not carry obvious clues to the direction of the modulation. In this case the entire melody must be analyzed carefully to determine the over-all progression and the function of each individual phrase. In this way the harmonic implications of the melody will reveal themselves. The natural modulation from I to III in minor often has this noncommittal characteristic. An example follows.

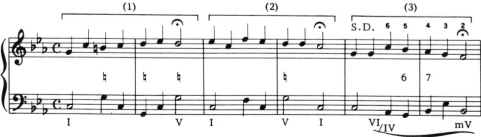

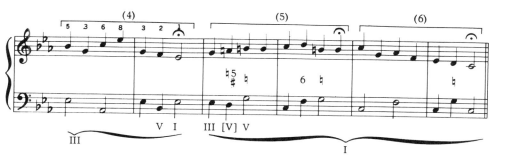

Phrase 3 is somewhat ambiguous if considered alone. But when grouped with Phrase 4 it is seen to be the first phrase of a modulatory period whose goal is III. The chorale as a whole thus has the following harmonic design:

I	III	I
2 phrases	2 phrases	2 phrases

When ascertaining the goal of a modulatory progression one must follow the same principle as when selecting an individual chord: context determines appropriateness. The harmonization exercises follow.

exercise 163.   *Franklin is fled away.* Modulation from I to II in major

Moderato

exercise 164.   Chorale. Modulation from I to III in major. For keyboard

exercise 165.   Chorale. Modulation from I to IV in major. For keyboard

exercise 166.   Chorale. Modulation from I to V in major. For SATB

exercise 167.   *The Baffled Knight.* Modulation from I to VI in major. For solo
voice with keyboard accompaniment

exercise 168.   *John Anderson, my Jo.* Modulation from I to III in minor. For solo
voice with keyboard accompaniment

(mV)

exercise 169.   Chorale. Modulation from I to IV and from I to VI in minor.
For SATB

exercise 170.   Chorale. Modulation from I to V in minor. For keyboard

E.   Unfigured Basses, Soprano Given

INSTRUCTIONS

In all cases the soprano is to be regarded as a solo voice and the bass is to be set out as a four-part accompaniment.

The soprano line of the accompaniment should follow the simplest and most direct succession as determined by the voice leading, yet in accord with good melodic structure. It may often double the solo line, although this is not essential. Doubling of this kind is actually reinforcement, not doubling of the voice leading; therefore it does not constitute parallel unisons or 8ves. Once completed the realizations should be analyzed for modulations and for specific modulatory techniques.

exercise 171.   HANDEL: *Flute Sonata in E minor*

exercise 172.   RAMEAU: *Diane et Acteon*

(7)

F. Unfigured Basses, Soprano to Be Composed

INSTRUCTIONS
Realize the bass in four parts, paying special attention to the progression of the soprano voice. Supply figures where none are given and in all cases indicate modulatory progressions, using the symbols presented in this chapter.

exercise 173.   BONONCINI: *Sonata for Two Violoncelli*
Some figures are given at problematic points.

exercise 174. CORELLI: *Corrente* from *Trio Sonata in G minor*

Chapter 10

THE RHYTHMIC PROCESS OF CHORD GENERATION: SUSPENSION CHORDS

> Endeavor, moreover, to introduce suspensions now in this voice, now in that, for it is incredible how much grace the melody acquires by this means. And every note which has a special function is rendered audible thereby.
>
> Johann Joseph Fux, 1725

Thus far the development of the harmonic vocabulary has been examined in terms of two fundamental processes: the harmonic (inversion), which yields inverted triads, and the melodic, which produces 7th chords. The latter are also invertible.

The resources of harmony are further extended by still a third process, one that is essentially rhythmic. When applied to triads, 7th chords, and their inversions, this process creates a large and important class of dissonant harmonies. We can see the process at work even within a single composition. Consider the following excerpt.

284

example 374. GLUCK: *Orfeo*

The bracket in Example 374 indicates a note that is repeated over the bar line. The note marked by an asterisk is a dissonance which momentarily displaces the chord note from its normal metrical position above the bass. This submetrical embellishment does not affect the structure of the chord, however. The chord remains a passing $\frac{4}{3}$ as figured. In a subsequent repetition of this passage we find that the submetrical embellishment has been greatly expanded in duration:

example 375.

Now that the note repeated over the bar line has the value of the metrical unit it is more than a momentary displacement of the expected chord note and therefore must be regarded as a chordal element. Accordingly its interval relation to the bass is figured as shown. The figures reveal the structure of this new chord: it is a second inversion of a 7th chord, except for the 7 which displaces the 6. A note held over in this way from a previous harmony so that it displaces a note of the prevailing harmony is called a *suspension.** And the transient chord which is formed by this rhythmic process is called a *suspension chord.*

Another example of the suspension process at work within a single composition is provided in Example 376.

example 376.   BEETHOVEN: *Piano Sonata in C♯ minor, Op. 27/2*

*The suspended note may or may not be tied over from the previous chord. With or without tie the suspension is the same rhythmic and harmonic event.

Here the second eight-measure group repeats the first eight-measure group. The second group differs from the first only in that it has a suspension chord on the downbeat of each measure. Otherwise the progression remains the same. These and all other suspension chords are totally dependent for their existence upon the chords which they temporarily displace.

Thus, although suspension chords constitute a resource of great beauty they do not affect harmonic direction, order, function, or any other aspect of progression. Their purpose is to develop and intensify the rhythmic texture. Therefore they should be examined together with the more fundamental chords they displace, the triads, 6th chords, 7th chords and their inversions—the chords which were presented in Chapters 3, 5, and 6. We shall make a systematic survey of suspension chords in that way after having considered the basic conditions under which they occur.

169.   The Three Chords of the Suspension Formation

The suspension process always involves three chords: (1) the *chord of preparation,* a chord which contains the note or notes about to be suspended, (2) the suspension chord itself, which falls on a metrical accent, and (3) the *chord of resolution,* on an unaccented beat.

example 377.   GLUCK: *Orfeo*

Three important rules regarding the suspension formation are outlined below. All are illustrated in Example 377.

1   The suspended note must resolve stepwise to the note it has displaced.
2   The note of resolution should not be present in the suspension chord, otherwise the purpose of the suspension is negated.
3   Since the suspended note is always a dissonance, the general rule that dissonance cannot be doubled without causing parallel octaves must be observed.

DISPLACEMENT OF THE TRIAD

170.   Single Suspension Chords That Displace Notes of the $\frac{5}{3}$

All the notes that can be suspended to displace notes of the triad are shown as quarter notes in Example 378.

example 378.

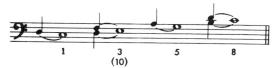

The bass can be displaced by the note above it, the 2nd. The 3rd can be displaced by the 4th. When the 3rd is expressed in its compound form, as a 10th, it can also be displaced from below by the 9th. The 5th may be displaced by the 6th. Finally, the 8ve can be displaced both by the 7th and by the 9th. We shall now examine these suspensions individually.

171. Displacement of the 3rd of the Triad (4 3)

A typical suspension of this type, called a "four to three" suspension is shown in Example 379.

example 379.

The figure 5 is sometimes placed above 4 in order to prevent one from assuming the double suspension $\frac{6}{4}$ (see Example 379). This precaution applies particularly to a figured bass alone. Another important detail: the dash above 3 means that the preceding 5th is still present. This saves writing out the 5 again and is standard practice in figured basses. An illustration follows.

example 380. MOZART: *Don Giovanni*

Both in Example 377 and in Example 380 the chord of preparation is a dissonant chord. We find that the chord of preparation can be either a consonant chord or a dissonant chord of any type except a suspension chord.

172.   Displacement of the 5th of the Triad (6 5)

Although normally a consonant interval, in this situation the 6th resolves to the 5th which it displaces and thus functions like a dissonant interval.

example 381.

This transformation of interval values is characteristic of suspension chords. Often such chords create illusory effects, as explained in the next section.

173.   Illusory Effects of Suspension Chords

It is extremely important to recognize that the structural meaning of the 6th chord by suspension differs altogether from that of the 6th chord by inversion. If the 6th chord in the previous example is incorrectly regarded as a first inversion which represents a parent triad (VI in that case) the harmonic direction of the passage make little sense. Here the supposed VI6 would have no harmonic function either as a tonic substitute or as a dominant preparation. Correctly regarded, the progression consists of the chord pair IV I; the suspension merely delays the appearance of the full tonic harmony.

Suspension chords often simulate triads or 7th chords with independent harmonic functions, misleading the untrained ear. We shall call such illusory harmonies false triads, or false 6th chords, false 7th chords, and so on.

Harmonic progression depends primarily upon consonant triads and their inversions, and secondarily upon the 7th chords that derive from triads. If the illusory harmonies sometimes created by the suspension process are taken to be those fundamental chords, the logical system of harmonic values and functions characteristic of tonal music is distorted beyond recognition.

We continue now with the suspensions that displace the triad.

174.   Displacement of the 8ve by the 7th (7 8)

This suspension chord simulates the major-7th chord presented earlier (section 93). However, the two chords differ basically. The 7th of the true major-7th chord resolves downward over a change of bass. The major-7th chord by displacement of the 8ve, a false 7th chord, resolves upward over the same bass. The first has some degree of independence; the second is entirely dependent upon the chord of resolution. Example 382 shows the major-7th chord by suspension in a typical context. In order to make clear the harmonic structure of the passage we present first its chordal succession without displacement by suspension (a), then with displacement (b), and finally the complete passage with all its rhythmic activity and melodic embellishment (c).

example 382.   CHOPIN: *Prelude in F♯ major*

175.   Displacement of the 8ve by the 9th (9 8)

A typical context for the suspension chord of the 9th is shown in Example 383.

example 383.

The bass note of the suspension chord is C, the note to which the suspended 9th subsequently resolves. This appears to contradict the rule given in section 169 which says that the note of resolution should not be present in the suspension chord. The bass, however, is always a special voice. And in this instance it carries the fundamental note of the triad, which cannot be omitted without changing the harmony altogether.

176. Ascending Resolution of the 9th (9 10)

The 9th also serves to displace the 10th. It should be borne in mind that the 10th is a compound interval which represents the 3rd of the triad.

example 384.

The suspended 9th chords are completely dependent upon the chord of resolution. They differ fundamentally from the quasi-independent 9th chord explained in section 199.

177. Double Suspension Chords

Thus far we have dealt only with the suspension of the single note. When more than one chord note is displaced by suspension we speak of double, triple, and quadruple suspension chords, depending upon the number of suspended notes.

Each note of the multiple suspension chord resolves exactly as it would if it were a single suspension.

The notes of a multiple suspension may resolve one at a time, providing an additional means of rhythmic elaboration. For the sake of uniformity only simultaneous resolutions will be shown here.

A familiar chord, the $\frac{6}{4}$, often occurs as a double suspension chord:

example 385.

Here both 5th and 3rd of the cadential dominant are displaced. Compare this with the single suspension $\frac{5}{4}$ shown in Example 379.

Another typical double suspension is shown in Example 386 below.

example 386.

In this cadential succession the notes that form the tritone of the V^7 are suspended over the bar line to displace the 8ve and the 3rd of I.

The double suspension that follows consists of the 9th and 4th. These notes resolve to the 8ve and 3rd of a triad, forming a succession of parallel 6ths marked by brackets.

example 387.

In the case of suspended 9ths, as here, the figure 2 is never used in place of 9 since the complete figuring would then read $\frac{4}{2}$ and the suspension chord might be mistaken for the third inversion of a 7th chord.

178.   Triple and Quadruple Suspension Chords

A representative triple suspension chord is the $\frac{9}{7}$, which combines the suspensions illustrated in the two preceding examples.

example 388.

Since each suspended note resolves to the triadic note which it displaces, both 7 and 9 resolve to the 8ve, leaving the final tonic triad without a 5th.

The quadruple suspension chord shown below is a five-note chord which combines all the intervals that displace notes of the triad: 9, 7, 6, and 4. Figures for triple and quadruple suspensions are always one digit higher than those of the chord they replace, unless the note must ascend in accord with the law of the half step, as 7 in Example 389.

example 389.

In Example 389 only the bass of the triad is not displaced. The reverse situation often occurs: the bass is suspended while all the other voices progress as expected.

179. Displacement of the Bass

When the bass of the triad is displaced by suspension a chord is formed which contains the intervals of a 7th, 4th, and 2nd.

example 390.

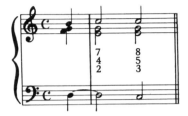

Bass suspension figures are easily remembered since they are always one digit lower than those of the chord they displace.

DISPLACEMENT OF THE SIXTH CHORD

180. The Available Suspensions

The available displacements of the notes of the consonant-6th chord are summarized in Example 391.

example 391.

Observe that only the 6th can be displaced both from above and from below. Each of the other notes can be displaced only by the note that lies directly above it.

181. Displacement of the 6th by the 5th (5 6)

This suspension formation is of particular interest since here the suspended 5th, normally a consonant interval, behaves like a dissonance. The suspension chord in this case is a false triad. Compare the false 6th chord in Example 381.

example 392.

182.   Displacement of the 6th by the 7th (7 6)

A series of 7 6 suspensions is shown in Example 393 at (*a*).

example 393.

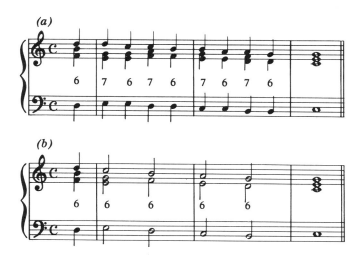

Example 393(*b*) shows the series of descending 6th chords that are displaced by the suspension chords.

   The suspended 7th chords shown above in Example 393 are entirely dependent upon the 6th chords to which they resolve over a stationary bass. They are false 7th chords. In contrast, the authentic 7th chords shown in Example 394 are far more independent since they are derived from a succession of $\frac{5}{3}$'s at (*b*) by the enlargement and assimilation of descending passing notes.

example 394.

(a)

(b)

183. Triple Suspension Displacing the 6th Chord

Every note of the triple suspension chord shown in Example 395 is dissonant against the bass.

example 395.

184. Displacement of the Bass of the 6th Chord ($\frac{5}{2}$)

When the bass itself is suspended while every note above it moves to a note of the 6th chord we have an instance of the $\frac{5}{2}$ chord. Albrechtsberger has supplied the following illustration.

example 396. ALBRECHTSBERGER

C. P. E. Bach explains the $\frac{5}{2}$ chord in this way: "This chord consists of the 2nd and the 5th. One of these two notes is doubled to become the fourth voice [in four-part harmony]. The $\frac{5}{2}$ chord always sounds empty, whether it be in four parts or in three. The resolution makes it full." To this we may add the reminder that the bass is never doubled, since it is dissonant. The figures for this suspension chord are easily remembered if we observe that like all bass suspension figures they are one digit lower than those of the chord of resolution: $\frac{5}{2}\,\frac{6}{3}$.

DISPLACEMENT OF THE 7th CHORDS AND THEIR INVERSIONS

185. An Important Limitation

Suspension chords displace not only consonant chords but also the first class of dissonant chords, 7th chords. However, an important limitation is placed upon such suspension chords: neither the 7th of the parent chord nor the note which represents the 7th in the inversion can be displaced by a suspended note. A moment's reflection will indicate why this is so. Displacement of the dissonant note reverses the dissonance-consonance succession which characterizes the suspension formation. The effect of this is illustrated in Example 397.

example 397.

Here the 7th is displaced by the 6th. As shown, this has the harmonic meaning I III⁶ I, not I V⁷ I, and the effect is ambiguous. The 7th appears to be only a dissonant upper-auxiliary note to the 6th of the consonant-6th chord, III⁶, as shown. From this demonstration we can understand the following general rule for suspension chords which displace 7th chords: only the consonant notes of the 7th chord or its inversions can be displaced by suspension.

Nor can the bass note of the parent 7th chord be suspended. This is because displacement by the second above creates a $\frac{4}{2}$, which has a different progressional tendency. Displacement by the second below doubles and thus conflicts with the 7th of the chord.

186.   Displacement of the 5th of the 7th Chord

In the passage quoted below, the suspension is prepared by a dissonance, by the 7th of a major-7th chord.

example 398.   CHOPIN: *Scherzo in Db major (Bb minor), Op. 31*

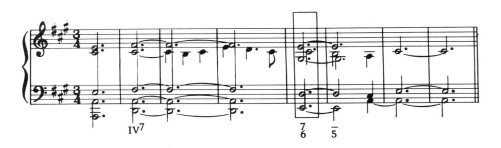

This suspension formation is entirely dependent upon the chord of resolution, the V⁷, for its structural meaning. It is not the fictitious "13th chord" which stems from the erroneous theory of chord generation by successive superposition of 3rds (see Example 417).

187.   Displacement of the 3rd of the 7th Chord

Here the suspended 4th resolves exactly as it would within a triad. The following passage permits us to compare the two.

example 399. BRAHMS: *Sonata for Violin and Piano in G major, Op. 78*

188. Displacement of the 6th of the $\frac{6}{5}$

An example of the suspended 7th displacing the 6th of the $\frac{6}{5}$ is provided below in a reduction that shows succinctly the context in which the suspension arises.

example 400. SCHUMANN: *Schöne Fremde* (reduction)

Two aspects of this passage should be remarked. First, the progression from III to I by modified sequence is unusual, especially here at the beginning of the composition (see section 262). Second, we have here an instance of the half-diminished-7th chord, VII[7], as a 7th chord by suspension, a false 7th chord.

    Sometimes the true 7th chord is incorrectly regarded as a suspension chord. This is apt to occur if the 7th is prepared as a suspension, for example in the sequence $\frac{4}{2}$ 6 $\frac{4}{2}$ 6, . . . Consider the following situation, in which the 7th of the II[7] is prepared in the preceding chord.

example 401.   PERGOLESI: *Trio Sonata in E minor* (continuo part only)

Here and elsewhere one can easily test the authenticity of the 7th chord by determining whether or not it can be omitted without affecting the progression in some marked way. If it cannot be omitted, as is the case here, it is authentic. If it can be omitted it is a transient suspension chord, a false 7th chord. As explained above, the distinction between the two kinds of chord is crucial since it reflects the difference between fundamental harmony, as derived from the triad, and various degrees of orderly harmonic development by melodic and rhythmic means.

189.   Displacement of the 6th of the $\frac{4}{3}$

The 3rd is always the dissonant note in the second inversion of the 7th chord since it represents the 7th of the parent chord. Therefore, this note cannot be displaced by suspension. Example 402 presents one of the possible suspensions that displace the $\frac{4}{3}$.

example 402.   WOLF: *Schlafendes Jesuskind*

The parallel 8ves in the upper part of the second measure are not voice-leading 8ves. They come about with a shift to three voices, one of which is doubled at the 8ve for reinforcement.

190.   Triple Suspension Chord Which Displaces the $\frac{4}{2}$

When the bass of the $\frac{4}{2}$ progresses in accord with the strict metrical pattern while the other notes of the chord are suspended the following formation results.

example 403.

The false major-7th chord here is easily recognized.

191.   Displacement of the Bass Note of the Inversions

It has been seen that neither the bass note of the parent 7th chord not the bass note of the third inversion can be displaced by suspension. This leaves two forms of the 7th chord, the first and second inversions, whose bass notes can be displaced. They are both illustrated in the next example.

example 404.

Of the two, the displacement of the bass of the first inversion occurs more frequently. As in the case of the $\frac{5}{2}$, above, the seemingly complicated figuring is easily memorized if one observes that each numeral of the suspension chord is one less than the subsequent numeral in the chord of resolution.

192.   Change of Harmony at the Point of Resolution

Sometimes a suspension is formed, but because of the requirements of the metric-rhythmic pattern or the harmonic progression the harmony changes at the point of resolution. This does not affect the actual suspension. It resolves as usual. However, the chord of resolution is not the expected one.

example 405.   PERGOLESI: *Trio Sonata in G major* (continuo part only)

In the third measure the suspended 7th itself resolves as usual. However, the expected chord, 6, is not heard. Instead, the harmony changes to a $\frac{6}{4}$. (Actually this chord is a $\frac{4}{2}$, but the 2nd is omitted from the three-voice realization.) A similar occurrence is the change of bass at the point of resolution, explained in the next section.

193.   Change of Bass and Harmony at the Point of Resolution

Occasionally the bass as well as the harmony may change just as the suspension chord resolves. Two examples of this follow.

example 406.   MOZART: *Quintet for Clarinet and Strings in A major, K.581*

In this instance the suspension chord is prolonged for an additional beat so that it resolves over the bass of the succeeding chord. The normative resolution is shown at (b). A more complicated instance is shown below.

example 407. BRAHMS: *Sonata for Violin and Piano in A major, Op. 100*

The second measure carries a double suspension. The suspended 4th is more prominent than the 9th, which appears only in the accompaniment. Just as the 4th resolves (arrow) the bass ascends instead of remaining stationary as expected. The 4 3 suspension in the last measure of the excerpt is normal except that the resolution occurs one eighth note sooner.

194. Interrupted (Embellished) Resolution

Direct stepwise connection from suspended note to resolution may be interrupted by submetrical embellishments. In the following case, the direct progression from the suspended 4th to its resolution is interrupted by a submetrical auxiliary note.

example 408. Chorale: *Lobt Gott, ihr Christen allzugleich.* Setting by Bach

A more intricate embellishment is shown below.

example 409. SCHUMANN: *Winterszeit (Jugendalbum)*

This excerpt contains two suspension formations. The first, a 7 6, resolves in the usual way. The second, a triple suspension, is embellished.

195.   Abbreviated Resolution

Normally the suspension is resolved by a note at least equivalent to itself in duration. If the note following the suspension is shorter than the suspension it may well be an embellishment of the resolution, not the resolution itself, as illustrated in the foregoing section.

However, it sometimes happens that the resolution takes place on an isolated short note which stands in place of a longer note. In such a case, illustrated below by an excerpt from Schumann, the suspension is effectively resolved.

example 410.   SCHUMANN: *Bunte Blätter, Op. 99/2*

The resolution of the suspended 9th (asterisk) is modified in two ways. First, the note of resolution is shorter than the suspension, as explained above. Second, the bass changes at the point of resolution, so that the 9 8 is represented by 9 6.

196.   Anticipation Chords

Like the suspension chord, the anticipation chord is purely rhythmic in origin. We have seen that suspension chords arise when the full change of harmony is delayed. Anticipation chords arise in precisely the opposite circumstance, that is, when a partial change of harmony occurs before it is expected. Such chords occur very rarely in actual composition. Kirnberger's illustration is quoted below.

example 411.   KIRNBERGER

EXERCISES

A. List of Some Important Terms to Define and Memorize

Suspension chord

Chord of preparation

Chord of resolution

Bass suspension

False 6th chord

Triple suspension chord

Interrupted resolution

Abbreviated resolution

Anticipation chord

B. Basic Keyboard and Aural Exercises

exercise 175.   Basic Chord Pattern 1

We have expanded and elaborated the basic chord patterns in several ways: by introducing 6th chords, 7th chords, and inverted 7th chords. The basic chord patterns can be elaborated still further by suspension chords, as shown below. Only a few of the many possibilities are included here.

exercise 176.   Basic Chord Pattern 2

C. Figured Basses, Soprano Given

INSTRUCTIONS

The first and second basses in this group are to be regarded as keyboard pieces. The third bass should be realized as a continuo accompaniment to the solo voice which is given.

exercise 177. FÖRSTER: Exercise in suspension chords

exercise 178.   After LOEILLET

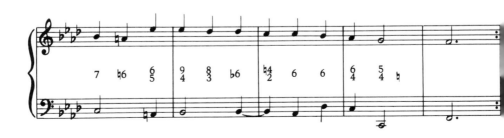

exercise 179. MARCELLO: *Sonata in B minor for Violin and Continuo*

D. Figured Basses

INSTRUCTIONS
Realize in four parts. For maximum effect the suspensions should be placed in the upper voice wherever possible.
The basses by Albrechtsberger are to be supplied with a metric-rhythmic pattern, then transposed to all keys.

exercise 180. ALBRECHTSBERGER: Diatonic Progressions in the Major Mode

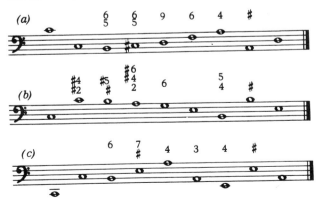

exercise 181. ALBRECHTSBERGER: Diatonic Progressions in the Minor Mode

exercise 182. HANDEL: *Sonata for Violin and Continuo in G minor*

E. Unfigured Basses

INSTRUCTIONS

Realize in four parts as continuo accompaniments. Plan out main harmonic progressions first, then elaborate wherever possible by introducing suspensions, either in the soprano, in the inner voices, or in the bass itself.

exercise 183. BACH: *Trio Sonata in E♭ major*

Largo

exercise 184. LULLY: "Le héros que j'attends" (*Alceste*)

Andantino

exercise 185. CORELLI: *Trio Sonata in G minor*

Adagio

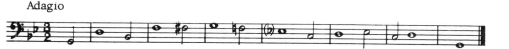

F. Soprano Voices to Harmonize

INSTRUCTIONS

Three folk songs are given below to provide practice in identifying suspension contexts from the soprano alone. The suspension is always either a prolonged auxiliary note or a prolonged passing note, generally the latter. It is prepared on a weak beat, dissonates on the following strong beat, and resolves on the next weak beat. Thus, the clue to suspension in a given melody is the passing or auxiliary note repeated from weak to strong beat. These are bracketed in the first two melodies below.

exercise 186. Welsh

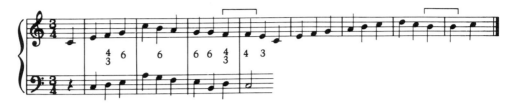

exercise 187. Czech

exercise 188. Welsh

Slowly

For the three exercises below only the soprano is given. The harmonizations are to be arranged for mixed voices (SATB). When working out the final harmonization suspensions should be introduced where appropriate. Any note that meets the melodic-rhythmic and harmonic requirements of the suspension formation may be suspended. To review these requirements:

1   The suspended note must be the repetition of a passing or auxiliary note. It must fall on a strong beat.
2   The chord it displaces must have a coherent harmonic function. The suspension must not destroy the identity of the chord of resolution.

exercise 189.   Chorale: *Was ist mein Stand, mein Glück*

exercise 190.   Chorale: *Ach Gott, erhör mein Seufzenmund*

exercise 191.   Chorale: *Ach Gott vom Himmel sieh' darein*

Chapter 11

LINEAR CHORDS AND INTERVALLIC PATTERNS

> In addition, there are various chords
> which are neither dependent upon a fun-
> damental chord, nor are they suspensions
> or anticipations. For the most part they
> occur in passing, over a stationary bass.
> Since these chords owe their existence
> only to embellishment of the melody and
> since they are not completely authentic
> chords in the harmonic sense they are
> called Deceptive Chords.
>
> Daniel Gottlob Türk, 1791

197. Linear Chord Defined

We come now to the third and last class of dissonant harmonies. In the first class, 7th chords, the melodic process of chord generation was witnessed. In the second class, suspension chords, we saw the formation of new harmonies by the displacement of consonant chords and 7th chords, a rhythmic process of chord generation. The third class contains chords that do not fall into either of the two other categories. We shall call them *linear chords* since they are described most easily in terms of the linear, or melodic, functions of their notes. To the linear chord, horizontal context is of first importance. The vertical arrangement of its intervals has secondary significance.

Not all linear chords are dissonant from the standpoint of vertical structure but since all are transient chords whose meanings are derived from more funda-

314

mental harmonies they function like transient dissonances with, for the most part, only local effect upon harmonic direction.

Linear chords are of two main types, diatonic and chromatic. We begin with a survey of representative diatonic linear chords.

DIATONIC LINEAR CHORDS

198. The Diatonic Linear Chord by Unaccented Passing Note

Examples have been seen of dissonant-7th chords and even of consonant chords that arise in the service of passing notes. The linear passing chord differs from both of these in that it is of a more transient nature. For example, it occurs often between two different forms of the same chord, as shown below.

example 412.

At (a) we see a 7th chord followed by its first inversion. At (b) the skips of a 3rd in both soprano and bass are filled by metrical passing notes, creating an additional chord. The vertical structure of this new chord would require a rather complicated figuring. However, we need not concern ourselves with describing the vertical intervals. We need only know that the chord is produced by passing notes.

The transient nature of the linear chord in Example 412 is further indicated by the dash after the 7. The chord does not represent harmonic change, nor does it influence harmonic direction. It serves only to increase the melodic content of the passage, which remains under the harmonic control of the dominant-7th chord.

Linear passing chords perform particularly valuable service in connecting dissonant chords, as in Example 412, where a consonant chord would be ineffective. Often linear chords are associated with dissonances in other ways. Example 413 contains a linear chord that serves to intensify the preparation of a dissonance.

example 413.   MOZART: *Piano Sonata in F major, K.280*

Here in the third measure the harmony is seen changing from 8 to ♭7. The linear chord arises on the second beat of the measure as a combination of descending passing note in the soprano and ascending double passing notes in the lower voices. It should be emphasized again that the meaning of this chord resides entirely in its linear function.

The chord in the following example arises when an ascending passing note connects two different soprano positions of the dominant-7th chord. This linear-9th chord is not to be confused with the quasi-independent 9th chord explained in section 199. Here the "9th" chord is entirely dependent upon the two 7th chords that enclose it.

example 414.   SCHUBERT: *German Dances, Op. 33/16*

The asterisk in the second measure marks another type of linear chord, an appoggiatura chord. This type is explained in section 201.

199.   The Diatonic Linear Chord by Accented Passing Note

Our first example of this type is figured 9. Since the 9th in this instance resolves over a change of bass, it gains a degree of independence not shared by the suspended 9th chord in Example 384, and therefore may be termed a *quasi-independent 9th chord.*

example 415.   SCHUBERT: *Waltz, Op. 50/2*

Very often 9th chords, whether suspension chords or linear chords, are created when the 7th is accompanied at the interval of a 3rd above, as here. Melodic parallelism of this kind is characteristic of waltzes and other forms of light music.

The accented passing note in the next example resolves to the 5th of a dominant-7th chord. The linear chord which it creates contains both a 7th and a 6th.

example 416.   CHOPIN: *Sonata in B♭ minor, Op. 35*

In some treatises this chord would be regarded as a "chord of the 13th." This designation stems from the viewpoint that the vertical structure of the chord is its most important aspect, and consequently that all chords can be regarded in terms of successive superpositions of thirds. Thus, the 7th chord is regarded as a triad plus a 3rd, the 9th chord is regarded as a 7th chord plus a 3rd, and so on. This thesis is illustrated in the following example.

example 417.

In contrast, we have taken the position that so-called 9th, 11th, and 13th chords are more adequately explained as suspension chords or as linear chords—chords that are always dependent upon triads or authentic 7th chords. Thus, with the exception of the quasi-independent 9th chord we do not recognize independent dissonant chords larger than the 7th. The so-called 11th is actually a 4th; the so-called 13th is actually a 6th. The use of compound intervals here is an unnecessary encumbrance.

Accented passing notes in the bass frequently create linear chords. Two types are illustrated in Example 418.

example 418.

In both instances the unaccented passing eighth note is enlarged in value to a quarter note, displacing the actual bass note from its metrical position. The figures for the linear chords thus produced are identical with certain bass suspension chords explained above. However, the context is quite different, as here. In the case of suspension chords the dissonant bass note is prepared. Here it occurs without preparation.

200. The Diatonic Linear Chord by Auxiliary Note

In addition to their harmonic functions triads, 6th chords, 7ths and inverted 7ths often serve auxiliary notes. Linear-auxiliary chords, to borrow Türk's words, "owe their existence only to embellishment of the melody." Two examples follow. First is a sequence of linear-9th chords created by accented upper auxiliary notes which embellish secondary dominant triads.

example 419. BRAHMS: *First Symphony*

Next, Example 420 shows an auxiliary note chord arising by parallel motion in the outer voices of a V_5^6.

example 420.

201. The Appoggiatura Chord

When an auxiliary note is not preceded by the note it embellishes it is called an incomplete auxiliary note. By tradition an incomplete auxiliary note that receives metrical or rhythmic accent is called an appoggiatura. Consequently a linear chord that features an appoggiatura is called an *appoggiatura chord.* Such chords always stand out in the musical texture, as in the following excerpt.

example 421. CHOPIN: *Mazurka in A♭ major, Op. 24/3*

Here the auxiliary note, F, is introduced in the melody without stepwise preparation. Since it receives the rhythmic accent characteristic of the mazurka we call both it and the entire chord an appoggiatura chord.

The following passage contains an instance of an appoggiatura chord brought about by the bass.

example 422. SCHUBERT: *Piano Sonata in Bb major*

202. Diatonic Linear Chord by Combined Auxiliary and Passing Notes

Particularly in nineteenth-century music we find many unusual linear chords created by a combination of auxiliary and passing notes. A remarkable example from the works of Schubert is given below.

example 423. SCHUBERT: *Waltz, Op. 77/8*

203.   The $\frac{6}{4}$ as a Linear Chord

From the preceding discussion of linear chords it is evident that many can be described most effectively in terms of their linear contexts. Certainly this is the case
with the $\frac{6}{4}$. This chord is sometimes described as the second inversion of a triad.
However, since the $\frac{6}{4}$ contains a dissonant interval, the 4th, it cannot represent the
parent triad, which is a consonant chord. There is one apparent exception to this
rule which will be explained now.

204.   The Consonant $\frac{6}{4}$

The $\frac{6}{4}$ extends the parent chord and therefore is consonant whenever it is immediately preceded by the parent chord, as in the following example.

example 424.   C. P. E. BACH: *Minuetto* from *Kurze* und *Leichte Klavierstücke*

Directly below the excerpt is the succession of basic harmonies that it represents. By comparing the two we realize that the bass of the $\frac{6}{4}$ is a result of arpeggiation. It does not represent an actual change of harmony but merely an extension
of the parent harmony. Thus, it is not a dissonant $\frac{6}{4}$ since the 4th does not require
resolution to the 3rd as in the other $\frac{6}{4}$ chords. This type of $\frac{6}{4}$ is called the consonant $\frac{6}{4}$ to distinguish it from the other types of $\frac{6}{4}$ described below, all of which
are dissonant chords.

Another example of the consonant $\frac{6}{4}$ is quoted below.

example 425. WAGNER: *Die Meistersinger*

The IV$\frac{6}{4}$ here obviously represents the parent triad, with the bass skip to C providing melodic emphasis. Compare the IV$\frac{6}{4}$ in Example 429.

205. The Cadential $\frac{8}{6}\!\!_4$

The cadential $\frac{6}{4}\,\frac{5}{3}$ progression is very familiar. However, we have not yet considered an important form of the cadential $\frac{6}{4}$, the $\frac{8}{6}\!\!_4$. This figuring indicates that the octave is in the soprano.

example 426.

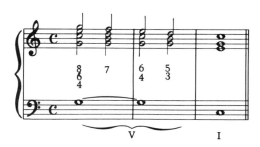

As is seen in Example 426, the octave position of the soprano serves to extend the cadential progression melodically. The $\frac{8}{6}$ does not progress to the V$\frac{5}{3}$ as does the $\frac{6}{4}$ but moves through a dominant-7th passing chord to the actual cadential $\frac{6}{4}$.

206.   The Passing $^6_4$

This chord often connects a sixth chord with its parent chord.

example 427.   BEETHOVEN: *Piano Concerto in C major, Op. 15*

Compare this passing $^6_4$ chord (a "V$^6_4$") with the passing V$^4_3$ and the VII^6. To a certain extent these three chords are interchangeable. The choice of one or the other depends upon the harmonic direction of the particular chord succession.

The next example shows a passing $^6_4$ between two dissonant chords.

example 428.

207.   The Auxiliary $^6_4$

This chord often occurs as a IV$^6_4$. We can accept the convention of inversion theory here as a convenience in labeling the chord, but we must bear in mind that the chord is actually a linear chord created by upper auxiliary notes moving in parallel motion. Its relation to the parent triad is tenuous.

example 429.   MOZART: *Don Giovanni*

"IV"

In this instance submetrical auxiliary notes (asterisk) embellish the resolution of the $\frac{6}{4}$. As in the cadential $\frac{6}{4}$ the bass is doubled at the 8ve, while the 6th and 4th descend in parallel 3rds.

LINEAR CHORDS of the 6th

208.   The Linear 6th as Distinct from the 6th by Inversion

In Chapter 10 it was demonstrated that the 6th chord by suspension bears no relation to a parent $\frac{5}{3}$. It results from the rhythmic process alone, not from the harmonic process of inversion, and functions like a dissonance. A similar case is the linear 6th chord, the 6th chord which arises from the action of an auxiliary note or a passing note. Like the 6th chord by suspension this chord is not derived from a parent $\frac{5}{3}$. Example 430 illustrates.

example 430.

In order to demonstrate the lack of relation between the linear 6th and a hypothetical parent chord Example 430(*b*) substitutes the hypothetical chord for the

6th chord. This proves to be VI, a dominant preparation, and is clearly not appropriate in this context. An example of the linear 6th chord is given below.

example 431.   SCHUBERT: *Du bist die Ruh'*

The first 6th chord (asterisk) arises by the action of an incomplete auxiliary note symbolized by the familiar figures 5 6. The second 6th chord is a 6th chord by inversion. It represents the parent $\frac{5}{3}$, a tonic chord. Again, we can test the derivation of the linear 6th chord by substituting the hypothetical parent chord:

example 432.

As shown in Example 432 the supposed parent chord tends to fulfill its normative function as dominant preparation and leads quickly to the cadential succession II$\frac{6}{5}$ V^7 I. The effect of the entire progression thus differs radically from the original, which extends the tonic triad, referring only briefly to the dominant at the end of the phrase.

When a chord can be read as a functional part of a harmonic progression it may be said to have *harmonic value.* When it is solely the result of linear processes, as in the case of the linear 6th chord, it does not have harmonic value, and it is incorrect to interpret it as a harmonic event. In section 220 the notion of harmonic value will be used to interpret an important feature of tonal compositions, linear intervallic patterns.

209.   Linear-6th Chords in Parallel Motion

Thus far only the single 6th chord has been considered. When linear-6th chords occur in direct succession and in parallel motion, they serve one of two purposes: (1) they neutralize an otherwise dissonant passage; (2) they expand a single harmony or a harmonic connection in a highly fluent way. The first of these functions is illustrated below.

example 433.   CHORALE: *Straf' mich nicht in deinem Zorn*

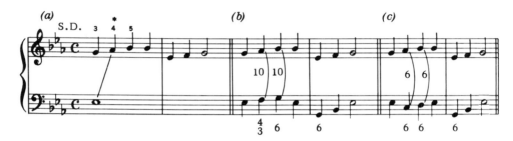

At (a) we see the familiar ascending scale degree 4, which requires harmonization in order to overcome the descending attraction of the half step. A common dissonant harmonization is shown at (b). A common consonant harmonization is shown at (c). There the parallel 6th chords effectively neutralize the dissonant 4th. Another example follows.

example 434.   Chorale: *Lobet den Herren*

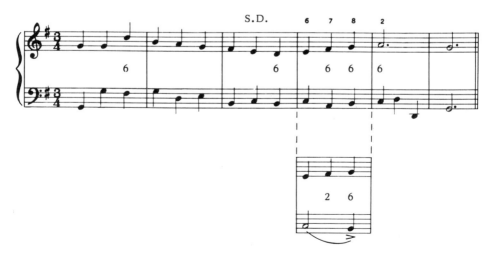

This example shows the function of a succession of three linear-6th chords in carrying the soprano fluently to the point of melodic emphasis, scale degree 2. The alternative harmonization sketched in below the fourth measure is unsatisfactory because it places harmonic emphasis upon the last beat and thus interferes with the forward motion of the soprano line.

The second function of parallel 6th chords—the extension of a single harmony or harmonic connection—is illustrated by the following extracts.

example 435. LOEILLET: *Sonata in C major for Flute and Continuo*

Here the bracket marks the linear 6th chord as an embellishment of the first inversion of the dominant triad. In this context and in many others the 6th chord is realized in three parts only. In four parts alternate doublings would be required in order to avoid parallel 8ves.

The asterisk in Example 435 draws attention to the dissonant bass note. The harmony on this beat is V, supporting ascending scale degree 2 in the soprano. However, the bass line is imitating the soprano in canonic fashion so that the contrapuntal device takes precedence over the harmonic progression at this point.

Our final example in this section shows a series of parallel 6th chords which connects one main harmony to another.

example 436. HAYDN: *Fantasy in C major for Piano*

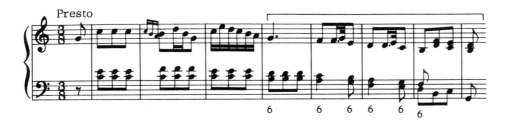

This entire succession (bracketed) lies within the control of the dominant triad. The large connection, as illustrated below, is from V[6] to V at the end of the phrase.

example 437.

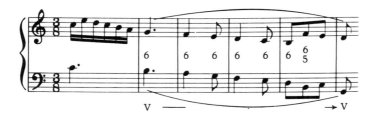

An alternative harmonization of the same soprano line is offered below.

example 438.

The rhythmic-harmonic effect of this harmonization is entirely different from the original. Here the long line achieved by the 6th chords of the original has been broken up into three smaller segments, indicated by slurs in Example 438. And whereas the original line began on G, this line begins on F, since G is defined harmonically here as the end of the first group, not as the beginning of the second.

CHROMATIC LINEAR CHORDS

210.   Chromatic Linear Chord Defined

By chromatic linear chord is meant simply a chord entirely of linear origin which contains one or more chromatic notes. A great many of these chords are to be found in the literature. Here we shall cover only certain representative types which, by virtue of their association with the primary triads, have become sufficiently universal to have attained an identity. In each instance we shall demonstrate how these chords derive by linear motion from more familiar diatonic chords.

The various chromatic linear chords all share one characteristic: They exploit half-step melodic progressions in one or more voices and thus intensify the motion of the diatonic chords from which they derive and which they often represent.

211.   The Augmented Triad and the Altered 6th Chord

The augmented triad arises when a chromatic passing note ascends from the 5th of the triad, creating the interval of an augmented 5th with the bass, as here:

example 439.   BEETHOVEN: *Third Symphony,* First Movement

A chord of similar sound arises when a chromatic passing note ascends from the 3rd of a 6th chord:

example 440.   SCHUBERT: *Pause*

The augmented triad and the altered 6th chord occur in similar contexts and almost invariably follow the consonant chord from which they derive. Sometimes the augmented triad is classified with the major, minor, and diminished triads. Although this may be convenient for textbook authors it is extremely misleading regarding the origin and function of the augmented triad. This triad is entirely the result of chromatic linear motion; it is not an independent diatonic triad.

212. The Diatonic Origin of the Augmented-6th Chord

In the minor mode the chord pair formed by the dominant and one of the dominant preparations, II, IV, or VI, is sometimes expanded to a three-chord group by the inclusion of a chromatic passing chord, a special type of linear chord known as the *augmented-6th chord*. There are three varieties of this chord, all closely related. We shall consider each separately.

213. The Italian 6th (+6)

The form of the augmented-6th chord called the Italian 6th derives from the dominant preparation IV⁶ by the melodic process of chord generation. Its evolution is demonstrated in the following example.

example 441.

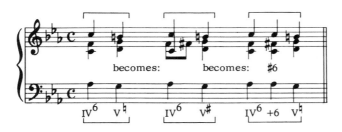

This example first shows the basic progression IV⁶ V. A chromatic passing eighth note then connects the 6th of the IV to the 8ve of the V. Finally, the passing note is enlarged metrically and assimilated by the harmony to form a new chord. This chord is characterized by the interval which the chromatic passing note forms with the bass, the interval of an augmented 6th. In all cases the two notes that form this dissonant chromatic interval expand outward to resolution on the 8ve. The chord is figured by indicating the alteration of the 6th, ♯6 in this case. We shall also find it convenient to indicate the augmented-6th chords in general by the sign +6.

The effect of all the augmented-6th chords is to intensify the progression to V. This is illustrated by the Italian 6th in the following passage.

example 442. C. P. E. BACH: *Sonata in G major*

There are two important things to observe in this passage. First, observe that the +6 chord is not preceded by IV⁶, as in the model progression (Example 441), but stands in place of that chord. The +6 can represent the chord of origin, as here, or it can follow it, as in the model. Second, notice that the 3rd of the +6 chord is doubled. This is the only doubling possible, for the resolution both of the bass and of the augmented 6th are bound by the law of the half step and thus a doubling of either one would give rise to parallel 8ves.

214. The French 6th ($\frac{6}{4}$)
$_3$

The basis for the assignment of nationality to each augmented-6th chord remains obscure. Nevertheless, the terms have a certain usefulness in designating the somewhat different structure of each type. The so-called French 6th derives from II$\frac{4}{3}$, as shown below.

example 443.

Again, as in the case of the Italian 6th, a chromatic passing note ascends from the 6th of the first chord to the 8ve of the second chord. The difference between the two chords is this: whereas the Italian 6th derives from a consonant chord, IV⁶, the French 6th derives from a dissonant chord, II⁴₃. In the French 6th no notes are doubled, no notes are omitted. An example follows.

example 444.   SCHUBERT: *Am Feirabend*

Here the French 6th stands between a suspension chord ($^5_4$) and its resolution, illustrating again the unique role the linear chords play in connecting dissonant harmonies.

215.   The German 6th ($^6_5$)

This chord derives from IV$^6_5$, as shown in the next example.

example 445.

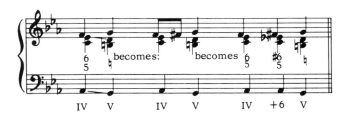

Again the chromatic linear chord arises when a chromatic passing note is enlarged and assimilated by the harmony. A voice-leading peculiarity of this chord is indicated by the diagonal lines: parallel 5ths occur when the chord resolves to V. Often these 5ths are avoided by interpolation of the $^6_4$ between the +6 and V:

example 446.

Since the augmented-6th chords derive from dominant preparations they themselves serve as dominant preparations. And because the dissonant interval of the augmented 6th always expands outward to resolution on the 8ve of the dominant harmony, the augmented-6th chords are even more specific indicators of direction toward the dominant triad than are the diatonic dominant preparations from which they originate. Observe the effect of the German 6th chord in the following modulatory sequence. Here, typically, it is in a prominent, metrically accented position.

example 447.   BEETHOVEN: *Piano Sonata in E♭ major, Op. 7*

Only with the augmented-6th chord does the direction of the sequential progression become specific.

The German 6th is sometimes prepared by the triad on VI, as shown below.

example 448.

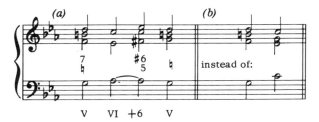

The progression from V⁷ to VI here resembles a deceptive cadence. Its effect is to avoid the progression from V to I shown at (*b*) and to extend V instead. As part of that extension the VI is converted to a German 6th by the addition of an augmented 6th (F♯). A more elaborate illustration of the same technique is given in the next example.

example 449.   HAYDN: *Piano Sonata in G minor*

Like the Beethoven and C. P. E. Bach excerpts (Examples 442 and 447) this passage is part of a modulatory progression. Here the ultimate goal of the progression is III in minor (the B♭ major triad). Again we note that the augmented-6th chord occurs in a harmonic context that suggests the parallel minor mode (B♭ minor).

216. Summary of the Augmented-6th Chords

Any of the three forms of the +6 chord may be located easily in the following way. The bass of the chord is found a half step above the dominant note. Above the bass we place the augmented 6th and major 3rd. This is the Italian 6th. We can then easily locate the other two forms from the Italian 6th. The French 6th adds an augmented 4th above the bass; the German 6th adds a perfect 5th. The procedure is illustrated in Example 450.

example 450.

217. The Linear $\frac{4}{2}$

The linear $\frac{4}{2}$ is a chromatic dominant preparation that simulates the third inversion of a dominant-7th chord, a particularly striking harmonic effect. Two of the linear contexts in which it originates are shown in the following examples.

example 451.

In Example 451 the linear $\frac{4}{2}$ comes into existence as a chromatic passing chord between IV[7] and the $\frac{6}{4}$ that precedes the dominant (b). At (c) the linear $\frac{4}{2}$ usurps the position of IV[7] and receives the full metrical accent.

The following example, in the major mode, shows the linear $\frac{4}{2}$ as it may arise from another dominant preparation, $II\frac{6}{5}$.

example 452.

Here the linear $\frac{4}{2}$ results from the motion of three chromatic passing notes which connect $II\frac{6}{5}$ with the cadential $\frac{6}{4}$. Both here and in the previous example the linear $\frac{4}{2}$ is characterized by the diminished 3rd between the bass and one of the upper voices. This interval contracts to resolution on the 8ve, recalling the augmented 6th, which expands to resolution on the 8ve. Sometimes the linear $\frac{4}{2}$ is spelled like an authentic $\frac{4}{2}$, as in the following example:

example 453.   CHOPIN: *Nocturne in B major, Op. 32/1*

The linear $\frac{4}{2}$ occurs where the final tonic is expected and introduces a long, recitativelike close, finally resolving to the cadential $\frac{6}{4}$. The bass note of the linear $\frac{4}{2}$ would normally have been spelled as E♯. In this case it is spelled as F♮, possibly in order to simplify the notation of the upper parts, which feature E.

218. The Neapolitan Chord as Dominant Preparation Derived from IV

Like the augmented-6th chords this chromatic linear chord originates in the minor mode.

example 454.

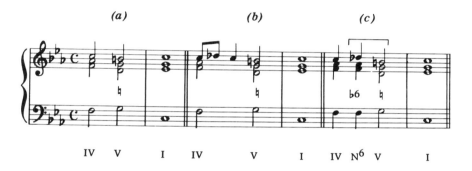

Example 454 illustrates its evolution from IV in three stages: (a) the basic progression IV V I. (b) the submetrical embellishment of the 5th of the IV by its chromatic upper auxiliary note. (c) the enlargement and assimilation of that note into the harmony, forming the chord of the lowered 6th known as the *Neapolitan 6th* (presumably because it was characteristic of music by the late Baroque Neapolitan composers).

This chord serves as a dominant preparation. Its hallmark is the horizontal interval of a diminished 3rd (bracketed in Example 454), a dissonant interval which comes about when the chromatic auxiliary note does not return to the main note (C in the present case), but instead progresses directly to the 3rd of the dominant triad. The Neapolitan 6th is also another instance of false consonance, for although it contains only consonant intervals it functions as a dissonance in the linear context. Here again, as in all linear chords, inversion theory does not apply. The Neapolitan chord is not the first inversion of a hypothetical triad on the lowered 2nd degree of the scale.

The example below contains both Neapolitan and its chord of origin, IV.

example 455.   BEETHOVEN: *Bagatelle, Op. 119/5*

219.   Pedal Point Chords

When the bass note of either I or V is sustained below moving chromatic and diatonic harmonies we call it a pedal point and describe the harmonies as pedal-point chords. Since they do not influence progression these chords are regarded as linear chords within the control of a more fundamental chord, either I or V depending upon which is the pedal point.

example 456.   RAMEAU: *Traité de L'Harmonie* (Rameau's figures)

In this instance the controlling harmony is I; its bass note remains stationary throughout the passage. The chords above the pedal point commence with the tonic itself and descend chromatically to measure 4 where, disregarding for a moment the stationary bass, we find a V^4_2. This chord resolves to I^6, which is followed by a II^6_5 V^4_2 I^6 succession. Thus, the pedal-point chords are not as unfamiliar as they might seem to be at first glance. Usually pedal-point chords are cadential chords, chords closely associated with I and V, as in this instance.

In the next excerpt a series of pedal-point chords is found at the beginning of a composition.

example 457.   BACH: *Prelude in B♭ minor, WTCI*

Example 458(*b*) is a harmonic sketch from which rhythmic and melodic detail has been eliminated. This reduction reveals the familiar chords that underlie the succession: I and VII⁷.

In section 111 the diminished-7th chord was explained as an altered inversion of V⁷. Example 458 shows the diminished-7th chord formed by auxiliary notes above the sustained bass note, G. As indicated by the figures, this linear chord occurs in the context of the succession $^6_4$ $^5_3$.

example 458.   MOZART: *Piano Sonata in C major, K.545,* Second Movement

220.   Linear Intervallic Patterns

Thus far, we have dealt with individual chords, the origins of which are linear, and with series of linear chords (the linear 6th chords and pedal-point chords). The final section of this chapter is concerned with linear formations of somewhat larger scope which will be called *linear intervallic patterns:* repetitive patterns formed by the outer voices. Characteristically, such formations contain chords without harmonic value (section 208). Example 459 will serve to introduce the concept.

example 459.   HAYDN: *Farewell Symphony,* First Movement

Shown at (*a*) is a reduction of the orchestral passage, a transition to the second theme of the exposition. At (*b*) is a representation of the underlying progression. This begins with V in m. 49 and ends with the same harmony in m. 53, as indicated by the long slurs. The linear intervallic pattern in this instance consists of the succession 10-7*, the intervals formed by the outer voices. Although some compo-

---

*Patterns of this kind are sometimes called sequences (cf. section 140). The term linear intervallic pattern is preferred, however, since the melodic detail may change while the pattern remains constant. Example 461 provides a clear demonstration of this.

nents might be said to have harmonic value—in particular, the last three in the progression (II-V-I)—the linear intervallic pattern is the predominant bearer of motion, carrying the progression to its goal in m. 53. Within the pattern the succession of parallel 10ths is of primary importance, and, indeed, the linear intervallic pattern consisting of 10ths alone (10-10) is commonly found in tonal music of all periods.

Closely akin to the linear intervallic pattern 10-7 is the pattern 10-5. Example 460 provides an instance.

example 460. BACH: *Fugue in A minor, BWV 947*

In this passage, the close of a fugue by Bach, the 10-5 pattern is used to effect the connection from I to V in the bass with a corresponding motion in the upper voice from scale degree 3 down to the leading note, G♯. Again, the underlying pattern of (a), the complete notation, is shown at (b). At (c) is shown the equivalent 10-7 pattern.

Example 460 permits a comparison of figured bass notation and the notation for linear intervallic patterns. Obviously, the figures represent the complete voice-leading, whereas the notation of the linear intervallic pattern extracts only the numerals that represent the outer voice intervals. The correspondence is spelled out at (a), where the succession 3-5 matches the linear pattern 10-5 at (b).

Finally, at (d) in Example 460 the correct analytical interpretation of the closing passage is given. This shows that the upper voice progression from C to G♯ is a motion from the outer to the inner voice. The return to the outer voice B is then supported by the bass motion C-D-E. Since this motion to B in the upper voice is not actually stated, but only implied by the bass, B is enclosed in parentheses in the representation at (d).

Example 461 shows the 10-5 pattern over a still longer span of music. Again, from the full notation at (a) is extracted the basic pattern shown at (b). An interesting feature of the pattern is the passing note in the bass in m. 26 and again in m. 28. With the acceleration of the pattern that begins in m. 29 the passing note is omitted.

Example 461 is a clear instance of change in melodic pattern (m. 29) of the upper voice, while the linear intervallic pattern 10-5 continues. For this reason the term *pattern* is preferred to "sequence."

Example 461 also illustrates what might be called a truncated linear intervallic pattern. As shown at (c), the continuation of the pattern after m. 31 would have led to the same melodic-harmonic goal. The braces at (c) enclose the part of the pattern that is truncated.

The main harmonic components of Example 461(a) are shown schematically at (d); they comprise a progression from VI to V, as indicated.

example 461. BACH: *Prelude in E♭ major, WTC II, BWV 876*

Example 462 presents one of the many beautiful instances of linear intervallic patterns to be found in the symphonic literature, the passage leading to the closing theme in the exposition of Schubert's *Unfinished Symphony.* Here the prominent motive of the second theme is carried by the bass and imitated by the upper part (m. 74), while the slower moving parts on the uppermost staff (woodwinds) carry the basic voice leading of the soprano and inner voice, with chromatic passing notes (A♭ and E♭) joining each occurrence of the pattern.

The linear intervallic pattern in this case is $\frac{6}{5}$-5, a more elaborate variant of the basic pattern 6-5. As shown at (c) the pattern as a whole effects a connection from secondary dominant to dominant within VI. The representation at (c) differs from that at (b) with respect to the upper voice beginning in m. 81. Whereas (b) shows E in the upper voice at that point, (c) gives C♯, which more directly represents the continuation of the upper voice of the linear intervallic pattern.

example 462. SCHUBERT: *Unfinished Symphony,* First Movement

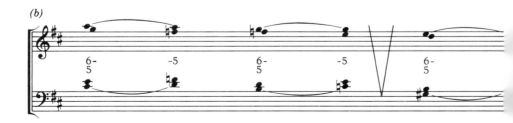

A more complicated instance of the linear intervallic pattern $^6_5$-5 is provided by Example 463.

example 463. MOZART: *Piano Sonata in F major, K.280,* First Movement

(a)   Allegro assai

(b)

(c)

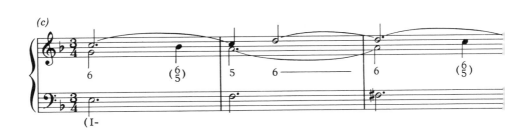

For the sake of precision and clarity the analysis is shown in three stages. At (*a*) the notation is given in full. At (*b*) embellishing notes are systematically eliminated to show the descending lines and arpeggiations.* The voice leading underlying the latter is shown at (*c*). There the descending lines spanning the 6th are shown as inner voice 3rds (e. g., G down to Bb becomes G up to Bb). Further, the arpeggiations are reduced as follows: the ascent to the octave is represented by a single note in the lower register in each case (e. g., A in the second space represents A on

---

*Although the treatment of embellishing notes is not undertaken until Chapter 12 it is hoped that the reader will be able to follow the analysis here.

the first leger line above the staff), while the second quarter note is shown in its correct voice-leading context as the 6th above the bass. As indicated at (*d*) the entire pattern is an elaboration of a succession of linear 6ths.

Example 464 presents an excerpt from the development section of the first movement of Beethoven's *Piano Sonata, Op. 78.* Here the linear intervallic pattern 6-5 is stretched out over some five measures.

example 464.   BEETHOVEN: *Piano Sonata in F♯ major, Op. 78,* First Movement
(Development)

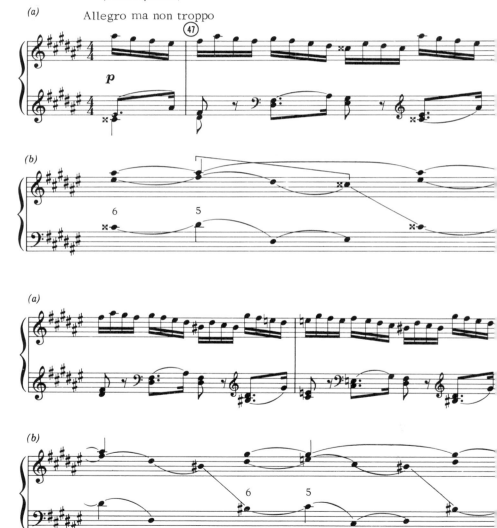

Notice that in each case the outer voice 5th is embellished by inner voice auxiliary notes—perhaps most clearly shown at (c).

The over-all stepwise progression of both outer voices cannot be interpreted analytically without reference to the beginning of the development section (and, ultimately, to the exposition). Therefore, suffice it to say that the harmonic goal of the progression is IV, as indicated. It is especially evident in this example that any effort to assign harmonic value to the $\frac{5}{3}$'s over the span of the entire passage will lead to absurd results; the linear pattern is the predominant bearer of motion.

The detail of this excerpt warrants two additional comments. Notice, first, that the rhythmic figure of the left-hand part effects an obvious association with the theme. (If the music is unfamiliar to the reader he should consult the complete score.) Not so obvious is the descending thematic motive carried by the 16th-note diminution. The first occurrence of this is bracketed in m. 47 at (b).

example 465. BEETHOVEN: *Piano Sonata in D major, Op. 28,* Third Movement

Example 465 requires minimal explanation. As shown at (c), the underlying pattern is a series of linear 6ths. The upper voice of the pattern departs from C♯ in the inner voice (m. 32) and leads up to G (m. 47), which is the continuation of the upper voice A at m. 32. Both A and G are shown in a single register at (c) in order to make the connection evident graphically. The lower voice of the pattern follows the upper voice in parallel 6ths, and, in this sense, has a dependent function. Although this aspect of linear intervallic patterns is not insignificant for the general case, further discussion at this point is not appropriate to the introductory nature of this section.

example 466.   F. COUPERIN: *Les Sylvains* (*from the Premier Ordre*)

In the passage from a keyboard piece by Couperin shown in Example 466 we find a mixture of linear intervallic patterns. As shown at (c), the pattern 8-10 occurs at the beginning of the passage. This is supplanted by 8-5 beginning at m. 40, and the passage closes with the 10-10 succession indicated.

The underlying patterns shown at (c) are given an elaborate setting in the music, as indicated at (b). Each 8-10 pattern is filled out with pairs of voices moving in parallel 10ths. The ultimate harmonic goal of the entire linear complex is V (m. 44), which leads to the restatement of the first part of the music.

Perhaps no other situation in tonal music so strikingly dramatizes the inter-action of linear and harmonic processes as the linear intervallic patterns. Although the present section is only a brief introduction to this structural aspect, some general observations can be made.

To sum up, two situations can be distinguished with respect to passages that exhibit linear intervallic patterns: (1) The chordal components have no harmonic value, as can be demonstrated by attempting to read them as elements of a har-monic progression, and only the point of departure and the goal are harmonic; (2) Some of the chordal components have harmonic value—as is often the case in the 10-7 pattern, by virtue of the 5ths progression—but the over-all linear pattern formed by the outer voices is a significant aspect of the motion and may even take precedence over the harmonic; (3) In all cases the linear intervallic pattern either extends a single harmony or effects a connection between two harmonies, with modulation a special case of the latter.

EXERCISES

A. List of Some Important Terms to Define and Memorize

Linear chord

9th chord

Appoggiatura chord

Consonant $\frac{6}{4}$

Passing $\frac{6}{4}$

Linear-6th chord

Parallel 6th chords

Italian 6th

French 6th

German 6th

Linear $\frac{4}{2}$

Neapolitan chord

Pedal point

Linear Intervallic Pattern

B. Basic Keyboard and Aural Exercises

Here the chords of the basic pattern are connected by inverted secondary dominant-7th chords. The latter, in turn, are connected by dissonant linear chords. As an exercise in analysis, to supplement those given later in this section, the basic chord patterns should be examined in terms of linear intervallic patterns.

exercise 192. **Basic Chord Pattern 1 in major**

exercise 193. **Basic Chord Pattern 1 in minor**

353

exercise 194.   Basic Chord Pattern 2 in major

This version of the basic pattern features appoggiatura chords and a linear half-diminished chord which prepares the dominant.

exercise 195.   Basic Chord Pattern 2 in minor

The minor version also features appoggiatura chords. However, the dominant here is prepared by an enharmonic $\frac{4}{2}$.

C. Chord Identification

INSTRUCTIONS

Identify all chords in the following excerpts. Linear chords made up of odd combinations of intervals should be labeled "lin." Those explained in the preceding sections should be identified by appropriate symbols. All excerpts are to be studied thoroughly for progression, especially modulatory progression, melodic structure, metric-rhythmic pattern, etc. After playing each as written, transpose to at least two other keys and sing the bass while playing only the upper parts.

D. Figured Bass, Soprano Given

INSTRUCTIONS
Realize in four parts. Identify all chords, paying particular attention to linear chords.

exercise 196. BACH: *Ihr Gestirn, ihr hohen Lüfte.* (Schemelli's *Gesangbuch*)

This soprano voice may be regarded as a solo line and the bass realized as a four-voice accompaniment.

exercise 197. BACH: *O Jesulein süss.* (Schemelli's *Gesangbuch*)

E. Unfigured Basses, Soprano Given

INSTRUCTIONS
Realize in four parts. Identify all chords, paying particular attention to linear chords.

exercise 198.   TELEMANN: *Fantasy* *

exercise 199.   BACH: *Bist du bei mir* (incomplete)

Realize the bass as an accompaniment for solo voice. Shift to three voices where advantageous.

*Occasional parallel 5ths and 8ves are unavoidable in these free compositions (for example, in the first and second measures).

exercise 200.   SCHUBERT: *Ländler*

F. Soprano Voices to Harmonize

INSTRUCTIONS
While constructing the minimal harmonization observe cues for linear chords, for
example, appoggiaturas, accented passing notes, passing or auxiliary notes within a
a dissonant harmony. Linear chords are required even for the harmonization of
many familiar songs.

exercise 201.   **German Folk Song. For SATB**

exercise 202.   Italian Folk Song. For vocal solo with piano accompaniment

exercise 203.   German Folk Song: *Es steht ein˙ Lind'*. Transpose to A♭ for SATB

exercise 204.   German Folk Song: *Mein Mädel hat einen Rosenmund.* Transpose
to A for solo voice with piano accompaniment.

Fast

exercise 205.   German Folk Song: *In Stiller Nacht*

G. Passages to be Analyzed for Linear Intervallic Patterns

INSTRUCTIONS
Using notation indicate the intervallic pattern(s) for each excerpt.

exercise 206.   F. COUPERIN: *La Diligente* (*Second Ordre*)

exercise 207.   MAHLER: *Fourth Symphony,* Third Movement

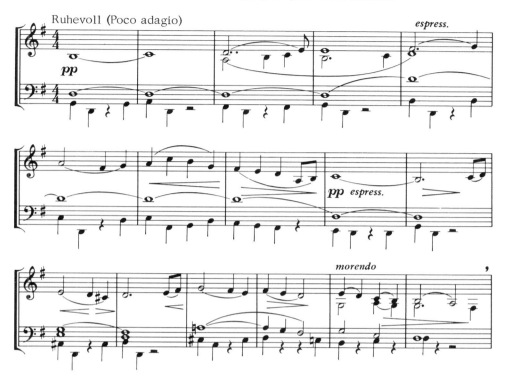

exercise 208.   MOZART: *Symphony in E♭, K.543,* Second Movement

exercise 209.   SCHUMANN: *Im Rhein, im heiligen Strome* (*Dichterliebe*)

Ziemlich langsam

exercise 210.   BACH: *Air* from the *Orchestral Suite in D major*

As an additional exercise supply figures and realize the continuo part.

Chapter 12

THE TECHNIQUES
OF MELODIC-RHYTHMIC
DEVELOPMENT

> Certainly no one doubts the need for
> embellishments. . . . They are indeed in-
> dispensable, for consider their uses. They
> connect notes, animate them, lend them
> a special effect and weight when required,
> make them pleasing and thus arouse a
> particular attentiveness. Embellishments
> help to clarify the content of the notes—
> be it sad, joyful, or of other nature. . . .
>
> C. P. E. Bach, 1753

221.   The Structural Role of Submetrical Embellishment

Chapter 7 considered the structure of the soprano voice and its relation to the
progression of the harmony. There the soprano voice was regarded as a special
case of melodic progression, and it was observed that any voice, including the bass,
can exhibit melodic characteristics. Let us review those characteristics here, giving
special attention to the relation between metrical and submetrical embellishment.

    A consonant harmony can be developed melodically in three ways: (1) by
auxiliary note (2) by arpeggiation (skip) (3) by a passing note which fills in an
arpeggiated harmonic interval. These three techniques are summarized in Example
467. Since the embellishments have full metrical value they require harmonization, as shown.

example 467.

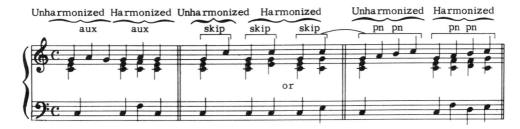

One of the most remarkable aspects of tonal music is that these basic techniques are applied both at the metrical and submetrical levels and over both short and long spans of music. An introduction to large-scale arpeggiations, passing and auxiliary notes is given in Chapter 13. Here we are concerned with the basic procedures as they apply to shorter spans of music.

The relation between metrical and submetrical embellishments is illustrated in the next example.

example 468.

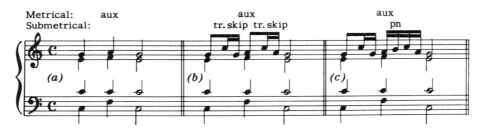

At (a) we see the harmonized metrical auxiliary note pattern. At (b) this basic pattern is developed melodically by transient skips—submetrical embellishments. At (c) further development has taken place with the filling of one of the skips by a submetrical passing note.

From this illustration it can be seen that metrical embellishment provides a means of *extending* a harmony to include other harmonies, whereas submetrical embellishment serves to elaborate and activate a single harmony.

Example 468 illustrates still another significant fact: submetrical embellishment necessarily means rhythmic as well as melodic development. For this reason the title of the present chapter uses the composite expression melodic-rhythmic.

Submetrical embellishments are sometimes called "unessential" notes, a term which suggests that such embellishments are superfluous, that they have no significant function in the tonal composition. This is an erroneous notion. Submetrical embellishments are no more extraneous than flesh on bone. If, occasionally, we omit them from illustrations in the present chapter it is in order to provide a clear view of underlying harmonic relations, not because we consider them superfluous.

We have seen that there are only three basic techniques of melodic-rhythmic development. However, these occur in various forms, producing diverse textures. For example, arpeggiations are complete or incomplete, auxiliary notes are accented or unaccented, and so on. One must be familiar with all these modes of occurrence and be able to recognize them immediately in order to achieve an adequate basis for the development of analytical as well as compositional technique.

The relevance of melodic-rhythmic embellishments to composing is readily apparent. In order to progress beyond the elementary level of note-against-note harmonization in close position one must exploit the resources offered by submetrical embellishment. In addition, an understanding of submetrical embellishing techniques is prerequisite to composition in two and three voices, and in free textures—all of which are introduced in Chapter 14.

222. Motive, Theme, and Figuration

These three terms are used frequently in connection with melodic structure and embellishment. We can draw illustrations of all from a single work.

example 469. BEETHOVEN: *Sixth Symphony* ("Pastorale")

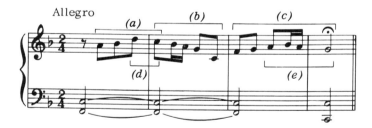

This opening melodic group consists of several segments marked off by brackets in Example 469. Each segment contains a distinct submetrical embellishment. When segments such as these are repeated during the course of a composition in such a way that they become characteristic features of its melodic structure they are called *motives.* Motives may recur in their original form or they may undergo transformations. For example, the identifying rhythmic pattern of the motive may be retained while its characteristic melodic shape is changed. Compare motive (*b*) in the following example with its original form in Example 469.

example 470. (BEETHOVEN: *Sixth Symphony*)

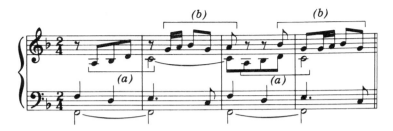

Here motive (*b*) has retained only the rhythmic shape of the original, whereas motive (*a*) recurs unchanged.

In contrast to the transformation of motive (*b*) just described, the characteristic melodic shape may be retained while the rhythm is changed, as in Example 471:

example 471. (BEETHOVEN: *Sixth Symphony*)

In this passage motive (*d*) has been expanded in duration so that it now occupies a complete measure. An expansion of this kind is known as an *augmentation.* Another example of augmentation is shown below.

example 472. (BEETHOVEN: *Sixth Symphony*)

As in the previous example the note values of the original motive have been doubled in this transformation. Observe also that there are two statements of the motive and that the second statement is extended.

The counterpart of augmentation is *diminution** of the original form of the motive. With this manipulation the original form is made proportionally smaller.

When the melodic shape of the original is turned upside down the motive is said to be *inverted.* Example 473 shows motive (*a*) in its original form combined with its inversion.

example 473.   (BEETHOVEN: *Sixth Symphony*)

Contour inversion of this kind has nothing whatsoever to do with harmonic inversion of intervals. Unfortunately, the same term has been applied to both.

Similar difficulty has beset the term *figuration.* If the term is used alone it usually refers to instrumental figurations such as those shown below.

example 474.   (BEETHOVEN: *Sixth Symphony*)

Typical instrumental figurations are bracketed at (*f*) and (*g*). The first of these is a type of arpeggiation found in many pieces and sometimes called the Alberti Bass. The second (*g*) is a repeated submetrical auxiliary-note pattern, a measured trill. These patterns are not distinctive, nor are they characteristic of this composition, for they may be found in a wide variety of works.

---

*Although the term diminution is current, the term *contraction* might be better since diminution is the traditional designation for embellishment in general.

The term figuration is also used to describe the general process of melodic embellishment. Thus, we often read of "figurated" melody or of chorale "figuration." The latter in particular is widely used and will be found in the present volume. Figuration has nothing to do with figured bass, except insofar as numerals often designate embellishing notes.

Finally, we come to the term *theme*. A theme, as distinct from a motive, is a longer and more complex melody which executes a complete progression of one of the types explained in Chapter 7. Example 469 may be regarded as the first statement of a theme. Like most themes it comprises several motives.

Themes and motives serve to enhance melodic and harmonic progression by preparing changes, by unifying and contrasting various phases of a composition, by signaling and intensifying climaxes, and by performing many other essential tasks. In large part they achieve this by virtue of the particular combinations of submetrical embellishments which they contain. These are discussed below in some detail.

THE AUXILIARY NOTE

223. The Complete Auxiliary Note

The complete auxiliary-note pattern consists of the main note, the auxiliary note or notes, and the restatement of the main note—in that order. The complete auxiliary-note pattern thus has four possible forms, summarized in Example 475.

example 475.

At both (a) and (b) we see a single auxiliary note embellishing a main note. At (c) upper and lower auxiliaries are combined in a formation of five notes. At (d) both upper and lower auxiliaries precede the final main note. This form of the auxiliary note is often overlooked, although it occurs very frequently in compositions. Excerpts from the literature follow.

example 476. BACH: *Chorale-Prelude, Wir danken dir, Herr Jesu Christ* (for organ)

The complete lower-auxiliary-note motive occurs in every voice except the soprano, which carries the chorale melody.

Auxiliary notes are altered chromatically when required in order to support the prevailing harmony and voice leading. For example, when the V is reached as a harmonic goal in the example below, C♯, not C♮ is the lower auxiliary note. C♮ belongs to the inverted V⁷ which follows, whereas C♯ belongs to the consonant-goal harmony.

example 477.   (BACH: *Chorale-Prelude, Wir danken dir*)

The following excerpt contains two auxiliary-note formations, the first metrical the second submetrical.

example 478. CHOPIN: *Prelude in F♯ major, Op. 28/13*

The first auxiliary-note formation is type (d) shown in Example 472. The second
is type (c), the five note figure, here distributed evenly over the first full pulse of
this compound metrical pattern.

The next example contains submetrical auxiliary notes of type (d) as well
as metrical auxiliary notes.

example 479. BRAHMS: *Third Symphony*

The first submetrical auxiliary note in Example 479 falls directly on the beat and
thus is relatively more accented than the auxiliary notes in Examples 476 and 477.
Our next excerpt contains an even more strongly accented auxiliary-note pattern.

example 480. BEETHOVEN: *Piano Sonata in C major, Op. 2/3*

The motive indicated by brackets is a variant of type (c) in Example 475.

224. The Incomplete Auxiliary Note

The incomplete forms of the auxiliary note are two-note motives, with one exception. In all cases the main note occurs only once, either at the beginning or at the
end, not in both positions as in the complete forms:

example 481.

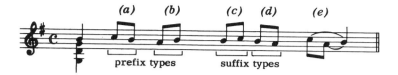

In types (*a*) and (*b*) the auxiliary note serves as a prefix to the main note, while in types (*c*) and (*d*) the auxiliary note is a suffix to the main note. Both auxiliary notes precede the main note in type (*e*).

When the prefix type receives the full metrical accent it is called an *appoggiatura* (section 201). An example follows.

example 482.   C. P. E. BACH: *Sonata in C minor*

Allegretto

The asterisks mark auxiliaries of type (*b*), the appoggiatura. Example 482 also offers a comparison between these incomplete patterns and complete auxiliary-note patterns (bracketed). In both cases the auxiliary note is accented.

The suffix type is illustrated in the passage below.

example 483.   BACH: *Chorale-Prelude, An Wasserflüssen Babylon*

Example 483(*a*), a reduction, contains only submetrical passing notes. Example 483(*b*), the complete version, contains incomplete auxiliary notes marked by asterisks. Thus, there are submetrical embellishments at two distinct rhythmic levels: passing eighth notes and their embellishments, the auxiliary sixteenth notes. The suffix type auxiliary note shown here is also characteristic of the embellished-suspension resolution (see section 194).

225.   The Secondary Auxiliary Note

Occasionally in very elaborate figurations a submetrical auxiliary note will be supplied with a still smaller embellishing auxiliary note—generally for rhythmic reasons. This smaller auxiliary note is called *secondary* to indicate its subordinate function in the embellishment as a whole. Example 484 shows how such notes may fit into an intricately ornamented melody.

example 484.   MOZART: *Symphony in C major, K.551* ("Jupiter")

The three stages of Example 484 show analytically the melodic-rhythmic development of a passage that serves to bring about a return to the tonic. At (a) may be seen a sequential progression of [V⁷]'s which leads to the final V⁷. At (b) the 7th of each chord is embellished by an upper auxiliary note. At (c), the complete version, the 7th of each chord is further embellished by a six-note group that contains a lower auxiliary note, the upper auxiliary note shown at (b) and a secondary auxiliary note marked by an asterisk. The reader will also recognize this passage as an instance of a familiar linear intervallic pattern (section 220).

ARPEGGIATION

226. Incomplete Arpeggiation (Skip)

Melodic lines are often embellished by submetrical skips above or below. Like metrical skips these may be purely of local effect, that is, transient skips, or they may represent the more elaborate technique of compound melody. An excerpt containing transient skips is quoted here:

example 485. SCHUBERT: *Ländler, Op. 67/2*

The submetrical skips in the second measure are activated harmonic intervals which can be represented as continuous lines moving in slower note values to form a succession of 3rds (b).

example 486. BACH: *Chorale-Prelude, In dir ist Freude*

(a)

(b)

The submetrical skip in the second measure are activated harmonic intervals which can be represented as continuous lines moving in slower note values to form a succession of 3rds (*b*).

227. Complete Arpeggiation

A complete arpeggiation involves all the intervals of a chord. Like the incomplete arpeggiation this may be merely a local embellishment of a note in the main line, or it may be a more extended activation of the full harmony, that is, compound melody. Example 487 illustrates the complete arpeggiation in its more transient role.

example 487. BRAHMS: *Deutsche Volkslieder,* "Ich stand auf hohem Berge"

The submetrical arpeggiation bracketed in Example 487 serves as embellishment above and below the main note, D. The melody contains two other forms of the arpeggio. The first two measures contain a metrical arpeggiation of the tonic triad. The next to last measure contains another metrical arpeggiation of the tonic triad. This time the arpeggiation is filled in by accented passing notes, as shown by the supplementary sketch.

A familiar example of complete arpeggiation which represents the technique of compound melody is given below.

example 488. BACH: *Prelude in C major, WTC I*

In Example 489 the arpeggiation shown at (*b*), a reduction, is embellished by auxiliary notes in the complete music shown at (*a*).

example 489. CHOPIN: *Waltz in B minor, Op. 69/2*

THE PASSING NOTE

228. The Unaccented Passing Note

Passing notes fill arpeggiated chordal intervals. Therefore it is not only convenient but also structurally correct to regard passing notes as embellishments of skips. The meaning of a passing note depends, then, upon the structural function of the skip which it fills. Consider the passing note in the following passage.

example 490. MOZART: *Piano Sonata in F major, K.280*

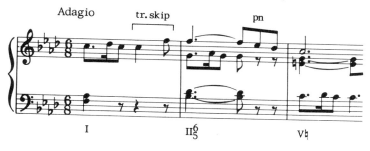

The soprano voice centers upon C in this excerpt. The transient skip away from C in the first measure is counterbalanced by the stepwise return in the second measure via the unaccented passing note, E♭.

In elaborate textures, passing notes may connect the notes of the harmony to form more complicated patterns such as those shown in Example 491:

example 491. BACH: *Chorale-Prelude, Heut' triumphiret Gottes Sohn*

The D in parentheses is understood from the harmony (I_3^5). Thus C is a passing note. Actual statement of D would be out of keeping with the characteristic motive of this prelude, which is a descending or ascending eighth-note succession preceded by a rest. Three of these motives fill the interval of a 4th and therefore contain two passing notes. The first motive traverses the upper 4th of the minor scale and therefore the two passing notes are altered chromatically, in accord with the melodic minor scale.

Passing notes are often of greater harmonic significance when they fill the intervals formed by a compound melody. Consider the following variational example.

example 492. HANDEL: *Gavotte and Double* (*variation*) from *Suite in G major*

The soprano at (a) is a compound melody which, together with the bass, outlines a succession of triads at the outset. At (b) two of the original skips are filled by passing notes (bracketed). These passing notes bring into play a 7th in each case, thus enhancing the original harmonic progression.

229. The Accented Passing Note

The accented passing note performs the same functions as the unaccented passing note and therefore does not require prolonged discussion. One aspect, however, does merit our special attention. The accented passing note displaces the main note from its metrical position. Several instances of this have already been seen. An additional example follows.

example 493. BRAHMS: *Es war ein Markgraf über'm Rhein*

Accented embellishing notes must be used with care if they displace dissonant notes, lest they inadvertently destroy the identity of the harmony. As a general rule they should not be used in connection with dissonant notes unless they too are dissonant against the bass and unless the harmony is identified by context as well as structure.

Here and in all cases of accented embellishments the bass and harmony define the main structural elements. One further example will serve as a reminder of this important principle, the principle of harmonic definition (section 142).

example 494. HAYDN: *Symphony in D major, No. 104*

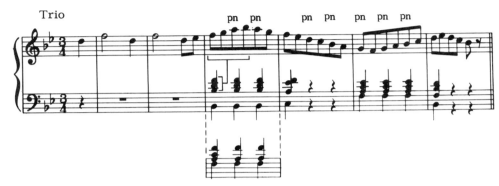

The bass and harmony of the third measure define F-B♭ as the chordal interval in the upper voice. Accordingly, A is an accented passing note within that interval. If, however, the bass and harmony were those shown in the sketch the harmonic interval in the upper voice would be F-A and B♭ would be an auxiliary note, not a passing note.

230. Submetrical Suspensions and Anticipations

Sometimes submetrical passing notes and auxiliary notes occur as suspensions in miniature. Since they do not retard the progression of the harmony and have only embellishing significance, they are not considered full-fledged suspensions. Three examples are quoted below. The first shows a submetrical suspension in combination with an actual suspension chord.

example 495. BRAHMS: *Intermezzo in E major, Op. 116/6*

The submetrical suspension in the second measure occurs directly below a suspended 4th. Observe that this submetrical suspension resembles an appoggiatura and could indeed be considered as such if the note were not present in the preceding chord.

In the next example the apparent submetrical suspension is better described as an accented auxiliary note embellishing A.

example 496.   MOZART: *Don Giovanni*

Similarly, the submetrical suspensions in the next excerpt are perhaps better regarded as special cases of the accented passing note.

example 497.   BEETHOVEN: *Piano Sonata in D minor, Op. 31/2*

The eighth notes form pairs, as indicated by the brackets. The second note of each pair is consonant, but is immediately repeated to become a dissonant, accented embellishing note. The two-note quasi-suspension motive prepares the suspension chord which displaces the dominant triad at the asterisk.

Submetrical anticipations occur quite often, especially in late eighteenth-century music. Example 498(*a*) shows a rhythmically simplified version of a passage which contains two anticipations. Example 498(*b*) presents the passage in full.

example 498.   HAYDN: *Piano Sonata in E major*

The anticipations are marked by asterisks in Example 498(*b*). The first of these embellishes a metrical passing note. The second embellishes the suspension resolution.

231. Interrupted Passing Notes

As explained in section 131, melodic notes need not be in immediate succession in order to be closely related. Relations of this kind are called nonconsecutive relations. Submetrical as well as metrical embellishments may serve to interrupt consecutive notes and thus bring about nonconsecutive relations. Consider the following excerpt.

example 499.   MOZART: *Piano Concerto in D major,* First Movement

Here the passing note E in the second measure is interrupted by the submetrical skips.

A more unusual situation is quoted below.

example 500.   CHOPIN: *Mazurka in A minor, Op. 67/4*

At first glance D in the soprano of the second measure appears to be an auxiliary note standing between two C's. However, the bass and harmony assign it a different role. As the figures 8 7 indicate, the D is actually a passing note. Here the C on the second beat is somewhat misleading. Although it appears to be a main note, the harmony defines it as an accented-metrical passing note which effects a stepwise return to D after the descending skip away from E on the first beat.

The concept of nonconsecutive relations is essential to the understanding of progressions of larger scale. The latter will be introduced in the following chapter, Chapter 13.

232.   Obligatory Chromatic Passing and Auxiliary Notes

Chromatic passing and auxiliary notes perform valuable functions of many kinds. For instance, the submetrical F♯ in the following passage (asterisk) serves to repeat and intensify the previous metrical F♯, as indicated by the dotted line.

example 501.   MOZART: *Quintet in C minor, K.406,* First Movement

The F♮ of the alternative embellishment sketched in below the fourth measure is "correct" from the standpoint of voice leading, but since it does not express the motivic relationship of the original F♯, it is defective from the standpoint of coherent melodic detail.

In certain instances such chromatically-altered auxiliary and passing notes are obligatory, for their diatonic counterparts would interfere with the melodic progression. Consider the following theme.

example 502.   MOZART: *Symphony in D major, K.385*

Example 502(*b*) is a reduction of Example 502(*a*). The submetrical embellishments have been omitted in order to show the basic melodic progression more clearly and the necessity for the chromatics. The first four measures contain a repeated arpeggiation; the second four contain an ascending line which ends with a skip to scale degree 5. Every chromatic embellishment in the complete version is obligatory. The reason for this can be seen if we compare an alternative version which substitutes diatonic embellishments for chromatic.

example 503.

(a)

(b)

Example 503(b), a reduction of Example 503(a), reveals that this purely diatonic version is in conflict with the original at every point where the chromatic embellishment has been exchanged for a diatonic embellishment. Thus G♮ in the third measure sounds like an interrupted passing note here, whereas in the original version its chromatic form G♯ is an auxiliary note. Even more striking is the change which the diatonic substitutes bring about in the second part of the theme. The line no longer ascends in the sixth measure since E now sounds like an upper auxiliary note embellishing D, a reversal of the original relationship.

This demonstration of obligatory chromatic embellishments indicates the many ways in which embellishments of all kinds influence the more fundamental aspects of musical texture: harmonic progression, voice leading, and metric–rhythmic pattern. The following sections examine these influences in more detail.

THE EFFECTS OF MELODIC DEVELOPMENT UPON HARMONIC PROGRESSION, VOICE LEADING, AND METRIC–RHYTHMIC PATTERN

In general, submetrical embellishments may displace metrical elements from their normative positions, shorten them, delay them, or interrupt them. Embellishments

of this kind provide some of the most beautifully refined details in tonal compositions. At the same time they are often difficult to decipher because they tend to
conceal the more fundamental elements upon which their structural meaning
depends. Perhaps the most obvious instances of such concealment occur with extended embellishments of the bass.

233. Concealment of Bass Progression by Embellishment

The bass can be developed by arpeggiation to such a degree that it becomes a self-
contained compound melody, as in the following case.

example 504.   PURCELL: *A New Ground*

(a)

(b)

Here the composer himself has deciphered the compound melody for us. At (a)
we see the first statement of the recurring bass theme or "ground," as it was called.
At (b) the second statement of the theme is seen. There the bass is sorted out
from the other lines in this compound melody and notated as a continuous,
uninterrupted line.

Sometimes a transient skip below the bass momentarily interrupts the
progression.

example 505.   BACH: *Little Prelude in D minor* (Wilhelm Friedemann Bach
Büchlein)

Allegro

The transient skips marked by asterisks here are not part of the bass progression. In this case the bass figure as a whole imitates the soprano of the first
two measures.

The accented passing note frequently conceals the actual progression since it momentarily displaces the bass note. An example follows.

example 506. BACH: *Chorale, Ihr Gestirn', ihr hohlen Lüfte*

Two forms of notation are used in Example 506 to indicate the accented passing notes. In the first measure the slant marks the accented passing note; the actual bass note which follows is figured. In the second measure the dash following 5 means that the notes above the bass remain unchanged. These are much simpler procedures than figuring the intervals upward from the accented submetrical passing note as though it were the real bass note. Only if an accented passing note in the bass has full metrical value are the intervals above it figured, for example, the linear passing chord $\frac{5}{2}$ which displaces a 6th chord.

234. Embellished Suspension Resolutions

Section 194 examined resolutions that are interrupted by embellishments. More extended submetrical embellishments such as those under discussion in the present chapter sometimes delay the resolution to an even greater extent than those shown there. In the next example an arpeggiation intervenes between suspension and resolution. As a result both suspension and resolution are stated only as sixteenth notes. Of course they are implicit in the chords, as indicated by dotted lines in the illustration.

example 507. BACH: *Prelude in F minor, WTC II*

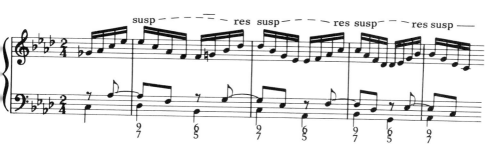

This passage contains a further complexity caused, in this case, by harmonic development. The $\frac{9}{7}$ suspension chord normally resolves to a 6th chord. Here both bass and harmony change before the upper voice resolves.

Another instance of delayed resolution is quoted below.

example 508. SCHUBERT: *Die liebe Farbe*

The suspended 9th in the third measure does not resolve immediately as do the submetrical suspensions in the second and fourth measures. Instead, the soprano skips down to an inner voice and returns to resolve the suspension only on the last sixteenth note in the measure.

235.   Parallel 5ths Involving Submetrical Embellishments

The following example contains parallel 5ths between soprano and alto as marked.

example 509.   Chorale: *Ach lieben Christen, seid getrost* (after Bach)

However, one of the notes involved is a submetrical auxiliary note and therefore the parallelism does not affect the harmonic succession. Such 5ths (or 8ves) are called *5ths by embellishment* to distinguish them from *voice-leading 5ths* which involve metrical notes essential to the progression.

Composers differ in the extent to which they tolerate parallelisms of this kind. One finds occasional examples even of parallelisms involving metrical embellishments, such as the two passages that follow.

example 510.   MOZART: *Piano Sonata in C major, K.279*

The parallel 5ths between the outer voices here are not voice-leading 5ths. As indicated, F♯ is an auxiliary note which embellishes the actual harmony note, G.

In the next passage the parallel 5ths are the incidental result of transient skips below the actual bass progression E-F-G.

example 511.   BEETHOVEN: *Piano Sonata in C major, Op. 2/3*

A rare case of voice-leading 5ths is quoted below

example 512.   BACH: *Chorale, Herr, wie du willst*

EXERCISES

A. List of Some Important Terms to Define and Memorize

Motive	Complete auxiliary-note pattern
Theme	Incomplete auxiliary-note pattern
Figuration	Secondary auxiliary note
Augmentation	Concealed passing note
Diminution	Obligatory chromatic auxiliary note
Inversion	

B. Preliminary Keyboard Exercises

These exercises are of two types: (1) sequential progressions and (2) short figured and unfigured basses. In both cases the soprano is to be embellished and, if possible, the bass. The first exercise is worked out in some detail to demonstrate the procedure.

exercise 211.

(a) An unembellished realization, beginning from the soprano position of the 3rd, but incorporating the line which begins from the soprano position of the 5th:

(b) Passing notes fill the skips in the soprano:

(c) Passing notes fill bass skips in imitation of soprano:

(d) Soprano of chords on even beats embellished by submetrical skips:

(e) Auxiliary notes embellish submetrical skips and submetrical skips added to chords on odd beats:

(f) Auxiliary notes embellish submetrical skips on every beat:

(g) Passing notes fill skips on even beats while bass of odd beats is embellished by combination auxiliary and passing-note motive:

(h) Beginning from the soprano position of the 8ve a bilinear melody is created by ascending skips:

(i) On the odd beats passing notes connect the two lines; submetrical skips occur on the even beats:

(j) Compare this further embellishment with (e):

*Skip necessary to avoid impending 8ves brought about by the submetrical embellishment.

(k) Beginning from the position of the 5th we obtain the descending line which was incorporated in the melody at (a):

(l) Upper auxiliary notes embellish the soprano progression while the bass is embellished by the motive used at (g) and by a new motive which moves within a 3rd (filled transient skip):

exercise 212. **Sequential Progression in Major**

exercise 213. **Sequential Progression in Minor**

exercise 214. **Sequential Progression in Major**

exercise 215. **Sequential Progression in Minor**

exercise 216. **Sequential Progression in Major**

exercise 217. **Figured Bass. (Mattei)**

exercise 218. **Figured Bass. (Corelli)**

exercise 219. **Figured Bass. (Mattei)**

C. Embellished Melodies to Harmonize

INSTRUCTIONS

The first step in harmonizing an embellished melody is to analyze it carefully until the relation between the basic metrical soprano line and the submetrical embellishments is clear. Minimal harmonization of the metrical soprano is the next step. The usual procedure can be followed thereafter, except that one should consider possibilities for introducing submetrical harmonies—especially if the tempo is slow.

Other styles of accompaniment and figuration can be used now. In almost all cases specific styles have been suggested. Parallel 8ves sometimes occur between the accompaniment and the soprano in these freer styles. These are acceptable if the bass is not involved. Avoid parallel 5ths between any pairs of voices.

exercise 220. *German Folk Song*

exercise 221. *Italian Folk Song*

exercise 222. *Swedish Folk Song*

exercise 223. *Swedish Folk Song*

exercise 224. *English Folk Song*

D. Longer Figured Basses

INSTRUCTIONS
Each bass is to be realized as an embellished solo melody for treble instrument or
voice with four-part continuo accompaniment. Until one achieves fluency it is wise
to limit the ratio of submetrical to metrical melodic notes. Embellishments which

move 2:1 against the metrical unit should be worked out before attempting 3:1 or 4:1.

In all cases the motivic aspect of melodic development should be heeded so that the detail has both consistency and clarity. Motives and themes must articulate harmonic groups and coordinate with the metric-rhythmic pattern. If they establish independent patterns the result will be loss of coherence. Thus it is important to mark off the harmonic units, large and small, and take care that the melody does not run past or fall short of them.

Since compound melody is usually the most difficult to construct, it should not be attempted until a certain degree of facility with single lines has been attained.

A final admonition: However attractive its submetrical embellishments may be, the effectiveness of a melody ultimately depends upon its basic metrical structure. In this regard Kirnberger has written:

The true basis of beauty in an aria [embellished melody] always lies in the basic melody which remains when all notes which belong to the embellishment have been taken away. If this is incorrect with respect to declamation, progression, or harmony, the errors cannot be concealed by embellishment.

exercise 225. **Passacaglia bass (after Handel)**

At least five solo soprano voices should be written as variations upon this bass and harmony, beginning with slow note values and becoming progressively faster with each variation.

Bear in mind here and elsewhere that since the continuo carries the complete harmony the soprano will inevitably double one of the continuo voices at the 8ve. This is perfectly normal. The only doubling prohibited is 8ve doubling of the bass by the soprano.

exercise 226. **LOCATELLI**

After the fundamental version of the continuo has been worked out, embellishments can be introduced into its soprano voice. These may double the solo soprano at the 3rd or 6th, may imitate the embellishments of the solo soprano, or otherwise enhance the progression of the solo part.

exercise 227. **BACH**

The slants in this exercise, for example in the eighth measure, indicate accented passing notes in the bass. The chord which belongs to the next bass note is to be played over the accented passing note in such cases so that, in effect, the chord precedes its bass note. (See section 233.)

Chapter 13

LARGE-SCALE ARPEGGIATIONS, PASSING AND AUXILIARY NOTES

The arpeggiation of a chord remains a harmonic event, despite its successive nature. The passing note, in contrast, is a melodic event, always dissonant, even though through transformation it may be expressed as a consonance. The same holds for the auxiliary note. . . .

Schenker (*Tonwille*)

236. Introduction

In Chapter 12 the various functions of arpeggiations, passing notes and auxiliary notes were discussed and illustrated. It was shown that these procedures serve to develop or expand musical content. This development of content occurs not only in short spans of music, such as those given in the examples of Chapter 12, but also—and more importantly—in larger musical contexts. The present chapter develops this basic concept.*

---

*Although the influence of Heinrich Schenker is apparent in other portions of the present volume, it is most explicitly evident in this chapter. The author's indebtedness, which extends over a period of many years, is gratefully acknowledged.

237. Arpeggiations of Longer Span

Of the three basic procedures, arpeggiation in the upper voice is perhaps the least common within the entire repertory of tonal music, with respect to occurrences of longer span. Two examples are given below.

example 513. CHOPIN: *Nocturne in C minor, Op. 48/1*

The full notation of the opening of a work by Chopin is shown in Example 513 at (*a*). The reduction at (*b*), which omits much of the detail, reveals a long arpeggio that descends from the opening melodic note, G. When the arpeggio reaches C, the bass and harmony change, bringing in the dominant preparation VI, followed by II⁶, then V, as shown. Thus, with the unfolding arpeggio there is a corresponding development of the harmony as well. To sum up, the structure of this passage may be described as a *prolongation* (Schenker's term) of the tonic harmony, with G as the main structural note in the upper voice.

example 514. BACH: *Sinfonia 15, BWV 801*

(b)

(c)

Whereas Example 513 shows an arpeggiation of large scale, each component of which is supported by auxiliary notes or skips, Example 514, from the last of the so-called three-part inventions, shows arpeggiations over two different spans. Each beat (dotted eighth note) carries an arpeggio, while just below the surface of these obvious patterns (*a*) is projected an arpeggiation of longer span, as shown at (*b*). The observant reader will notice that this latter arpeggiation is brought about by the subdivision of the six-note pattern into groups of two—an instance of *hemiola.*

As in Example 513, the arpeggiation in Example 514 prolongs the tonic triad. In the latter instance, however, the main upper voice note is clearly the third of the triad, as shown in Example 514 at (*c*). (Compare Example 517.)

Although arpeggiation is only infrequently the underlying structure over longer spans in the upper voice, it is commonly found in the bass, where it serves to unify sections and even complete movements. Example 515 provides a typical instance from the rondo movement of Beethoven's *Pathetique* Sonata. The large-scale bass motion progresses from I (Theme 1) to III at m. 25. The mediant harmony is then prolonged through the statement of Theme 3, with the dominant returning before m. 62 to complete the arpeggiation and prepare the return to I at m. 62. The example also provides an illustration of a large-scale auxiliary note in the bass, corresponding to the prolonged VI that serves as dominant preparation.

example 515. BEETHOVEN: *Piano Sonata in C minor, Op. 13,* Third Movement

238.   The Passing Note over Longer Spans

It is probably safe to say that every well-constructed tonal composition employs the passing tone to create longer unified spans of music. It operates over the longer span just as it does in the detail of the music: connecting two "more important" notes. Another, and perhaps better, way of saying the same thing is that the passing note fills an intervallic space and performs a connective function. Example 516 illustrates.

example 516.   BEETHOVEN: *Piano Sonata in C minor, Op. 10/1,*
Second Movement

In the upper voice of the first two measures we see that Ab, scale degree 1, is prolonged by means of the descending third, C-Ab. (Compare (a) and (b).) In the next two measures the upper voice prolongs the large-scale passing note Bb, scale degree 2, again by means of a descending third. The ascending motion is concluded on the downbeat of m. 5, as the upper voice reaches C, scale degree 3, harmonized by the tonic triad. The essential motion is shown at (c): the entire first phrase consists of the ascent from scale degree 1 (Ab) through the passing note Bb to scale degree 3 (C).

In the present chapter we shall concentrate on the passing note as a connector that fills out a consonant interval, as in Example 516. The passing note can also operate within a dissonant interval, but this type of motion involves a different level of structure, as will be evident in the discussion of Example 518.

Example 517 is similar, in its application to the motion of longer span, to the passage shown in Example 516.

example 517. BACH: *Sinfonia 15, BWV 801*

(a)

(b)

(c)

Here the right-hand part consists of a compound melody, the upper voice of which carries a line that ascends from scale degree 1 (B) through the passing note C♯ (scale degree 2) to the melodic goal, scale degree 3. The lower component of the compound melody consists of the sustained F♯, embellished by its upper auxiliary note, G. The latter embellishing motion is shown in parentheses here to signify that it does not affect the melodic progression of longer range—the ascent from B to D. A condensed version of the basic structure is shown at *(c)*. The melodic goal, D, in Example 517 is the note which is then prolonged by the arpeggiation, as shown in Example 514.

The two previous examples of passing notes involved an ascent to the main melodic note through a passing note that traversed the interval of a 3rd. In contrast, the next example, Example 518, shows a motion that prolongs the main melodic note, C, by a descent through the passing note B♭ to scale degree 3.

example 518. MOZART: *Piano Sonata in C major, K.279,* Second Movement

The summary of the over-all motion at (*c*) shows the simplest version of the basic progression, while the analytical representation at (*b*) provides more detailed information. Perhaps the most important aspect of (*b*) is the descent from B♭ to E (m. 2–3), indicated by notes with downward stems. This is a motion that traverses a dissonant interval, namely, the tritone formed by the 7th and the 3rd of the dominant-7th chord, a motion that serves to prolong the large-scale passing note Bb. Notice that, within the line that descends from Bb to E, A is a passing note. Further, that A is supported by an F-major triad. This triad, however, is not a functional tonic; to label it as such would be incorrect in terms of harmonic progression, for the direction here is toward V⁷, through II⁶.

A secondary, but significant aspect is the exchange of voices indicated by the crossing lines in (b) at m. 3. (See section 241.) Here the exchange clearly supports the reading of an implied A, indicated by parentheses, in the soprano at the close of the passage.

Thus far, we have seen examples of passing notes filling out intervals of the 3rd and 5th. The next example, Example 519, shows the passing note within a still larger interval, the 6th.

example 519. CHOPIN: *Waltz in C# minor, Op. 64/2*

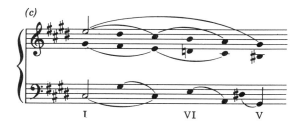

(c)

I   VI   V

At this point the reader should be capable of reading a notational display of this kind. A few comments are perhaps in order, however. The prolongation of E in the upper voice through a descent of a 6th to G♯ traverses the corresponding descending minor-scale segment; at m. 6, however, the chromatic passing-note B♯ occurs in order to permit mm. 5 and 6 to replicate mm. 1 and 2. That is, only the chromatic note B♯ is available as a passing note connecting C♯ and B. The only interruption of this descending pattern occurs at mm. 3—4 and 7—8, and consists of the skip to the inner voice in each case. As shown at (c), the harmonic progression corresponding to the descending 6th is a progression from I to V, and the latter is prepared by VI. More specifically, the first 3rd, from E to C♯, unfolds over the tonic triad, with V^7 as a passing chord. The next 3rd, from C♯ to A, corresponds to the progression to VI through its dominant. The final motion to G♯ coincides with the change of bass and harmony to V. At this point, as shown in (b), the parallel octaves of the outer voices are broken up by the 5th which is formed by the bass skip to D♯, producing the outer voice pattern 8-5-8. One other detail should perhaps be pointed out: the elegant ascending passing motion from E to A in the inner voice mm. 5—8, which coincides with the upper-voice motion from C♯ to A.

A final instance of passing notes over a long span of music is provided in Example 520.

example 520.   BACH: *Twelve Short Preludes, No. 1, BWV 924*

(a)

(b)

10   10

I-

(a)

(b)

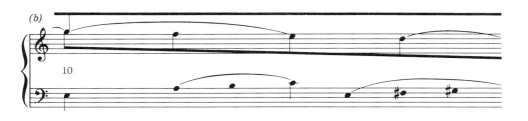

(a)

(b)

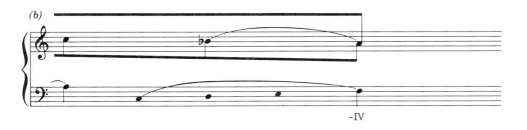

-IV

(c)

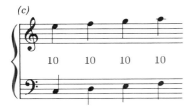

At (c) the fundamental progression is shown: an ascending line in the upper voice, accompanied by the bass moving in parallel 10ths. The connection from G to A in the upper voice is prolonged, as shown at (b), by a secondary prolongational line, the onset of which is signaled by the change in bass pattern in m. 3. This descending line brings in the final note of the pattern, A, an octave lower than the register established in the upper voice at the beginning of the piece—an instance of *transfer of register* (after Schenker).

Before proceeding to the next section, the reader should take time to convince himself that the detail shown in Example 520 at (a) reduces to the more fundamental structure shown at (b). This may also be regarded, in part, as a review exercise in suspensions (Chapter 10).

239. The Auxiliary Note over Longer Spans

In this section instances of prolonged auxiliary notes will be presented and discussed. First, however, let us consider an example of an unprolonged auxiliary note.

example 521.   CHOPIN: *Waltz in F minor, Op. 70/2*

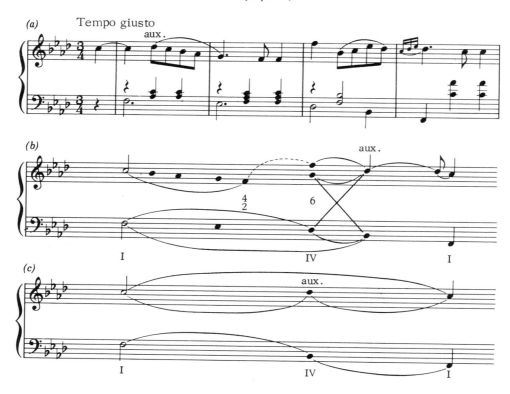

In the excerpt from the Chopin Waltz provided by Example 521 the auxiliary note is introduced in a somewhat complicated way. The analysis shown at (b) is intended to clarify the situation. Following the initial prolongation of C in the upper voice by means of a descent to F over $\frac{4}{2}$ there is an exchange between bass and soprano that brings the auxiliary note D♭ into the soprano voice. Although the exchange, as well as the transfer of register of F, may be regarded as prolonging the auxiliary note (in the manner of a preparation), once stated, the auxiliary note resolves immediately. The simplest version of the passage is shown at (c). It is important to notice that here, and in many such instances, the harmonically supported auxiliary note (m. 3) is an enlargement of shorter auxiliary notes (m. 1 and m. 4).

Subsequent examples all deal with prolonged as distinct from the unprolonged auxiliary note shown in Example 521.

example 522.   BRAHMS: *Variations on a Theme by Haydn, Op. 56*

The middle section of a well-known composition is given in full notation at (a) in Example 522. The analysis at (b) shows, first, an ascent from the inner voice F over V to the upper voice D over I. The auxiliary note E♭ then enters and is prolonged through the descent to A. Here it is essential to realize that the upper voice D in m. 16 is a passing note in the descending prolongational motion and does not represent a resolution of the auxiliary note. The resolution occurs only with the return of D over the tonic harmony at the restatement of the main melodic theme in m. 19. As in the Chopin example (Example 521), the auxiliary note is an important motivic component of the music, and, indeed, is perhaps the most prominent melodic feature of the upper voice at the opening.

As a final example of the auxiliary note over a long span of music, Example 523 presents an analysis of the opening section of Bach's Two-Part Invention in D minor.

example 523.   BACH: *Inventio 4, BWV 775*

Because of the complexity of the music, the analysis is presented in four stages. At (b) is shown a metrical reduction of (a). The reader's attention is directed to m. 8, where the transfer of register of Bb (a) is undone, so to speak, in (b). The same analytical operation is performed at m. 12 and m. 14 in order to show the long-range progression in the upper voice more directly.

The analysis at (c) interprets the structural relations. The music begins with a prolongation of A in the upper voice through its upper auxiliary note, B . This is a small-scale prolongation of the auxiliary note, subsequently to be repeated, which prepares the long-span prolongation that begins in m. 8. The beams connecting Bb to G and F to A here represent what Schenker calls an *unfolding:* a motion to an inner voice and back out again.

The large-scale prolongation of the auxiliary note Bb is shown in detail at (c) beginning in m. 8. First, however, the reader's attention is directed to the condensed version of the melodic and harmonic progression as shown at (d). There the auxiliary note is introduced over the progression from II to V^7 of III, so that the return of the auxiliary note to the main note coincides with a change in harmony from I to III.

The details of the prolongation can now be read from (b). The prolongation consists of the descending bass progression G (II^7) to C (V^7) and the linear intervallic pattern (section 220) 10-7-10, as a result of which the upper voice moves in 10ths with the stepwise bass until it reaches F (m. 14). At that point Bb is brought in in the upper voice once more and immediately becomes the 7th of V^7 (m. 15). Once again there is an unfolding down to G and out to A, as in mm. 1—3 and 5—7, and the auxiliary note Bb resolves to an implied A on the downbeat of m. 18.

EXERCISES

A. List of Some Important Terms

Prolongation

Prolongational line

Transfer of register

Unfolding

B. Analyses

The following excerpts from compositions are to be analysed for arpeggiations, passing notes, and auxiliary notes, with special attention to large-scale structures such as those illustrated in the foregoing chapter. The student should endeavor to show more than one stage (as in the chapter examples) in order to clarify his reading. In some cases either the beginning of the analytical representation is given to aid the student in starting out correctly or a hint is given in order to avoid a mis-reading of the structure.

exercise 228.   HANDEL: *Sonata for Flute and Continuo in E minor, Op. 1/1*

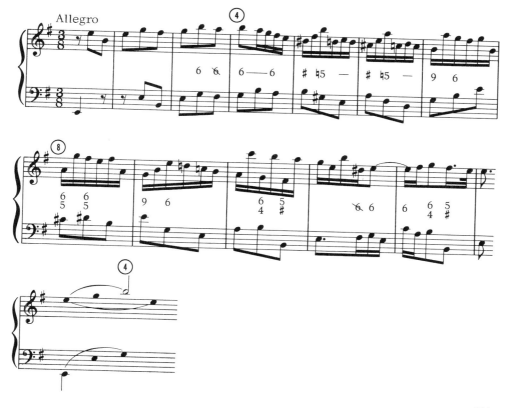

exercise 229.   BEETHOVEN: *Piano Sonata in C major, Op. 53* ("Waldstein"),
First Movement

exercise 230.   MOZART: *Piano Sonata, K.282,* First Movement

Notice that the upper voice motion Eb-D (mm. 1–2) does not interfere with the
basic progression of the upper voice. Those notes merely follow the bass progression C-B .

exercise 231.   MOZART: *Eine kleine Nachtmusik, K.525,* First Movement

Be sure to take into account the fact that the F♯ in the upper voice at the cadence is a temporary displacement of E ($^6_4$), and that therefore the main note in the upper voice at that point is E.

exercise 232.   HANDEL: *Air* from the *Suite in E major*
          ("Harmonious Blacksmith")

This passage features a prolongational line (passing notes) as well as an auxiliary note.

exercise 233. BACH: *Brandenburg Concerto V, BWV 1050,* First Movement
(Soprano and continuo only)

This famous opening utilizes the passing note as well as arpeggiations. One obvious
occurrence of the latter is evident in the upper part.

exercise 234. HAYDN: *Piano Sonata in F major*

It is advisable to make a metrical reduction of this first—i. e., reduce to three
quarter notes in each measure. This excerpt contains arpeggiations over two different time spans, as well as an instance of transfer of register and a somewhat
concealed exchange of voices.

Chapter 14

MULTIPLE MELODIC DEVELOPMENT

For as so many men, so many minds, so
their inventions will be divers and di-
versely inclined.

Thomas Morley, 1597

By *multiple melodic development* we refer to the simultaneous and extended embellishment of two or more voices. This kind of embellishment typifies many tonal compositions. Although we shall concentrate on one style of composition here, the figurated chorale of the Baroque period, the principles and techniques to be discussed are relevant to other styles as well, for they reflect a general concept of structural development that spans the entire tonal period.

240. Chorale Figuration

Chorale figuration is practiced at several levels of complexity. All involve orderly and sustained melodic development under the control of harmonic progression and in accord with the principles of voice leading. Clarity of rhythmic structure is the hallmark of the chorale figuration. Let us consider examples of two different levels of melodic development in that style—first the relatively uncomplicated chorale phrase below.

example 524. BACH: *Chorale, Lobt Gott ihr Christen, allzugleich*

This excerpt illustrates well two characteristic features of chorale figuration. First, it contains a single motive which is used consistently throughout. In this instance the motive is derived from the chorale melody itself (brackets). Second, it exhibits perfect rhythmic clarity. The motive begins in the alto, passes to the tenor, which is then joined by the bass. The tenor then continues alone, to join with the soprano at the close of the phrase. Rhythmic continuity is provided by the overlapping of each motivic statement on the next.

A much more elaborate figuration of the same chorale phrase is given in Example 525.

example 525. BACH: *Chorale-Prelude, Lobt Gott, ihr Christen*

This extract is typical of the short chorale-prelude. It features a distinctive embellishment carried in the inner voices. The soprano carries the melody, and the bass has its own figuration. With melodic elaboration of this kind, particularly the embellishment of the bass, the harmonies of the original chorale setting are modified to a considerable degree. Here almost every triad of the original is replaced by a 6th chord.

Some of the detailed problems in chorale figuration will be considered in connection with the exercises. At this point we turn to certain general aspects of multiple melodic development.

241.   Representative Kinds of Linear Interaction

The embellished voices may combine in various ways. Often they move in parallel 3rds, 6ths, or 10ths. All three of these parallel patterns are illustrated in the following excerpt.

example 526.   BACH: *Chorale-Prelude, Lob sei dem Allmächtigen Gott*

When two voices move in contrary motion traversing the same interval we call their interaction an *exchange of voices.* Three such exchanges occur in the following example.

example 527.   BACH: *Chorale, Herzliebster Jesu, was hast du verbrochen*

The diagonal lines in Example 527 indicate the voices involved in the exchange. Since the voices traverse the same interval, but in opposite directions, they literally do exchange positions.

Exchange of voices is a valuable technique for obtaining melodic motion within a harmonic interval. It is found in many styles of composition, often disguised by embellishments, as in the passage quoted below.

example 528.   BRAHMS: *First Symphony*

If an exchange of voices occurs in the same register, the voices cross and momentarily exchange registral positions as well:

example 529.   BACH: *Fugue in G minor WTC I*

Immediately after the exchange here the soprano returns to the upper register, thus restoring the normative arrangement of the voices. A more elegant type of exchange is shown in Example 530. Here the voices interchange in successive measures, creating the intervallic pattern 6-6 10-10. This is by no means an isolated instance of this pattern, for it occurs throughout the instrumental and orchestral repertory.

example 530. MOZART: *Piano Sonata in A minor, K.310,* Third Movement

(a) Presto

(b)

A special kind of chromatic interaction between two voices is called *cross relation.* This term refers to the successive statement in different 8ves of a diatonic note and its chromatically altered form. An example follows.

example 531. BACH: *Fugue in C minor, WTC I*

This passage contains a series of cross relations indicated by asterisks. Normally the diatonic note and its chromatic form would occur in the same voice. When they are distributed between two voices, as here, we still tend to regard the progression in terms of a single line, now expressed in two registers. This is particularly so in the passage quoted since the lower line does actually carry the complete chromatic succession (note dotted lines). In each instance, however, the chromatic note is stated first in the upper voice.

242. The Effects of Multiple Melodic Development On Basic Elements of the Structure

The changes brought about by multiple melodic development are of the same nature as those brought about by development of the single line, with one exception: multiple melodic development often creates submetrical harmonies.

Multiple melodic development may affect the resolution of dissonant chords. For example, the resolution of a bass suspension may coincide with an embellishing motion in another voice that normally would have remained stationary.

example 532. SCHRÖTER

More startling effects are obtained when one voice completes a motive at the expense of the harmony, as in the following passage.

example 533. BACH: *Chorale-Prelude, Wir danken dir, Herr Jesu Christ*

The asterisk in Example 533 marks the point at which the bass completes its motive, creating a 7th chord in place of the expected $\frac{5}{3}$ and carrying the progression through the cadence to the beginning of the next phrase.

EXERCISES

A. Figured Chorales to Be Realized for Four-Part Vocal Performance

INSTRUCTIONS

These figured-outer-voice exercises provide preliminary experience in chorale embellishment (and multiple melodic development in general). Each exercise should be notated in full, played at the keyboard, and sung. Here and elsewhere the figures do not indicate the voice that is to contain the embellishment. This will depend upon the disposition of the inner parts in each case. The figures also do not indicate the rhythm of the embellishment, but usually this can be determined without difficulty.

exercise 235. Chorale: *Mach's mit mir, Gott* (setting by Rinck)

exercise 236. Chorale: *Wie soll ich dich empfangen* (setting by Kühmstedt)

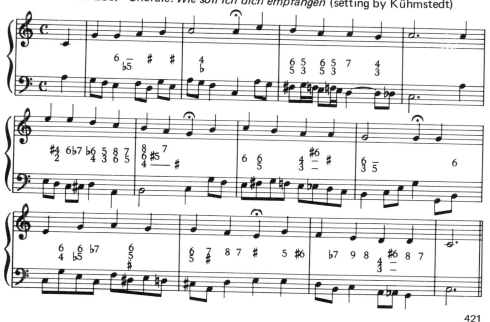

B. Exercises in Chorale Figuration

INSTRUCTIONS
These exercises in multiple melodic development may be notated for performance
on a single keyboard, for two-manual organ with pedals, for piano duet, or for an
instrumental ensemble of one bass and three treble instruments.

As long as the embellished single line follows the voice leading and satisfies the
essential conditions of progression, it can move without restriction. Similarly, two
voices can be embellished simultaneously provided each remains clearly under the
control of the melodic and harmonic progression.

The only additional limitations apply to the interval succession formed by
the embellishments. These are set forth below. When the embellishing voices move
together note for note in parallel motion the familiar prohibition of 5ths and
8ves is effective. For example, this sequence should not be embellished in the
following way:

And successions of parallel imperfect consonances often change the harmony,
as below:

Here the voice in the treble staff moves in 10ths with the bass and brings into play
a dissonant note, the 5th, which transforms the original 6th chord into a $\frac{6}{5}$. In this
context the change is not incorrect; indeed it enhances the progression and therefore is a genuine development of the harmony. In other contexts a motion of this
kind might very well confuse harmonic and melodic progression.

When three embellishing voices move simultaneously they create submetrical harmonies. These are difficult to control, particularly if they move in a

ratio greater than 2:1 against the metrical unit since they then obscure the constant underlying harmonic pulse. Consider the effect of the following multiple embellishment:

To demonstrate the procedure for working out the exercises we begin with a four-voice setting of the first phrase of a famous chorale melody: *Alle Menschen müssen sterben*:

It is of the utmost importance that the basic setting be uncomplicated harmonically, as it is here. Minimal use of dissonances should be the rule since they are the products of melodic motion. If we begin with a partially developed setting there are that many less opportunities for active development by submetrical embellishment. If a 7th is already present in a chord it cannot be unfolded melodically. In contrast, consonant settings are "open" and lend themselves to development.

Our first step, then, is to study the setting for specific opportunities to embellish. The skips in alto and bass at the outset and again at the beginning of the second measure suggest the passing note as a basic motive. We begin by embellishing the alto alone:

Merely filling in the available intervals in this way proves unsatisfactory. There is motion, but no distinctive melodic direction. The embellishment is enclosed within a single interval at the very outset and does not suggest a continuation. This brings us to a fundamental principle of chorale figuration and of melodic development in general: In order to exploit more fully the possibilities for figuration one must provide effective interval contexts. This means that a four-voice setting cannot be embellished effectively and yet retain its original form in all respects. One must rearrange intervals or, if necessary, substitute other chords. In the present case we can extend the passing note motive and give it a more interesting progression by changing the doubling of the third chord so as to open another 3rd between alto and soprano:

We must now consider how to continue the figuration. Since it is based upon the passing eighth note which fills the interval of a 3rd, that interval must either be available in the basic setting or it must be made available. A glance at the basic setting, below at (a), tells us that a 3rd is not available in any voice. All voices move stepwise from the third to the fourth chord. The doubling of the third chord cannot be changed without sacrificing the alto figuration, and a change in the doubling of the fourth chord offers no advantage.

At (b), however, we see a solution that maintains the passing eighth-note motion: by submetrical skip the tenor opens a 3rd which is then filled in. With the tenor skip the chord lacks one note, D, on the second half of the beat. This is corrected by the bass, which skips down to D, exchanging voices with the tenor as marked. Beginning on the fourth chord the alto moves in parallel 10ths with the tenor, and the exchange on the first beat of the second measure enables both voices to continue the passing note figuration.

This somewhat detailed explanation was intended to demonstrate that chorale figuration (and melodic development in general) involves not merely the application of embellishments to given chords wherever they happen to fit, but rather the manipulation of intervals and voice leading so as to **create** contexts for the continuation and development of figuration.

The following example contains a 4:1 figuration in the alto of the chorale setting discussed above. Compare this with the 2:1 figuration above and observe the changes in voice leading which are required to accommodate this more elaborate embellishment and yet maintain complete harmony.

The asterisk calls attention to a skip in the bass which serves to break impending 5ths between bass and alto. The dissonant F♯ in the alto above it also helps to conceal the 5ths.

Given below are chorale melodies to be figurated. Following these, more difficult figurations are suggested for chorale melodies which are given in full.

exercise 237.   Chorale: *Dies ist der Tag, zum Segen eingeweihet*

exercise 238.   Chorale: *Der Himmel jetzt . . . .*

exercise 239. Chorale: *Cum luce*

exercise 240. Chorale: *Meinen Jesum lass ich nicht* (after Bach)

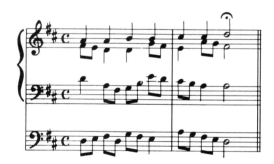

Remainder of chorale melody:

exercise 241.   Chorale: *Straf' mich nicht in deinem Zorn* (from Rinck manuscript collection, anonymous)

Since the chorale melody is somewhat concealed by the embellishment in the upper voice, it is given in its entirety below.

Chapter 15

INTRODUCTION TO COMPOSITION IN TWO AND THREE VOICES

It is far easier to create a harmony in four voices than to condense it into two. . . . and the ability to say much with little does not become completely one's own until he has developed—nor can wine be made until the grapes are mature.

Abt Vogler, 1803

243. Preliminary: Interval and Triad

Before the advent of tonality the interval was the basic structural element in composition; harmonies were formed by combining intervals. For example, the 3rd and the 5th combined to form what we recognize as a triad:

example 534.

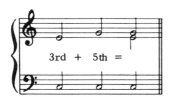

It is important to understand that at that period each of these intervals was regarded as complete in itself, implying no other interval.

During the tonal period the triad, not the interval, became the basic structural element in compositions. Thus, in tonal music an interval does not stand alone; it always implies at least one other interval. For example, the 3rd alone may imply the 5th which completes the $\frac{5}{3}$ or the 6th which completes the $\frac{6}{3}$.

example 535.

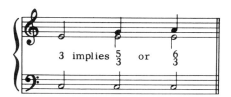

Thus the two voices in Example 535 may imply a third note to complete a consonant harmony, as indicated. Obviously, to avoid ambiguity in this instance it would be preferable actually to state the third note. With four-voice harmony there is no difficulty of this kind since complete harmonies can be stated at any point in a progression.

It is possible, however, as indicated in Example 536, to express the complete harmony, either implicitly or explicitly, in fewer than four voices. The present chapter explains how this is done and also indicates the extensive compositional resources which the techniques of two and three voice composition afford. Here will be considered also the special characteristics of compositions in one voice and in five voices, as well as combinations of various kinds, which we will call free textures.

THREE-VOICE COMPOSITION

244. Complete and Incomplete Chords in Three Voices

Let us examine first the ways in which a single consonant chord can be expressed in three voices. These are summarized in Example 536.

example 536.

(a) Complete *(b)* Incomplete   *(c)* Complete   *(d)* Incomplete *(e)* Complete

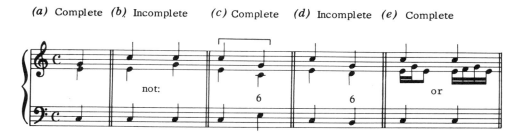

At (a) is the complete triad in three voices. At (b) the triad is in the soprano position of the 8ve; therefore it cannot be complete in three voices. Either the 3rd or the 5th must be omitted. Here and in all three-voice consonant triads in the soprano position of the 8ve, the 3rd is included and the 5th omitted. In such cases the 5th must be implied by harmonic context.

The complete statements shown at (c) and (e) are of most importance to us here. Example 536(c) shows that the triad can be stated completely in three voices by metrical arpeggiation. The complete statement therefore requires two metrical units. In an actual composition it may be impossible to retain the same harmony for that duration and a change of harmony may occur, as shown at (d). In that situation the missing 5th is clearly implied by the harmonic context.

And finally, turning to Example 536(e), we see that a complete statement can be obtained within the metrical unit by submetrical arpeggiation. There the inner voice skips up to add the missing 5th to the harmony.

The foregoing explanation can be summarized as follows:

1   If three voices move metrically (note against note) those notes are extracted from the complete chord which most effectively represent the harmonic progression. Often the progression of the soprano or the progression of the bass may render impossible the statement of the complete chord on each metrical pulse. In that event the missing notes should be implied by the context.
2   If it is desirable or necessary to state the complete harmony this can be done in two ways: by metrical arpeggiation or by submetrical arpeggiation.

Let us now apply this information to the composing of a three-voice chorale setting. Example 537 shows first the four-voice setting which serves as a guide, then three ways in which the three-voice setting may be composed.

example 537.

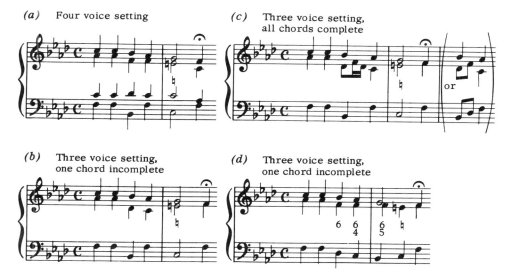

Examples 537(a) and 537(b) require no explanation. At (c) the third chord is stated completely by means of submetrical skip. If the bass skips also, as shown in parentheses, the rhythmic pattern of the inner voice is simplified since it need not return to the 3rd (Db) before progressing to C. Example 537(d) shows still another setting. This one uses inversions but no submetrical embellishments. All chords are complete except the $\frac{6}{5}$.

At this point it is evident that three-voice composition always requires careful consideration of the relation between metrical and submetrical notes as they state or imply the harmonic progression. The following sections examine this relation in more detail.

245. Single and Multiple Melodic Development in Three Voices

As in four-voice compositions, submetrical melodic development can occur in a single voice while the others progress metrically, or it can occur in more than one voice simultaneously. The excerpts quoted below in Example 538 illustrate some of the possibilities.

example 538.   HANDEL: *Variations on Air in D minor*

(*a*) Four-voice realization of the *Air:*

(*b*) First variation (submetrical embellishment of soprano only):

(*c*) Second variation (embellishment of bass only):

Observe the changes here that the bass embellishment brings about in the original harmony.

(*d*) Third variation (embellishment of inner voice and bass):

In the Baroque trio sonata, which in many respects is an apex of three-voice composition, all voices may develop simultaneously in different rhythms, creating a complex texture such as that illustrated here:

example 539.   BACH: *Trio Sonata* from *The Musical Offering*

In this passage, which confirms the modulation to the dominant, may be seen extended and elaborate development in all voices. The underlying four-voice harmonic succession is carried in full by the continuo, as shown by the realization below.

example 540.

246. Bass Arpeggiation to Complete the Harmony

Submetrical arpeggiation of the bass often has the specific purpose of completing the harmony. Instances of this are marked by asterisks in the following passage:

example 541. MARCELLO: *Psalms*

Of particular interest here is the overlapping of the thematic statements in the fourth measure, so that they form a 5th. The bass arpeggiation then completes the triad, adding the 3rd. Note that in every case the 3rd is introduced as quickly as possible—always on the second beat, not on the last.

247.   Dissonant Chords in Three Voices

If it is limited to a single metrical unit and not embellished, the dissonant four-note chord is necessarily incomplete in three voices. The question then arises: which notes should be selected to represent the chord most effectively? Since the bass is essential it cannot be omitted. Therefore only two notes may be selected. The general rule is this: always select the dissonant note or notes in preference to the consonant notes unless special melodic progressions make this impossible (section 248). Consider the II$^6_5$ at the cadence in the following passage. A four-voice version is supplied at (b) for comparison.

example 542.   PERGOLESI: *Trio Sonata in C minor*

The dissonant note of the II$^6_5$ is the 5th, which represents the 7th of the parent chord. The note against which it dissonates is the 6th. These two notes together with the bass identify the chord. Other combinations are ambiguous:

example 543.

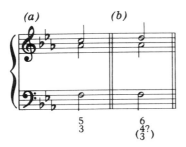

At (*a*) the 3rd is included instead of the 6th. The result is not the $\frac{6}{5}$ but a $\frac{5}{3}$. Similarly, omission of the 5th at (*b*) produces a 6th chord which might imply a $\frac{4}{3}$ as well as the $\frac{6}{5}$. The same principle applies to all the 7th chords.

Three-note suspension chords which displace triads and 6th chords present no new problems since their vertical structures are dependent upon chords of resolution discussed above. For example, the passage below contains a bass suspension which displaces a $\frac{5}{3}$.

example 544. MARCELLO: *Psalms*

In addition to the three-voice suspension chord marked by the asterisk this excerpt contains incomplete diminished-7th chords. The diminished-7th chord can be represented in three voices by bass, 7th, and either 5th or 3rd depending upon the melodic progressions of the voices involved. In this respect the diminished 7th is far more flexible than the other 7th chords, a characteristic discussed earlier.

In three voices suspension chords of four notes are expressed by omitting the note which is not required in the chord of resolution. In the next example the 5th is omitted.

example 545. MOZART: *Piano Sonata in A minor, K.310*

When the duration of the four-note chord is more than one beat it can be stated completely by metrical embellishment or by an inversion which extends the parent chord. In the following example the required dissonant note is brought in by the inner voice just before the change of harmony.

example 546. HAYDN: *Piano Sonata in A major*

(b)

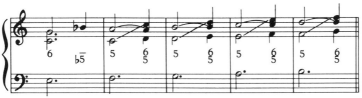

The four-voice version of the passage, shown at (b), reveals more clearly the interaction of the various lines. In the 5 6/5 sequence, with which we are mainly concerned here, the tenor introduces the 6th on the last beat of each measure. At the same time the soprano replaces the 5th which the tenor was carrying (note diagonal line). In the actual composition the soprano is displaced by syncopation so that it occurs one half beat later than the tenor, just before the change of harmony in each case.

We have already seen one instance in which the full dissonant harmony was stated by means of submetrical embellishment: Example 538(b), the 6/5 at the end of the first measure. Another example is given below.

example 547. BACH: *Prelude in D major*

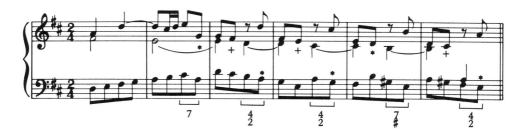

Complete four-note dissonances obtained by submetrical skips are bracketed and figured in Example 547. In each case the essential dissonant note is marked by an asterisk. The + marks a note which belongs to the chords on both beats in each measure and which would still be present on the second beat if the soprano did not suddenly skip away (transient skip) on the last eighth note before the change of harmony.

As an instance of the free treatment of dissonance in elaborate three-voice compositions another passage from Bach's works follows:

example 548. BACH: *Trio Sonata* from *The Musical Offering*

The complete realization of the continuo at (*b*) shows the 7 6 resolution in its normal form, whereas in the violin part the 7th is stated without preparation as part of an ascending arpeggiation and resolved in another register. Both points are marked by asterisks in the illustration.

248. The Influence of Parallel Melodic Lines on Chord Structure in Three Voices

It is a mistake to assume that complete vertical statement of the harmony is the only requirement of three-voice composition. Linear forces also influence the structure of individual chords. We have already seen an instance where the overlapping statement of a motive left the harmony incomplete (Example 530).

Other melodic factors cause similar deviations. Foremost among these are the parallel lines in 3rds, 6ths, and 10ths which are commonly found in three-voice compositions. For example, the best vertical arrangement of the dominant 7th chord retains the 3rd and 7th and omits the 5th. Yet, if the 5th is the main soprano note and if the 7th doubles it at the interval of a 6th below, the preferred vertical arrangement cannot be maintained. An instance of this is shown in the passage below.

example 549. BRAHMS: *Liebeslieder, Op. 52/9*

The succession of parallel 6ths bracketed in Example 549 clearly represents a linear technique that takes precedence over the vertical structure of the individual chords. A similar situation occurs in the next example.

example 550. BACH: *Trio Sonata in G major*

Here the $\frac{6}{5}$ of the full harmony (Bach's figures) is represented by a $\frac{5}{3}$ in three voices. If vertical structure were the only consideration this chord should consist of the 6th and the 5th above the bass. Here again the parallel 6ths between the two upper voices take precedence over the vertical structure of the individual chord.

To close this section a familiar example is quoted—a linear chord which results from parallel 10ths in the outer voices.

example 551. MOZART: *Piano Sonata in A major, K.331*

The bass and soprano move in parallel 10ths throughout. Mozart retains this parallel succession even in the third measure where it creates a linear chord, a false 7th chord in this case.

249. The Selection of Appropriate Passing Notes

Submetrical and metrical arpeggiations in three-voice settings are often filled by passing notes. The selection of passing notes is particularly crucial here since an unwanted change of harmony may be implied by the wrong passing note. (See section 232.)

The general rule for passing notes is as follows: they must fill the intervals of the chord without changing its structure and function. Thus the prevailing diatonic scale may serve as a guide to appropriate passing notes—unless a particular diatonic passing note might be assimilated as a note that would change the harmony. This situation is illustrated below.

example 552.   HANDEL: *Chaconne with 64 Variations*

(a)

(b)

The C♯ is required in the second measure since the diatonic note C♮ would be assimilated as a chord note and thus change the structure and function of the chord as shown at (b).

Passing notes of course must not contradict dissonant chord-notes and therefore again C♯, not the diatonic C♮, is required in the third measure.

When a minor triad is involved special care must be taken with ascending passing notes. These must follow the pattern of the melodic minor scale, otherwise an unwanted change of harmony will be effected. Consider the situation illustrated in the next example.

example 553.

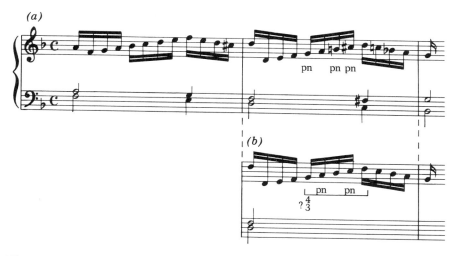

The chromatically altered passing notes at (a) belong to the melodic minor scale of D, the chord that is being embellished. If these alterations are not made, there is a strong conflict between harmony and embellishment since the unaltered passing notes imply the change of harmony shown at (b).

TWO-VOICE COMPOSITION

The principles of three-voice composition apply to two-voice composition as well. However, the two-voice composition must depend even more upon submetrical arpeggiation (and filled arpeggiation) to state or imply the harmonic progression. In general this means that two-voice compositions are more active rhythmically. Both voices, bass and upper voice (usually soprano), need not be active. Often the upper voice moves slowly against a faster pattern in the bass which fills out the harmony. Or if the bass is unembellished the soprano moves quickly and is usually a compound melody. Examples of three rhythmic relationships between soprano and bass are provided below.

250. Submetrical Bass Arpeggiation against Metrical Soprano

In the example following, the soprano moves almost entirely in metrical durations or larger, while the bass arpeggiates and fills in the harmonic intervals.

example 554. MENDELSSOHN: *Italian Symphony*

(a) Andante

(b)

Example 554(*b*) presents a portion of the repetition of the thematic statement shown at (*a*). The repetition harmonizes fully the two-voice outline of (*b*), even including several submetrical harmonies.

In the following example the lower voice figuration of the chord succession (the familiar Alberti bass) achieves full statement of the harmony.

example 555. MOZART: *Piano Sonata in G major, K.283*

Allegro

The harmony can also be fully stated if the relationship above is reversed so that the soprano is active rhythmically while the bass moves more slowly. This relationship is illustrated in the following section.

251. Compound Soprano against Metrical Bass

Just as a three-voice composition can state four-voice harmony by means of submetrical embellishment so a two-voice composition can state three- and even four-voice harmony by the same means. Kirnberger has provided us with a clear illustration of this.

example 556. KIRNBERGER

At (a) is a two-voice passage in which the bass moves metrically against submetrical arpeggiations in the soprano. Kirnberger tells us that this two-voice passage sounds like the three-voice passage at (b). One of the chords, the $\frac{6}{5}$, is a four-note chord whose 3rd has been omitted. The first chord lacks a 3rd, but is stated fully over two beats.

Complete statements of four-note chords are achieved by means of elaborate submetrical arpeggiations such as those shown in the following example.

example 557.   BACH: *Short Prelude in C minor*

The compound soprano voice at (*a*) states the complete succession shown at (*b*). Only the V⁷ is not given in its entirety. All the other harmonic strands are woven into the melody. In contrast to this a soprano voice may be very active and yet only hint at the changes of harmony, as in the passage below.

example 558.   BEETHOVEN: *Fifth Symphony*

Arpeggiation in the soprano voice may occasionally conceal the basic line. For example, the basic line of the following upper voice centers upon the 3rd of the tonic triad. This line is covered by two harmony notes arpeggiated above it. The sketch at (b) reveals the line by rearranging the voices so that the basic line is uppermost.

example 559. BACH: *French Suite in B minor*

252. Arpeggiation in Bass and Soprano Simultaneously

If both voices are arpeggiated, each usually has its own rhythm. In the following example the soprano moves in a ratio of 2:1 against the bass.

example 560. HANDEL: *Suite in F major*

In the second measure of this excerpt the compound soprano includes a suspension. Here and elsewhere the suspension is treated like any other chord note. It may be approached or left by skip but its function in the voice-leading pattern must be fulfilled.

253. Parallel 5ths and 8ves in Compositions of Fewer than Four Voices

There is a venerable rule that says: "The fewer the parts, the stricter the voice leading." It is true that parallel 5ths and 8ves are more exposed in three- and two-voice compositions than in four voices. This is particularly the case if they progress metrically. And since submetrical embellishments may also carry important notes of the harmony, as has been seen, one must take care to see that they do not form parallelisms. This is easily done if compound melodies are consistently regarded in terms of vertical harmonies, in the way demonstrated by Kirnberger (Example 556). The distinction between voice-leading parallelisms and parallelisms by embellishment remains the same as in four-voice composition (section 235).

254. One-Voice Compositions

The term one-voice composition does not include short unison or 8ve passages such as those illustrated in Example 561:

example 561. MOZART: *Symphony in C major, K.551* ("Jupiter")

Passages of this kind are unharmonized lines.

The true one-voice composition is a single voice of compound structure which, harmonically as well as melodically, is self-contained. Seldom is this texture used throughout an entire work. The Chopin *Prelude* quoted below is an exception, for the entire composition consists of a single voice in one hand doubled at the 8ve by the other for reinforcement.

example 562. CHOPIN: *Prelude in E♭ minor, Op. 28/14*

The triple subdivision of each beat here permits a complete statement of the harmony in three voices.

Perhaps the most remarkable one-voice compositions in the musical literature are those for solo violin by J. S. Bach. An excerpt follows.

example 563. BACH: *Sarabande and Double in B minor for Solo Violin*

Example 563(*a*), the *Sarabande,* is played in chordal fashion—insofar as the technique of the violin permits. Example 563(*b*), the *Double,* is an arpeggiated version of the *Sarabande* progression. Like the Chopin example above it is a compound melody which expresses a three-voice structure.

255. Composition in Five Voices

It is important to distinguish between a temporary shift to five voices and extended composition in five voices. For the purposes of reinforcement voices are sometimes added to the normal four-voice texture. Doubling of this kind is the rule rather than the exception in orchestral works, but we find it often in other media also. Here is an example drawn from a keyboard work:

example 564.   HANDEL: *Suite in D minor*

The extra voices in this passage have nothing to do with voice leading. Both harmonic progression and voice leading can be fully expressed in four voices as shown at (*b*). Neither have the added voices individual melodic structures; they are merely 8ve duplications of other lines.

Only when the added voices affect voice leading and when they have an independent function do we speak of harmony in more than four voices. Let us confine our discussion here to harmony in five voices since this is the most frequently used number of voices beyond four and since the principles governing larger numbers of voices remain the same as those governing the single additional voice.

Harmony in five voices occurs temporarily in four-voice settings when it is required in order to complete a chord or in order to satisfy the requirements of voice leading and complete harmony at the same time. In Example 565 below, the 8ve soprano position of the $\frac{4}{3}$ requires that an extra voice be added in order to complete the chord and assure stepwise voice leading. In such situations the temporary addition of another part is a valuable technique.

example 565.

The actual composing of five individual voices, called "real" voices, requires constant shifts, alternate doubling, and crossings, in order to avoid parallelisms. This is shown in the following example, which offers a comparison of two almost identical harmonic successions drawn from the same work.

example 566. MOZART: *Quintet in C minor, K.406*
(Last movement: variations)

The four-voice passage (*a*) and the five-voice passage (*b*) are shown in condensed score rather than in the customary open score in order to show more clearly the arrangement of the voices. Slight rhythmic simplifications have been made for the same reason.

The specific instrumental registers are not shown, but doubling and voice leading are exact. The four-voice passage does not require comment. It serves here merely as a basis for examining the five-voice version.

The diagonal lines in the five-voice passage indicate skips that the fifth voice must make in order to avoid parallel 8ves (represented here as unisons). The numbered comments below refer to the numbers between the staves at (*b*).

1   Here the doubling is in the outer voices. Consequently the bass cannot resolve stepwise, in accord with the stepwise resolution of the diminished-7th chord, but must skip down to G. Compare (*a*) at this point.

2   Here the fifth voice skips away from the unison but returns to it immediately.

3   The five voices permit full statement of the cadential succession as well as stepwise voice leading.

256. Variable Texture

A great many compositions consist of what may be called *variable textures,* that is, combinations of four-voice, three-voice, two-voice, and unison passages, with occasional excursions into five voices. Voice-leading principles still apply to these textures but the continuity of individual voices may occasionally be interrupted. Voices are dropped out and added depending upon a number of compositional factors: register, instruments or voices involved, type of progression, position in the progression, and so on. There is one primary restriction upon the abandonment of a voice, however. A voice is never abandoned on a dissonant note, so that the dissonance is left unresolved, nor is it abandoned before it has completed its function in the harmonic progression. Examples of typical variable textures follow.

example 567. BEETHOVEN: *Second Symphony*

example 568. BRAHMS: *Intermezzo, Op. 76/6*

example 569. C. P. E. BACH: *La Stahl*

Often the texture of a work changes by abandoning the bass temporarily. An example follows.

example 570.   SCARLATTI: *Sonata in A major*

In many cases the bass may be abandoned for even longer periods while attention is focused on the melodic or rhythmic development of the upper voices. However, the bass is always implicit in such cases.

EXERCISES

A. Melodies to Set in Two or Three Voices with Figuration

INSTRUCTIONS
Beginnings of the figurations are given. Complete the setting in the same style.

exercise 242. **Chorale melody and figurated bass (from Rinck manuscript collection—anonymous)**

exercise 243. **Chorale:** *Meinem Jesu lass ich nicht* (from Rinck manuscript collection—anonymous)

exercise 244.   Chorale: *Jesu, Leiden, Pein und Tod* (from Rinck manuscript collection—anonymous)

exercise 245.   HUMMEL (in classical period style). Extend to a sixteen-measure variation theme, including a modulation to V and return. Write three variations.

exercise 246.   HUMMEL (in classical period style). To be used as a basis for a set
of three variations.

Each of the following chorale melodies may be set in one of three ways:
1   as a three-voice composition with embellished bass and inner voice
2   as a two-voice composition with embellished bass
3   as a two- or three-voice composition with embellishment in all voices either
singly or in combination.
The latter possibility is particularly attractive since by this means the chorale can be
transformed into a number of freer forms. The excerpt below indicates the wide
variety of styles one can obtain without forsaking the basic harmonic and melodic
progression.

First phrase of *Jesu, meine Freude:*

Walther's variation on this phrase:

exercise 247.   Chorale: *Dein Heil, o Christ*

exercise 248.   Chorale: *Vater unser im Himmelreich*

exercise 249.   Chorale: *Wie gross ist des Allmächt'gen Güte*

The folk songs that follow may be arranged for voices in various combinations, for example, tenor and bass, or two tenors and bass (if the melody is transposed to fit the tenor range), soprano-alto-baritone. Embellishment may occur in any voice except the upper.

exercise 250.   **English song:** *All in the Downs*

exercise 251. Scotch song: *On a Bank of Flowers*

exercise 252. English song: *Thou soft flowing Avon*

B. Basses to Realize as Two- and Three-Voice Compositions

INSTRUCTIONS
These basses are to be realized as instrumental compositions in two or three voices. In addition, one or two may be realized as solo voices with two- or three-voice accompaniment.

SPECIAL ADDITIONAL INSTRUCTIONS FOR THE TRIO SONATA
Those who are more advanced may realize a bass as a trio-sonata movement. It is important to bear in mind that the trio-sonata movement is actually two compositions in one. The two solo voices form a three-voice composition with the bass, and the continuo accompaniment is also complete in itself, usually in four, but possibly in three or in two voices. The solo voices can double any note in the harmony, except the bass, at the 8ve.

exercise 253. **TÜRK**

exercise 254. **LOCATELLI**

exercise 255. **HANDEL**

Largo

exercise 256. **MARCELLO**

Moderato

Chapter 16

FURTHER TECHNIQUES OF HARMONIC DEVELOPMENT

> Little by little, human reason has suc-
> ceeded in understanding all conceivable
> harmonic combinations . . . , the entire
> harmonic fabric of the composition as
> well as the individual parts.
>
> Heinrich Koch, 1802

We may not share Heinrich Koch's confidence in the capability of human reason to understand the artistic products of the human mind, particularly because we are in a position to survey a vast and complex musical development which Koch in 1802 could hardly have foreseen—the period that begins with the mature works of Beethoven and extends through the late works of Brahms.

Nevertheless, in this final chapter we shall examine some of the techniques that characterize the music of that period as well as certain extended practices in earlier periods. All these are techniques which in some way deviate from the normative harmonic and melodic procedures discussed in previous chapters. Although we shall examine both diatonic and chromatic techniques, the latter are of particular interest since they enable us to understand many aspects of the music composed during the last part of the tonal period. For although the resources of chromaticism were sampled earlier, only with Beethoven and his successors were they exploited to achieve harmonic extension on a large scale in ways consistent with the logic of tonality.

The techniques to be discussed apply not only to small contexts of a few chords but also to larger contexts, including complete sections of compositions. Accordingly, the chapter is divided into two parts: the first deals with small, the second with larger contexts.

TECHNIQUES COMMONLY APPLIED TO SMALLER CONTEXTS

257. Chromatic Substitution

The chromatic expansion of tonality which characterizes much of nineteenth century music is illustrated in miniature by the substitution of a chromatic harmony for an expected diatonic harmony. This technique resembles the deceptive cadence, which involves the substitution of another diatonic chord for the expected diatonic goal harmony. The following passage contains a clear instance of chromatic substitution.

example 571.   WOLF: *Zur Ruh, zur Ruh*

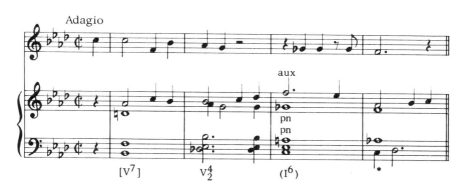

Here a chromatic-appoggiatura chord replaces I⁶, as indicated. In all other respects the passage is normative, with the possible exception of the bass suspension marked by the asterisk (see section 173). Substitution of a single chromatic chord like this of course cannot be regarded as large-scale harmonic extension. In represents linear development which affects only the local context. Of far more importance to the longer span is the substitution of a chromatic consonance, since it may be established as a quasi-tonic and thus extend indefinitely. We shall discuss this harmonic resource in a later section. Here let us consider the substitution of chromatic consonances in small contexts. In the major mode a substitute chromatic consonance often proves to be a triad which has been taken from the parallel minor mode. This process, described below, is called *mixture of mode* or simply *mixture.*

258.   Mixture of Mode: a Special Case of Chromatic Substitution

Example 572 surveys the possibilities for the assimilation by the major mode of consonant triads from the parallel minor mode.

example 572.

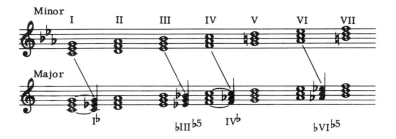

Example 572 shows that four consonant triads from the minor mode may replace their counterparts in the major mode. These we call *chromatic triads by mixture.* The amount of harmonic change wrought by a particular mixture depends upon the extent to which the borrowed triad differs from the triad it replaces. Example 572 shows that in two cases, I♭ and IV♭, only the 3rd of the borrowed triad differs from that of the diatonic triad, while in the other two cases both the fundamental and the 5th differ. (The alteration of the fundamental note is indicated before the Roman numeral.) In the latter cases the harmonic change is far more marked.

    Two examples of mixture of mode follow.

example 573.   BRAHMS: *Third Symphony*

IVb

In the first measure of Example 573 is seen the diatonic upper-auxiliary-note figure, G A G. In the third measure this is replaced by the chromatic figure, G Ab G and the chromatic auxiliary note is harmonized by the VI from the parallel minor mode. The other chromatic triad in this passage, IVb, is also taken from the parallel minor mode and also harmonizes the chromatic auxiliary-note Ab.

The second example of mixture in a small context offers a comparison between a diatonic chord and its chromatic substitute, as did Example 573.

example 574. LISZT: *Der du von dem Himmel bist*

This excerpt contains the III from the parallel minor mode in alternation with the diatonic III. The chromatic substitute finally serves as preparation for the cadential V_3^4.

TECHNIQUES COMMONLY APPLIED TO LARGER CONTEXTS

259. Multiple Chromatic Substitution

We have considered examples of chromatic substitution in small contexts. The remarkable effect of extended or multiple substitution is illustrated in the composition below. For study purposes the diatonic harmonies of the variation theme are placed above the chromatic substitutions.

example 575. C. P. E. BACH: *Variation* on *La Folie d'Espagne*

Aligned are: (*a*) variation theme, and (*b*) variation.

Two relations between theme and variation are obvious immediately: (1) the melody of the theme is retained almost intact in the variation; (2) chromatic dissonances are present in addition to the chromatic substitutes. Of most interest to us here are the latter. These mainly involve the primary triads I and III. In

order to preserve the basic tonal outline no substitution was made for V throughout or for I when it occurred at the close of the harmonic unit. Perhaps the most
remarkable aspect of this variation is that, despite the elaborate chromaticism, the
basic harmonic direction of the original is retained. Without exception the substituted chromatic chords or chord pairs have the same direction as the I or the
III they replace. However, in three instances the progression of the substitute is
not completed. At the last moment an irregular resolution of dissonance occurs.
Thus, the $\frac{4}{2}$ in the second measure should resolve to a 6 over bass E; the $\frac{4}{2}$ in the
fifth measure should resolve to a 6 over bass F; and the 7 in the seventh measure
should resolve to a $\frac{5}{3}$ over bass C. Nevertheless, of these three instances only the
first radically affects the harmonic direction of the progression.

260.   Extension from a Diatonic or Chromatic Substitute

The reader is familiar with the substitution of a diatonic chord for an expected
diatonic chord in the case of the deceptive cadence. A more elaborate example
of diatonic substitution occurs in the next example.

example 576.   MOZART: *Symphony in C major, K.551* ("Jupiter")

The two asterisks in Example 576 mark substitutions. At the first asterisk IV substitutes for the expected II^6, both being dominant preparations. At the second asterisk, VI (prepared by its secondary dominant) substitutes for the expected I. By means of these two substitutions the passage is greatly extended. After Beethoven not only diatonic chords but also chromatic chords were frequently used in this way. A striking example from Brahms is quoted below.

example 577.   BRAHMS: *Sonata for Violin and Piano in A major, Op. 100*

At the asterisk the substitution of the chromatic 6 over E for the expected diatonic 6 serves as point of departure for a long extension, only part of which is shown in Example 577. The relation of the chromatic substitutes to the harmonic axis cannot be demonstrated without quoting a much longer segment of the composition. Over a longer span the main chromatic harmony shown here, the G major triad, proves to be IV of the diatonic IV (D major triad)—an unusual extension of the subdominant relationship.

   In the next example the relationship between diatonic and chromatic harmonies is much more easily grasped since both the initial substitution and the chords that follow it are chromatic triads by mixture with the parallel minor mode (Eb minor).

example 578.   BEETHOVEN: *Piano Sonata in E♭ major, Op. 81a*

Still another type of chromatic substitution is illustrated in the next example. In this case the III with a raised 3rd replaces the expected I.

example 579.   WOLF: *Bedeckt mich mit Blumen*

The common note G serves as a link between the V⁷ and the substituted chord, III♮, and compensates for the abruptness of the change.

The relation between a chromatic chord and the harmonic axis may not be immediately apparent, as remarked earlier. In this instance we note that chromatic alteration of the 3rd alone, as in Example 579, does not affect the diatonic position or function of a consonant triad (unless the triad then serves as a secondary dominant). We must also distinguish clearly between this kind of chromatic chord (Example 579) and a chromatic chord by mixture. The technique of mixture is not used in Example 579.

261. Elision and Incomplete Progression

Elision affects larger contexts when it occurs where one expects a harmonic goal. Two examples of such elision are contained in the following passage.

example 580. WOLF: *Mignon* (*Kennst du das Land*)

Example 580(*b*) summarizes Example 580(*a*). It shows that the first part of the passage centers harmonically around the F minor triad (VII in the tonality of the song). Resolution to this triad is prepared by the V$^4_2$ and again by the linear $^4_2$. In both cases the expected chord of resolution is elided. The linear $^4_2$ then proves to be a returning dominant.

262. Nontonic Beginnings

Compositions normally begin with a statement of the tonic triad. Harmonic extension and melodic development follow from that primary element. But particularly in the nineteenth century we find many compositions that begin *in medias res* with chords other than the tonic. Often quite a long passage precedes the statement of the tonic triad, serving as a kind of extended harmonic upbeat. An example from Chopin is quoted below.

example 581.   CHOPIN: *Waltz in A♭ major, Op. 69/1*

Again, the harmonic sketch at (b) summarizes. The composition begins with the dominant preparation IV⁶. This chord progresses to another dominant preparation, II⁶, via a linear-6th chord and a passing diminished-7th chord. With the [V⁶₅] the direction toward V becomes even more specific. The V⁷ then arrives (preceded by ⁶₄) and finally the progression reaches its ultimate destination, I, after a harmonic prefix that has spanned seven measures. No sooner is I reached, however, than the prefix begins anew, as can be seen in Example 581(a).

In the example below, the tonic triad receives its definitive statement at the very end of the progression, but occurs in secondary roles earlier. The final chord has two functions. It serves as tonic and simultaneously as V leading back to IV at the beginning of the progression. The augmented-6th chord also has a unique dual role. It stands in place of V and at the same time serves as preparation for the [V].

example 582.   BRAHMS: *Fourth Symphony*

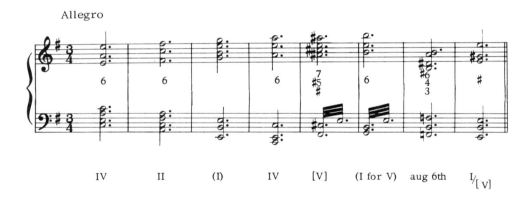

Since its end is simultaneously its beginning this ingenious progression is particularly appropriate to the passacaglia form, which is based upon successive variations of the same harmonic or bass pattern. Each variation carries forward to the next, creating a chain of repetitions. A comparison with the variation theme in C minor by Beethoven (*Thirty-two Variations*) sheds further light on Brahms' unique progression.

example 583.

For easier comparison we have transposed Beethoven's theme to E minor and represented only the most essential harmonic and melodic elements. In many ways it is remarkably similar to that of Brahms. Both span eight measures in $\frac{3}{4}$ meter; both sopranos ascend by step to scale degree 5, and both have the same harmonic goal. Yet no two measures correspond harmonically. The Brahms progression turns on the axis of the dominant preparation IV, while the Beethoven progression unfolds within the more normative succession I V I.

263. Modulation to Chromatic Triads

In Chapter 9 it was seen that any consonant diatonic triad could be established as a quasi-tonic and maintained for a long period without losing its relation to the main harmonic axis I V. Beginning with Beethoven chromatic triads also came to be treated as goals of modulatory progression and established firmly as quasi-tonics. This process, which greatly increased the resources of tonality, was utilized more and more by composers during the last part of the nineteenth century, mainly in longer works but also in short compositions such as songs. In these shorter works such modulations are often incomplete; the goal is prepared but never stated, as in the case of incomplete diatonic modulation (section 167). Similarly, the returning progression may be very brief or absent altogether.

A summary of the modulations to chromatic triads follows. Like the diatonic modulations, certain chromatic modulations offer harmonic and melodic advantages and therefore were favored by tonal composers. Others contain inherent structural problems and were rarely used. So that the chromatic triads may be more easily surveyed we have divided them into three classes, depending upon their relation to the diatonic scale. Each class contains two triads. In the first are two of the four triads by mixture. Included here are only the two triads with both chromatic fundamental and 5th.

We do not include in this summary the two triads with chromatic 3rd alone since as goals of modulation they do not differ significantly from their unaltered counterparts. The harmonic conditions essential for modulation are the same in both cases. In the second class we place the two remaining triads on chromatic scale degrees, ♭II and ♯IV. And finally we include in a special class the dissonant diatonic triads in both modes which become consonant chords by chromatic alteration of the fundamental or the 5th.

example 584. Summary of Consonant Chromatic Triads Available as Goals of Modulation

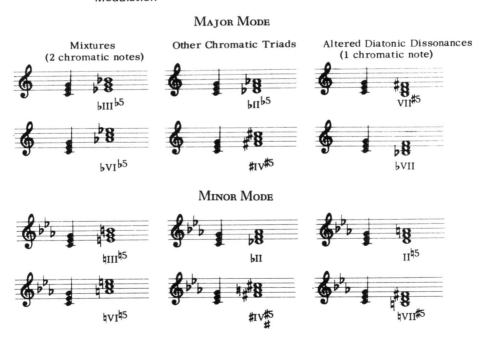

Examples of some of these modulations are given below. We begin with the first class, modulation to chromatic triads by mixture.

example 585.   BEETHOVEN: *Piano Sonata in C minor, Op. 13*

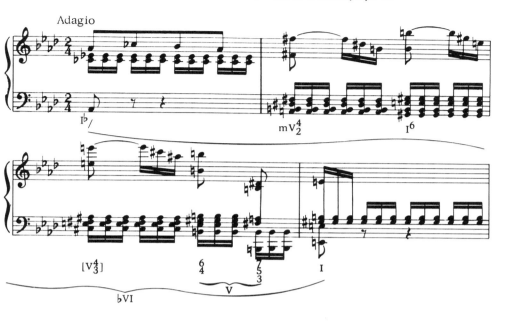

With lowering of the 3rd the tonic triad becomes identical in structure to III of the goal harmony, VI from the parallel minor mode. To make the notation more accessible, Beethoven has spelled the VI enharmonically. In A♭ minor, the parallel minor, it would be an F♭ triad. Here he has spelled it as an E major triad to avoid double flats in the other chords that make up the progression. From the standpoint of technique the modulation is conventional. Only the goal harmony is unusual.

    The most direct return from ♭VI to I is achieved by converting the ♭VI into an augmented-6th chord. However, for the movement illustrated in Example 585, Beethoven composed the more elaborate returning passage summarized in Example 586 below.

example 586.

The returning V is preceded by a II$^4_3$ which belongs to the parallel minor mode, A♭ minor. This chord, in turn, is introduced by a diminished-7th chord which stands in place of a [V$^4_3$].

The next two examples show modulations to the chromatic consonance on the tritone, ♯IV. Of all chromatic triads this lies the greatest distance from the tonic, measured in terms of the 5th relation. The problem of effective and coherent returning progression therefore is acute. A different solution is shown in each example.

example 587. BRAHMS: *Requiem* (harmonic reduction, rhythmic pattern not represented)

There is no pivot chord in this modulation to ♮IV. The modulating dominant is related to the preceding chord only by two notes which they hold in common. The returning progression is based on the same connection (asterisk).

This passage is particularly interesting because of its symmetrical harmonic design. It divides into two parts, each of which contains the progression I VI IV V I. The bass descends by 3rds in each part and the over-all progression ends as it began, with the ♮IV standing exactly in the middle.

The modulation to the tritone takes place in two stages in the next example.

example 588. BEETHOVEN: *Piano Sonata in A♭ major, Op. 26* (harmonic reduction, rhythmic pattern not represented)

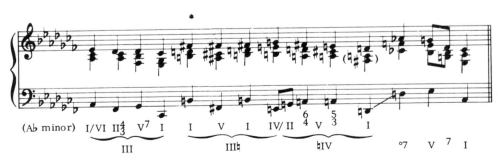

The passage begins with a modulation to the diatonic triad on III, carried out in the conventional way. The 3rd of III is then lowered and the triad is notated enharmonically as a B minor triad. This triad is then extended until its IV is reinterpreted as II, signaling the modulation to ♮IV, as shown by the symbols in Example 584. The return to I is effected by the diminished-7th chord, which represents a [V⁶₅] leading to the V⁷ of A♭ minor, the main tonic.

In Example 588 the altered 3rd of III (asterisk) is the key to the unusual extension, for it provides the pivot chord IV/II. This pivot is not available within the diatonic III, C♭ major.

We come now to two examples of modulation in the third class of chromatic triad, the diatonic dissonance made consonant by chromatic alteration. The goal is the same in both instances, but the techniques of progression differ. First, an excerpt from a work by Hector Berlioz.

example 589. BERLIOZ: *Harold in Italy*

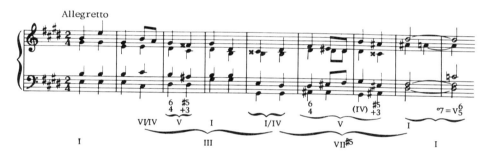

Like the Beethoven example above, this passage contains two modulations. The first is a conventional diatonic progression from I to III, in which VI serves as pivot. The second, which is of most concern to us here, is the modulation to the altered VII. The modulatory technique itself is familiar: the quasi-tonic chord, III, serves as pivot, becoming IV in relation to the new quasi-tonic. The goal of the progression, however, is unusual: the normally diminished triad on scale degree VII which is converted into a minor triad by a change of only one note. The altered note is of course the 5th of the triad. It is raised to change the diminished 5th into a perfect 5th. In Example 589 the return to the main tonic is effected by restoring the diatonic and dissonant form of VII and then adding a 7th. As shown in the example, the resulting °7 serves as a substitute for the returning V⁶₅.

This excerpt demonstrates clearly that no consonant triad, diatonic or chromatic, is far removed from the harmonic axis. If it is distant when measured in terms of the 5th relation, as is the altered VII in Example 589, it is close melodically, when measured in terms of the 2nd relation. We will call this *the principle of proximity.*

The next example of chromatic modulation also provides a convincing demonstration of that principle. In this case the dominant triad itself is the pivot chord, becoming the dominant preparation, VI, in relation to the modulating dominant. The return reverses the relationship: VI becomes the returning dominant.

example 590. SCHUBERT: *Auf dem Flusse*

264. Modulatory Progression without Diatonic Pivot Chord

We come now to another process of development which differs from the norm. As has been seen, diatonic modulations almost always utilize a pivot chord. The present section illustrates three other techniques by which the modulating dominant is prepared.

example 591. Preparation of the modulating V by chromatically altered chord.

SCHUBERT: *Mein!* (accompaniment only)

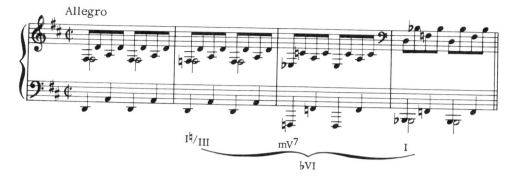

Here the 3rd of the tonic triad is lowered so that it becomes III of ♭VI.

example 592. Preparation of the modulating V by enharmonic reinterpretation of a dissonant embellishing chord.

BEETHOVEN: *Fifth Symphony*

The dominant-7th chord in the third measure at first seems to be an embellishment of a forthcoming IV. Subsequently, however, it is reinterpreted as a German 6th which resolves to the modulating dominant of III♮.

example 593.   Preparation of the modulating V by linear chords.

WAGNER: *Parsifal* (orchestral reduction only)

Because of the large number of chromatic embellishments in this passage we have represented the basic harmonic elements in the simplest possible terms. Both the modulating dominant and its preceding secondary dominant are embellished and prepared by complex linear chords.

265.   Linear Chords That Assume Harmonic Stability

Linear chords are normally only transient, dependent chords which lack stability and consequently harmonic significance. Occasionally, however, we find that they have been invested with harmonic meaning and that they play important roles in directing progressions. The Mozart passage below contains a linear chord which is reinterpreted as a quasi-tonic chord and extended for many measures.

example 594. MOZART: *Piano Concerto in A major, K.488*

From the outset the progression is directed toward VI. But at the cadence a linear 6th chord (asterisk) replaces the expected VI. This proves to be more than a temporary delay of the cadence. As can be seen in Example 594 the linear chord is redefined as a quasi-tonic by its own dominant and serves as point of departure for a new section of the piece.

Although the two linear 6th chords marked by asterisks in the following excerpt do not assume as much harmonic significance as the 6th chord in the Mozart passage, Example 594, they do assist in directing the progression, contrary to expectations when they first appear.

example 595. BRAHMS: *Requiem*

The familiar linear chord, the Neapolitan 6th, is temporarily stabilized by its own dominant in the passage quoted below.

example 596. BEETHOVEN: *Bagatelle, Op. 126/3*

This excerpt also illustrates the quasi-diatonic relationship which can be established between two transient chromatic chords. In this case the [V^7] of N^6 is associated enharmonically with the augmented 6th chord which prepares the main V^7 (asterisk)

266. Progression by Chromatic Sequence

In the music of Chopin and his successors we often find passages that move chromatically by intervallic pattern, the pattern itself being their sole rationale. Such progressions are essentially nonharmonic in that they do not depend upon the harmonic axis for coherence. (Compare section 220.) A famous instance is quoted below.

example 597. WAGNER: *Tristan und Isolde*

The second pattern is an exact duplication of the first, pitched a minor 3rd higher. Although the key signature as well as the harmony of the first measure indicate

Ab major, the chords in the sequence do not express that tonality. The coherence and direction of the progression depend upon the establishment of pattern by repetition, not upon the harmonic axis of tonality.

Another sequence from Wagner is given in Example 598.

example 598.   WAGNER: *Parsifal*

Here again the sequence as well as the chords within each pattern do not contain recognizable harmonic connections. Rather, their meanings lie entirely within the melodic and rhythmic figures and are established by repetition alone without reference to the harmonic axis which controls tonal music.

Procedures such as this foreshadow the abandonment of tonality and the consequent efforts to develop other ways of organizing musical elements, efforts which characterize the whole of music history. Thus in closing let us recall Riepel's words, which perhaps are the best possible final words for a technical book devoted to introducing a single phase of music:

> *Die Musik ist ein unerschöpfliches Meer.*
> (Music is an inexhaustible sea.)

EXERCISES

A. Some Important Terms to Define and Memorize

Chromatic substitution

Mixture of mode

Elision

Multiple chromatic substitution

Incomplete progression

Nontonic beginning

Chromatic modulation

Principle of proximity

Chromatic sequence

B. Short Chromatic Modulations

INSTRUCTIONS

All these short chromatic modulations have been notated as figured basses. They should be realized in four voices or in free texture at the keyboard, transposed, and supplied with various metric-rhythmic patterns. After the progressions have been analyzed and compared, one from each group should be memorized. In each instance it is assumed that the initial tonic chord has been established by a previous progression. Therefore, only the modulatory progression is shown in full.

The progressions by Mattei are shown in their original form. Both C. P. E. Bach and Albrechtsberger notated their progressions without rhythm, and they are presented in that way here. As a visual aid only, we have notated the point of departure and the goal as half notes, while the modulatory harmonies are shown as quarter notes. These need not be the actual durations, of course.

exercise 257.   **Modulation from I to ♭III**

C.P.E. BACH

ALBRECHTSBERGER

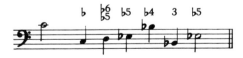

MATTEI

exercise 258.   Modulations from I to ♭VI

ALBRECHTSBERGER

C. P. BACH

MATTEI

exercise 259.   Modulations from I to ♭II

MATTEI

ALBRECHTSBERGER

C. P. E. BACH

exercise 260. Modulations from I to ♯IV

C. P. E. BACH

ALBRECHTSBERGER

MATTEI

exercise 261. Modulations from I to VII♯5

MATTEI

C. P. E. BACH

ALBRECHTSBERGER

C. Completion Exercises

INSTRUCTIONS

In each case part of a progression is given. You are then asked to complete the progression, following specific instructions. The initial task is analysis of the given part. The extension should then be sketched out over as large a span as possible. This can be done in several ways: by notating the essential harmonies in the form of bass and figures, by Roman numerals, by projecting the outer voices, or by sketching in the soprano voice alone. Working out of the voice-leading details then follows, as in a harmonization exercise.

exercise 262.   **From a composition by Wolf, adapted**

Fill in the upper voices in the blank measures and extend approximately eight measures to a close on I; use techniques consistent with those in the given part.

Adagio

exercise 263. **From a composition by Brahms, adapted**

Complete the bass and harmony in the blank measures and extend approximately eight measures to a close on I; use chromatic techniques.

exercise 264. **From a composition by Wolf, adapted**

Beginning with the final chord given here write a passage at least eight measures in length that returns to I by means of chromatic sequence.

exercise 265.   **From a composition by Chopin, adapted**

The metric-rhythmic pattern is not given, although general proportional relations are indicated by the notation. This passage is to be provided with a metric-rhythmic pattern, embellished, and extended harmonically at several points.

exercise 266.   **From a composition by Schubert, adapted**

This composition is in the key of C minor. Metric-rhythmic pattern is to be supplied. Elaborate the given succession melodically and harmonically, then extend it approximately ten measures, using techniques consistent with those given.

(VI)

exercise 267.   **HUMMEL**

Using multiple chromatic substitutes, write at least one variation on this theme.

D.   Melodies to Harmonize

exercise 268.   **LISZT** (adapted)

Con moto

exercise 269.   WOLF (adapted)

Moderato

exercise 270.   LISZT (adapted)

Poco adagio

INDEX
OF MUSICAL EXAMPLES

SUBJECT INDEX